INEQUALITY MATTERS

INEQUALITY MATTERS

The Growing Economic Divide in America and Its Poisonous Consequences

Edited by James Lardner and David A. Smith

Published in collaboration with Demos

THE NEW PRESS

NEW YORK
LONDON

Requests for permission to reproduce selections from this book
should be mailed to: Permissions Department,
The New Press, 38 Greene Street, New York, NY 10013

Published in the United States by The New Press, New York, 2005
Distributed by W. W. Norton & Company, Inc., New York

Portions of this book originally appeared, in slightly different form,
in the *American Prospect.*

LIBRARY OF CONGRESS CATALOGING-IN-PUBLICATION DATA

Inequality matters : the growing economic divide in America and its poisonous
consequences / edited by James Lardner and David A. Smith.
p.   cm.
Includes bibliographical references (p.).
ISBN 978-1-56584-995-2 (hc.)
ISBN 978-1-59558-175-4 (pbk.)
1. Income distribution—Social aspects—United States.
2. Equality—Economic aspects—United States. 3. United States—Economic
conditions—2001–   4. United States—Social conditions—1980–
I. Lardner, James. II. Smith, David A. (David Alden), 1956–
HC110.I5I525 2005
339.2'0973—dc22   22005052237

The New Press was established in 1990 as a not-for-profit alternative to the large,
commercial publishing houses currently dominating the book publishing
industry. The New Press operates in the public interest rather than for private gain,
and is committed to publishing, in innovative ways, works of educational, cultural,
and community value that are often deemed insufficiently profitable.

www.thenewpress.com

Composition by dix!
This book was set in Minion

Printed in the United States of America

4   6   8   10   9   7   5   3

CONTENTS

INEQUALITY MATTERS

THE FIGHT OF OUR LIVES
Bill Moyers

SOME THINGS ARE WORTH GETTING MAD ABOUT. These two stories from the same page of the same day's *New York Times,* for example. Under a six-column headline across the top, the *Times* of March 10, 2004, tells us that the annual tuition at Manhattan's most elite private schools has reached $26,000—for kindergarten as well as high school. Lower down the page, in a story with a two-column headline, we learn about a school in Mount Vernon, New York, just across the city line from the Bronx. Its student body is 97 percent black. Nine out of ten kids qualify for free lunches. One out of ten lives in a homeless shelter.

During Black History Month, a sixth-grader sets out to write a report on Langston Hughes but cannot find a single book about the man in the library. It's no fluke: this is a library with only one book on Frederick Douglass, and none on Rosa Parks, Josephine Baker, or Leontyne Price. In fact, apart from a few Newbery Medal books bought by the librarian with her own money, the shelves are filled with books from the 1950s and 1960s. A child's primer on work begins with a youngster learning how to be a telegraph delivery boy. In another book, the dry cleaner, the deliveryman, and the cleaning lady—in fact, all the characters—are white, as all the students in the school were at the time the book was written. A 1967 book about telephones points out that while most phones have dials, a few of the newer models have buttons. The library has no computer. It doesn't even have a card catalog.

And here's something else to get mad about: Caroline Payne has continually been turned down for jobs because of her appearance. Her Medicaid-financed dentures don't fit, and her face and gums are distorted. Caroline Payne is one of the protagonists of David Shipler's *The Working Poor: Invisible in America.* She was born poor, and though she once owned her own home and earned a two-year college degree, she has bounced from one poverty-wage job to another all her life. She has the will to move up, but not the resources to overcome a succession of unexpected and overlapping problems—a mentally handicapped daughter, a broken marriage, a sudden layoff that forces her to sell her few assets and give up her home. "In the house of the poor," Shipler writes, "the walls are thin and fragile and troubles seep into one another."

Here's something else: the House of Representatives, now a wholly owned subsidiary of the corporate, political, and religious right, has approved new tax credits for children. Not for poor children, but for families earning as much as $309,000 a year— the very families that have already been showered with tax cuts. The editorial page of the *Washington Post* calls this "bad social policy, bad tax policy, and bad fiscal policy. You'd think they'd be embarrassed," the *Post* says. "But they're not."

Nothing seems to embarrass the political class in Washington these days. Not the fact that more children are growing up in poverty in America than in any other industrial nation; that millions of workers are making less money in real dollars than they did twenty years ago; that working people are falling behind even as they put in longer and longer hours; or that while we have the most advanced medical care in the world, nearly forty-seven million Americans—eight out of ten of them in working families—are uninsured and cannot get basic care.

Astonishing as it seems, scarcely anyone in official Washington seems to be troubled by a gap between rich and poor that is greater than it has been in half a century—and greater than that of any other Western nation today. *Equality* and *inequality* are words that have been all but expunged from the political vocabulary. Poverty still gets mentioned every now and then, but in an airy, offhand way. Next to nothing is said, for example, about the profound shift in poverty that is under way in America today. For years we were told that those people down there at the bottom were single, jobless mothers. The poor themselves were counseled that if they wanted to move up the economic ladder, they had only to go to school, work hard, and get married. But now we see poverty where it was not supposed to be: among people who have followed the program to the letter—families with two parents, a full-time worker, and a head of household with more than a high school education. These are the newly poor, whom our political elites expect to climb out of poverty on a downward-moving escalator.

The Stanleys and the Neumanns come to mind. These two Milwaukee families—one black, one white—lost their breadwinners in the first wave of downsizing in 1991 as corporations began moving jobs out of the city and out of the country. In a series of documentaries over the next decade, my public TV colleagues and I chronicled their efforts to cope with wrenching changes and find a place for themselves in the new global economy. The Stanleys and the Neumanns are the kind of people my mother would have called "the salt of the earth." They love their children, care about their communities, go to church every Sunday, and work hard all week.

To make ends meet after the layoffs, both mothers had to take full-time jobs. Both fathers became seriously ill; when one father had to spend two months in the hospital, the family went $30,000 in debt because they didn't have adequate health coverage. We were present with our camera when the bank began foreclosure on the modest home of the other family because they couldn't meet the mortgage payments. Like millions of Americans, the Stanleys and the Neumanns were playing by the rules and getting stiffed. By the end of the decade they were running harder and slipping further behind, and the gap between them and prosperous America was widening.

They love America, and their patriotism turns a personal tragedy into a political travesty. When our film opens, both families are watching the inauguration of Bill Clinton on television. By the end of the decade, they have tuned out. They no longer believe they matter to those who run the country; they don't think their concerns will ever be addressed by the governing class. They are not cynical—they are too religious to be cynical—but they know the system is rigged against them.

And so do we. For years now a small fraction of American households have been garnering an extreme concentration of wealth and income while large corporations and financial institutions have obtained unprecedented power over who wins and who loses. In 1960, the gap in terms of wealth between the top 20 percent and the bottom 20 percent was thirtyfold. Four decades later it is more than seventy-five-fold. Such concentrations of wealth would be far less of an issue if the rest of society were benefiting proportionately. But that's not the case. The pressures of inequality on middle- and working-class Americans have grown more severe despite the general prosperity (which is why we called our documentaries about the Stanleys and Neumanns *Surviving the Good Times*). In the words of the economist Jeffrey Madrick, "The strain on working people and on family life, as spouses have gone to work in dramatic numbers, has become significant. VCRs and television sets are cheap, but higher education, health care, public transportation, drugs, housing, and cars have risen faster in price than typical family incomes. Life has grown neither calm nor secure for most Americans, by any means."

This is a stunning turn of events for a nation saturated with paeans to "the American Dream." Ours was not supposed to be a country where the winner takes all. Through a system of checks and balances, America sought to maintain a healthy equilibrium. Because equitable access to public resources is the lifeblood of any democracy, Americans made primary schooling free and universal. Because everyone deserves a second chance, state laws were changed to protect debtors, especially poor ones, against rich creditors. Charters to establish corporations were open to most if not all (white) comers, rather than held for the elite. Government encouraged Americans to own their own piece of land,

and even supported squatters' rights. Equal access, long a promise implicit in our founding documents, gradually became a reality for millions of us in the twentieth century. My parents were knocked down and almost out by the Depression and stayed poor all their lives. Nevertheless, I went to good public schools, and my brother made it to college on the GI Bill. When I bought my first car with a borrowed loan of $450, I drove to a subsidized university on free public highways and rested in state-maintained public parks. I was one more heir to a growing public legacy that shaped America as a shared project and became the central engine of our national experience.

Until now.

America is undergoing a profound transformation. The radical political elite that has gained ascendancy over politics has made inequality the objective of a sustained campaign, described by the (now defunct) Center for the Renewal of American Democracy as "a fanatical drive to dismantle the political institutions, the legal and statutory canons, and the intellectual and cultural frameworks that have shaped public responsibility from social harms arising from the excesses of private power." From land, water, and other natural resources, to media and the broadcast and digital spectrums, to scientific discovery and medical breakthroughs, a broad range of America's public resources is moving toward elite control, contributing substantially to those economic pressures on ordinary Americans that, says Jeffrey Madrick, "deeply affect household stability, family dynamics, social mobility, political participation, and civic life."

You could have seen it coming by following the Great Divider —money. After a long career covering Washington, the veteran reporter Elizabeth Drew concludes that "the greatest change in Washington over the past twenty-five years—in its culture, in the way it does business and the ever-burgeoning amount of business transactions that go on here—has been in the preoccupation with money." Campaign money has "flooded over the gunwales of the ship of state and threatens to sink the entire vessel," writes Jeffrey Birnbaum, who spent nearly twenty years as a political reporter for the *Wall Street Journal.* "Political donations determine the course and speed of many government actions that—though we often forget—will deeply affect our daily lives."

Senator John McCain describes elections in the United States today as nothing less than an "influence-peddling scheme in which both parties compete to stay in office by selling the country to the highest bidder." During his brief campaign for president in 2000, McCain was ambushed by dirty tricks from the religious right in South Carolina and drowned in a flood of cash from the wealthy cronies of George W. Bush, who was sworn in for a second term under a canopy of cash—$40 million to $50 million—supplied for his inauguration by the very corporations waiting offstage for the payback.

And what a payback! Here's how it works:

When powerful interests shower Washington with millions in campaign contributions, they often get what they want. But it's ordinary citizens and firms that pay the price and most of them never see it coming. This is what happens if you don't contribute to their campaigns or spend generously on lobbying. You pick up a disproportionate share of America's tax bill. You pay higher prices for a broad range of products from peanuts to prescriptions. You pay taxes that others in a similar situation have been excused from paying. You're compelled to abide by laws while others are granted immunity from them. You must pay debts that you incur while others do not. You're barred from writing off on your tax returns some of the money spent on necessities while others deduct the cost of their entertainment. You must run your business by one set of rules, while the government creates another set for your competitors. In contrast the fortunate few who contribute to the right politicians and hire the right lobbyists enjoy all the benefits of their special status. Make a bad business deal; the government bails them out. If they want to hire workers at below market wages, the government provides the means to do so. If they want more time to pay their debts, the government gives them an extension. If they want immunity from certain laws, the government gives it. If they want to ignore rules their competition must comply with, the government gives its approval. If they want to kill legislation that is intended for the public, it gets killed.

I'm not making this up. And I'm not quoting from Karl Marx's *Das Kapital* or Mao's *Little Red Book*. That was *Time* magazine. From the heart of America's media establishment comes the matter-of-fact judgment that America now has "government for the few at the expense of the many."

It is easy to understand why Franklin Delano Roosevelt feared a government by money as much as a government by mob. It is easy to understand why the Stanleys and the Neumanns were turned off by politics. They and millions like them have been the losers in a class war that disarmed them of political influence before defeating them.

The battle strategy was outlined a generation ago in *Time for Truth*, a powerful polemic by the wealthy right-winger William E. Simon, who had served as secretary of the treasury under President Richard M. Nixon. If the financial and business classes wanted to reclaim the power and privileges they had lost as a result of the Depression and the New Deal, "funds generated by business" would have to "push by the multimillions" into conservative causes, Simon wrote. They got the message and had soon put together a well-orchestrated, lavishly financed movement. *Business Week* put it bluntly: "Some people will obviously have to do with less. . . . It will be a bitter pill for many Americans to swallow the idea of doing with less so that big business can have more." The long-range strategy was to cut workforces and their wages, scour the globe in search of cheap labor, trash the social contract and the safety net erected to protect people from hardships beyond their control, deny ordinary citizens the power to sue rich corporations for malfeasance and malpractice, and eliminate the ability of government to restrain what editorialists for the *Wall Street Journal* admiringly call "the animal spirits of business."

Looking backward, it all seems so clear that we wonder how we could have ignored the warning signs. What has been happening to working people is not the result of Adam Smith's invisible hand but the direct consequence of corporate money, intellectual activism, the rise of a literalistic religious orthodoxy opposed to any civil and human rights that threaten its paternalism, and a string of political decisions favoring the interests of wealthy elites who have bought the political system right out from under us.

To create the intellectual framework for this revolution in

public policy, these elites funded conservative think tanks that churned out study after study advocating their agenda. To put muscle behind these ideas, they created a formidable political machine. Thomas Edsall of the *Washington Post* is one of the few mainstream journalists who has covered the class story. "During the 1970s," he writes, "business refined its ability to act as a class, submerging competitive instincts in favor of joint, cooperative action in the legislative area." Big-business political action committees flooded the political arena with a deluge of dollars. And the wealthy elites built alliances with the religious right—Jerry Falwell's Moral Majority and Pat Robertson's Christian Coalition—who gleefully contrived a cultural holy war as a smoke screen behind which the economic assault on the middle and working classes would be waged.

And they won. In Daniel Altman's recent book on the "neoconomy," he describes a place without taxes or a social safety net, where rich and poor live in different financial worlds. "It's coming to America," he announced. He's a little late; it's here. "If there was a class war," says Warren Buffett, the savviest investor of them all, "my class won."

Look at the spoils of victory:

- $2 trillion in tax cuts—tilted toward the wealthiest people in the country
- cuts in taxes on the largest incomes
- cuts in taxes on investment income
- cuts in taxes on huge inheritances

More than half of these tax cuts are going to the wealthiest 1 percent. In 2003, according to the *New York Times,* "nearly 3,400 of the tax returns of people earning $200,000 or more showed no federal income tax due—a rise of nearly 45 percent" over the previous year. You could call it trickle-down economics, except that the only thing that trickled down was the sea of red ink that overwhelmed our state and local governments, forcing them to cut services and raise taxes on those who live paycheck to paycheck.

Deficits are part of the plan. The late Senator Daniel Patrick Moynihan tried to warn us, when he predicted that President Reagan's real strategy was to force the government to cut domestic social programs by fostering federal deficits of historic dimensions. President Reagan's own budget director, David Stockman, admitted as much. The goal, according to Grover Norquist, the leading right-wing political strategist, is to "starve the beast"— with trillions of dollars in deficits resulting from trillions of dollars in tax cuts, until the United States government is so anemic and anorexic that it can be drowned in the bathtub.

There's no question about it: the corporate, political, and religious right are remaking American life according to a blueprint that only they fully understand, because they are its advocates, its architects, and its beneficiaries. In creating the greatest economic inequality in the advanced world, they have saddled our nation, our states, and our cities and counties with structural deficits that will last until our children's children are ready to retire; and they are systematically stripping government of its capacity to do much more than reward the rich and wage war. Every morning's news brings a litany of evidence: Tennessee is withholding Medicaid from three hundred thousand people, the poorest of the poor, because the state is deeply in debt. Florida is laying similar plans. Hearing this, the social reactionaries convened at Grover

Norquist's Wednesday Group in Washington will likely break into cheers. But long after George W. Bush has retired back to Texas, Americans will be struggling with shrunken resources to reverse the unraveling of our social contract which his radical and reckless policies deliberately hastened.

If instead of practicing journalism I were writing for *Saturday Night Live,* I couldn't make up some of the things said by "All This President's Men." His chief economic adviser assures us that shipping technical and professional jobs overseas is good for the economy. His Council of Economic Advisers classifies hamburger chefs in fast-food restaurants as manufacturing workers. His labor secretary tells us not to worry about stalled job growth because "the stock market is the ultimate arbiter." His Federal Reserve chairman expects the tax cuts to cause Social Security benefit reductions—but wants the cuts made permanent anyway. This may be the first class war in history where the victims will die laughing.

But what is being done to middle-class and working Americans and the poor—and to the workings of American democracy —is deadly serious. Go online and read the transcripts of Enron traders during the energy crisis four years ago, manipulating the California power market and gloating over their ability to rip off "those poor grandmothers." Read how they talked about making political contributions to politicians like "Kenny Boy" Lay's good friend, George W. Bush. You'll find more of these shenanigans from one end of the World Wide Web to the other: Citigroup, the nation's largest financial institution, being fined $70 million for deceptive home-mortgage practices; a subsidiary of the corporate computer giant NEC being fined over $20 million after pleading guilty to corruption in a federal plan to bring Internet access to poor schools and libraries; millions of dollars missing among contractors in Iraq; untraceable funds disappearing behind the facade of faith-based initiatives.

The unmitigated plunder of the public trust has spread a spectacle of corruption across America. For its equivalent one has to go back to the first Gilded Age, when the powerful and the privileged controlled politics, votes were bought and sold, legislatures corrupted, and laws flagrantly disregarded, threatening the very foundations of democracy. It was a time—now is another—when the great captains of industry and finance could say, with Frederick Townsend Martin, "We are rich. We own America. We got it, God knows how, but we intend to keep it."

And they will, unless, reading this book, you get mad—mad enough to get organized.

WHAT'S THE PROBLEM?

James Lardner

NATIONAL TRAGEDIES are not always sudden. This book is about one that has been going on for nearly three decades, changing America in profound ways, by slow degrees.

Many of us have memories of the postwar era, when the benefits of prosperity were broadly shared and millions of Americans climbed out of poverty into a middle class that was the envy of the world. Sometime in the late 1970s, our economy began to go a different way, sending most of its rewards to those who already had the most. The result is a concentration of income and wealth that is not only higher than it has been since the 1920s, but higher than that of any of the world's other developed nations.

A generation ago, America's distribution of income and wealth was similar to that of other rich countries. Today, the share of income going to the top 0.1 percent of Americans is twice the equivalent figure for Britain and three times that of France. While the United States remains a spectacularly rich country by any standard, we are drifting toward a Third World–like distribution of our riches. For tens of millions of Americans, the alternative to unemployment has become a dead-end job that may not even cover basic living expenses. Many who are doing better materially are paying a steep emotional price: in the struggle to keep up or avoid falling behind, Americans are commuting farther, borrowing more, working longer hours, and living with the knowledge that if something goes wrong, they stand to lose much of what they have. To put it another way, the American middle class is slowly coming apart, and we are learning, in the process, how essential it has been to economic opportunity and democratic government—perhaps the two ideals that come closest to defining our sense of national identity.

When the founders declared all men to be created equal, they gave America a long-term project as well as an argument for independence. For two centuries, we have clung to the notion of a society in which children start off on roughly the same footing regardless of origins or ancestry. Enunciated by a slaveholder, that idea was in Abraham Lincoln's mind when he ended slavery; it inspired the civil rights revolution and the resulting breakthroughs for people of color, women, the disabled, gays, and others who had lived outside the cover of the Constitution. Even in this age of deregulation and boundless faith in the market, the image of America as a land of escape from the rigid systems of class and foreordained lives of the Old World remains a vital piece of what Bruce Springsteen has called "the country we carry in our hearts."

Some authorities—economists and others—insist that America's commitment to opportunity is alive and well in our era of $300,000-a-year lobbyists and $30,000-a-year librarians. A more unequal society, they argue, is merely one with the good sense to reward invention and enterprise properly—in other words, a land of greater opportunity than ever. It's a consoling thought but a mistaken one, according to almost every expert who has taken the trouble to examine the evidence. When it comes to mobility as well as inequality, it turns out, the United States lags behind a good number of what we used to call the "class-ridden" societies of Western Europe. A poor German or Swedish child, the research shows, has a better chance of getting ahead than a poor American child. Poverty, in addition to being more widespread on this side of the Atlantic, casts a longer shadow.

Democracy, like opportunity, has always been a work in progress; and here, too, our progress has run aground on the shoals of rising inequality. A growing class divide means a diminished store of shared experience, common haunts, and inclusive institutions, feeding a politics of narrow interests that rely on money rather than popular support and involvement to assert their will. When people "are ranked in an irrevocable way according to their occupation, wealth, and birth," the Frenchman Alexis de Tocqueville wrote in 1835, lamenting how things were in Europe as opposed to America, "each caste has its opinions, its sentiments, its rights, its moral habits, its separate existence."

This book grew out of a conference held at New York University in June 2004. It was organized by Demos, a think-and-action tank committed to the pursuit of broader economic opportunity and a more robust democracy, and it was cosponsored by, among other groups, United for a Fair Economy, the AFL-CIO, ACORN, the Center for Public Integrity, the Center for American Progress, the Economic Policy Institute, the National Council of Churches, Common Cause, the NAACP, and the Center for the Advancement of Health. Reformers tend to think and work in policy silos; in the name of pragmatism, they focus on narrow issues where solutions seem possible, and steer clear of problems that appear overwhelming and intractable. Many of the more than three hundred people who attended the "Inequality Matters" conference were taking time away from their labors as activists, scholars, and community leaders concerned with education, health, poverty, racial justice, the workplace, the environment, and the integrity of public life. Their readiness to devote three days to such a large and daunting question stemmed from a belief that it had become a barrier to progress in all these areas, aggravating problems, making the political landscape less friendly to reform, and undermining the effectiveness of those reforms that, against the odds, are occasionally written into law. In that sense, perhaps, their experience mirrors that of the nation as a whole.

Pollsters and political scientists tell us that Americans do not care about the level of inequality. But if you stop to think about it, quite a few of the heated political debates of recent years have been about accumulations of advantage and disadvantage in realms of life, such as health care and education, where a great many Americans would like to preserve a threshold of rough equality, and where that has turned out to be a near-impossible task. We come across a situation that offends us, such as the use of "soft money" to give corporations and wealthy individuals a disproportionate say in the political process. We argue, we struggle, perhaps we eventually pass a law, and a few years later we're back more or less where we started.

In the late 1960s, Congress created a system of grants and loans designed to reduce the class divide in higher education by bringing college within reach of anyone who was academically qualified. It worked, for a while. But, in recent years, tuition has soared and funding has lagged, reducing the maximum student loan to a droplet in the bucket of what it costs to go to a four-year private college. Meanwhile, schools have taken to using precious financial aid money to compete with one another for a pool of top applicants who, in many cases, would have little difficulty paying the costs on their own. The net effect is an enrollment gap between low- and high-income Americans as wide as it was forty years ago—as wide, and much more meaningful, because of the greatly increased economic value of a college degree.

For as long as inequality has been growing and some people have been worrying about it, others have been telling them not to worry. The naysayers point out that this is a trend driven by enormous gains at the top, not by objective losses at the bottom. What possible reason, they ask—what reason other than envy or "class warfare"—could there be for anyone to worry about purely *relative* differences in a land of such abundance that even a have-not can have a VCR and a cell phone, and restaurant meals and air travel (luxuries in our parents' and grandparents' day) are marketed to the masses?

Although the focus of our book is on the problem, many of the contributors also respond to those who insist that it is *not* a problem. Some engage the naysayers on their own terms—growth, opportunity, liberty, efficiency, fairness. Others challenge the terms of argument, in particular the habit of measuring human well-being in money and things.

You don't have to be carrying a brief for envy or "class warfare" to be concerned about the emotional impact of rising inequality on those who are bombarded by advertising for things they will never be able to afford, or who find themselves on a career ladder that is going nowhere. In the real world, unlike the hothouse of right-wing economic theory, extreme economic differences rest on power relationships that are inimical to liberty as well as opportunity. In American workplaces today, employees can be compelled to listen to presentations on the evils of unions but forbidden to meet for the purpose of forming one.

Relative differences can have absolute consequences. When some people enroll their children in high-priced test-taking courses or hire "private guidance counselors," the landscape is changed for everybody, like it or not. When a small number of people have huge sums of money to spend on housing, prices skyrocket for whole communities, and people of far more modest means feel compelled to spend more than they should.

As money differences have grown, so has the sphere of life ruled by money. Other nations have marked their arrival in the first rank of prosperity by making health care a universal right; in the United States, millions of people who used to have employer-provided health insurance must now pay for their own care or go without. Physicians as well as patients resent the hurried and impersonal service that has become the norm for those fortunate enough to have health coverage and forced to depend on it. Worn down by the pressures of general practice in the age of managed care, a handful of enterprising doctors have made the leap into a new subspecialty known as "concierge medicine." Instead of battling to keep up with the needs of hundreds of patients (and their insurers), they dedicate themselves to a deep-pocketed few, who pay premium fees in return for relaxed appointments, home visits, and promptly returned phone calls.

What was once a health care *system* has made up its mind to be a health care *industry,* with an increasingly steep socioeconomic hierarchy of its own, from $10-million-a-year HMO chieftains to $8-an-hour home health aides. On the patient end, we see rising disparities not only in care, but also in health. In 1950, an African American baby was 1.6 times as likely as a white baby to die before her first birthday; by 2002, that ratio was 2.4. Class- and race-related gaps in spending, along with the huge sums of money that go to insurers and administrators, help make America a nation of also-rans in almost every basic measure of health, despite the highest per capita gross domestic product and the highest rate of per capita medical spending in the world.

Education is traveling on a parallel path. America has a loud message for those who worry about being caught on the wrong side of the technological tracks: "Go to school!" Yet we design our schools to keep some people up and other people down. Half a century after *Brown v. Board of Education,* poor children across the country are routinely, and increasingly, assigned to schools filled with other poor children—a practice with a long, proven record of failure. Almost every national politician has a pet remedy for the problems of American education; almost none has anything to say about this basic issue.

For much of our history, America has been an exemplar of democracy, inspiring people the world over to stand up to those who have declared them unfit to rule. In their global proselytizing, our country's leaders promote democratic values with undiminished fervor. Meanwhile, millionaires, who make up about 1 percent of the American people, hold close to half the seats in the Senate; and in the House, incumbents have used their fund-raising and redistricting powers to achieve the kind of reelection rate associated with banana republics. In every election from 1996 through 2004, at least 98 percent of incumbent candidates retained their seats in the House; in the watershed year of 2006, the reelection rate plummeted to . . . 94 percent! Much has been said about the voter apathy that supposedly explains why so many Americans fail to show up at the polls on Election Day. Surely some of that supposed apathy flows from the suspicion of many Americans that meaningful political representation, like regular doctor's visits and a four-year college, has been priced out of reach.

When it comes to inequality, too, a good deal of what gets called indifference is simply resignation. Americans may not care much about inequality in the stereotypical way that such an emotion is supposed to be felt: rage against the wealthy, romanticization of the poor, demands for redistribution. They may not care about inequality as a word or an abstraction. But they care deeply, when they are given an opportunity to show it, about work that doesn't pay enough to pay the rent; the exploding numbers of uninsured; the wave of corporate backsliding on pensions and retirement benefits; the growing class divide in higher education; the syndrome of middle-class working parents with no time for their children (to say nothing of church, the PTA, or the volunteer fire department); and the routinized and increasingly brazen power of money over the political process.

Our challenge, then, is not to create concern where none exists but to connect the dots. That means linking the supposed "non-issue" of inequality to the galaxy of problems that are, in large part, driven by inequality. It means, above all, making the connection between growing inequality and the policies, practices, and powerful forces that feed it. For if many Americans do not see it as an issue, that's because they see it as a given—a product of the deep and impersonal machinery of the "free market."

And if many Americans think that way, it's no accident. The corporate-funded right has worked long, hard, and very effectively to sell its vision of a world divided between a natural entity known as the market, and an unnatural, interfering entity known as government. But markets—functioning markets—are not free; they depend on elaborate structures of rules, practices, understandings, and enforcement mechanisms. These structures vary widely, and the differences matter profoundly, as America's recent experience proves.

During the past twenty-five years, tax rates and rules have been altered again and again in ways that favor corporations, financiers, and wealthy families and individuals. The Reagan and Bush tax cuts, moreover, are only the most obvious cases of a host of economic policy actions with effects on the distribution of income and wealth. Many, such as the weakening of accounting rules that once required corporations to count stock options as an expense (and might have discouraged CEOs and other executives from playing the market for quick personal gain), occurred with little public notice, and with scarcely any discussion of their inequality effects.

All of this and more has been done under the banner of "deregulation." But much of it is really *re-regulation*, designed to benefit the few at the expense of the many. In short, America has chosen to be more unequal; and as that fact becomes increasingly clear, it could be the key to a tectonic shift in perception. For it is human nature not to worry too much about things we consider beyond our ability to change. Once we stop thinking about growing inequality as a divine or natural thing, Americans can gain the ability to look at it squarely, and then to recommit ourselves to the work of making the country in which we live more like the one we carry in our hearts.

Part One

HOW UNEQUAL ARE WE, ANYWAY?

WHAT THE NUMBERS TELL US
Heather Boushey and Christian E. Weller

SOME QUESTIONS CANNOT BE ANSWERED with statistics. But some can. Economic inequality is rising in America. Except for a brief interruption in the late 1990s, it has been growing for nearly thirty years. What was at first widely dismissed as a temporary blip or a misreading of the data is now an undisputed trend—one that, most economists agree, sets the United States apart from other developed nations in addition to marking a sharp departure from the course set by this country in earlier decades.

The closest thing to a standard measure of economic inequality is the Gini coefficient, developed nearly a century ago by an Italian statistician of that name. The Gini coefficient ranges from 0 (where everyone's income is exactly the same) to 1 (where all the income goes to a single person, leaving the rest of the population with nothing). Between 1968 and 1992, the Gini coefficient for the United States rose from 0.388 to 0.434—an increase of almost 12 percent. There are other ways to measure inequality, but almost regardless of the one you choose, it is higher than it has been in many decades; most economists believe that the distribution of wealth as well as income is more unequal today than it has been since before the onset of the Great Depression.

A careful examination of the data is also chastening (or should be) to those who accept the fact of higher inequality but depict it as a matter of no importance in what they say is a context of constant upward (and downward) mobility. Free-market ideologues paint a picture of the American economy as a kind of madcap

DRIFTING APART
Share of total income received by highest-earning and lowest-earning 20 percent of population, 1967–2003

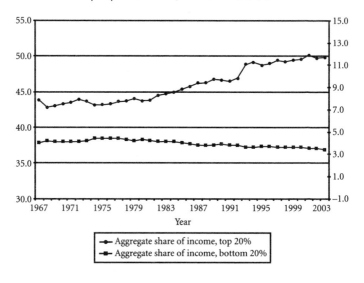

Year

- Aggregate share of income, top 20%
- Aggregate share of income, bottom 20%

Source: U.S. Census Bureau.

road race in which it would be foolish to care who's ahead or behind, because things can change in an instant. But the data paints a more predictable picture. The titles of two recent research papers capture the thrust of the latest work in this area: the first was called "The Apple Does Not Fall Far from the Tree"; the second, "The Apple Falls Even Closer to the Tree Than We Thought." The economist Thomas Hertz estimates that a child with parents in the bottom-earning fifth of Americans now has roughly a 7 percent chance of reaching the top fifth as an adult; by contrast, a child with parents in the top fifth has a 42 percent chance of winding up there.

In the early postwar era, mobility was the ace up America's sleeve—a powerful argument for a set of economic arrangements that, even then, generated higher inequality and insecurity than in some of the welfare-state economies of western Europe. Now the United States has even higher inequality and insecurity, with no such consolation. While mobility is a tricky thing to measure, and international comparisons are especially problematic (because countries collect data differently), hardly any economist considers the United States a world-beater in mobility today. Among the developed nations, we appear to be a middling performer at best—ahead of Britain and South Africa, perhaps, but behind Canada, Germany, and most of Scandinavia. When it comes to mobility as well as inequality, the United States in recent years has been moving slowly away from the orbits of the rich nations of Europe and the Pacific Rim, toward the trajectories of Russia, Brazil, and Mexico.

When pollsters want to find out what Americans think about growing inequality, they trot out an old proverb, "The rich get

richer, the poor get poorer," and ask their subjects to agree or disagree, approve or disapprove. It's a simple way to pose the question, but a poor way to portray the situation. The rich have
certainly gotten richer—steadily and immensely so—during the
past several decades. The fortunes of the poor are not so easily
summed up.

Their wages and incomes did show a decline, in the aggregate,
during the 1980s; for just that reason, the eighties were the decade that recorded the sharpest increase in inequality. From the
economic peak in 1979 to the next peak in 1989, workers at the
tenth percentile of the income distribution (that is, ten steps up
from the bottom) saw their wages fall by 14.1 percent, while the
wages of those in the ninety-fifth percentile rose by 8.1 percent.
Meanwhile, wages for the median worker were flat. In other
words, as the top and bottom pulled away from each other, the
middle, generally speaking, stayed put.

The pattern of the 1990s was different. Inequality kept increasing for much of the decade, but the trend was driven more
by a widening gulf between the top and the middle. From 1989 to
2000, the wages of the median U.S. worker rose by only 5.9 percent, while those of workers in the ninety-fifth percentile went up
16.6 percent. Compared to the 1980s, those at the bottom did a
better job of keeping up: wages increased by 13.1 percent for
those in the tenth percentile—only a little less than the increase
registered by those in the ninety-fifth percentile. The gains at the
bottom were especially strong in the tight labor market of the late
1990s, as the growth in wage inequality slowed and briefly halted.
Between 1995 and 2000, Americans at the bottom of the wage
distribution actually saw their wages rise faster in percentage

terms than did those at the top—for the first time in decades. Still, by 2000, the top 5 percent of households earned 25.4 percent of all wages, up from 17.6 percent in 1980. *Their* gains, moreover, were dwarfed by those of the top 1 percent of households, whose share of wages roughly doubled, going from 6.4 percent in 1980 to 12.6 percent in 2000. Breaking the numbers down even further, we find that most of the gains of households in the top 1 percent actually went to those in the top 0.5 percent.

Because most families get most of their income from wages, income and wage trends tend to move up and down in tandem. The biggest differences emerge when we look at high earners, because they are the people most likely to enjoy significant income from dividends, rents, business profits, and other nonwage sources. From 1979 to 2003, households in the top 20 percent, and in particular the top 5 percent, saw their incomes grow significantly faster than did other households. Recent research using data from tax returns has found that the average real income of the bottom 90 percent of American taxpayers declined by 7 percent between 1973 and 2000, while the income of the top 1 percent went up 148 percent. While the top earners were pulling away from the bottom, they pulled away from the middle as well. Today, households at the eightieth percentile have over twice the income of the median household; in 1967, that ratio was only 1.66. (The gap between households at the bottom and middle has remained relatively constant: it was 0.42 in 1967 and in 2003.) The income ratio of the top 5 percent of earners to the bottom 20 percent, similarly, increased from 6.3 in 1967 to 8.6 in 2003. The share of total income accruing to the top 20 percent of households rose from 43.8 percent in 1967 to 49.8 percent in 2003, while the share of income going to the bottom 20 percent of households fell from 4.0 percent to 3.4 percent.

Although some pieces of inequality data are debatable, the sheer persistence of the trend has given researchers an unusual amount of time to work out the methodological kinks and arrive at a degree of consensus concerning both what has happened and, perhaps more decisively, what has not happened. During the 1990s, for example, many accusing fingers were pointed at the personal computer. The PC, it was said, had expanded the influence and economic power of an elite of professionals, managers, and corporate strategists, while eroding the economic value and leverage of others.

But, after a comparatively brief vogue, the computer-did-it theory lost favor. One problem was timing: the beginning of inequality growth in the late 1970s and early 1980s predated the widespread use of computers in industry. By the late 1990s, the productivity benefits of computers were spreading to data entry clerks, cashiers, and others who were clearly not reaping great financial rewards as a result. Another lingering puzzle was why, if computers caused inequality, they had caused so much more of it in the United States than elsewhere.

While the computer is no longer a popular culprit, the search for a simple explanation of inequality has continued, with attention shifting from machines to people. Could what looks like a broad increase in inequality be attributed to a narrow segment of the population? Although a number of candidates have been proposed—African Americans, single mothers, immigrants— these theories all carry a similarly comforting message between the lines: the macrophenomenon is really a microphenomenon, caused by the increased presence or unfortunate decline of a single subgroup (perhaps because of its own behavior or character weaknesses). Our concern should therefore be with the subgroup, not the system. Some of the naysayers have incorporated more than one group into their hypotheses. But, of course, a string of exceptions is not very different from a sweeping trend; in any case, the evidence does not support the string-of-exceptions theory any more than it supports the various single-exception theories.

If there is a common denominator to some of the theories, there is also a common strategy for evaluating them. It begins by disaggregating the data in order to zero in on individual demographic groups and look, first, at differences between one group and another (or between one group and the population as a whole), and then, at differences within the group. Through these within-group and across-group comparisons, we can go a long way toward determining whether the larger trend can be traced to an increase or decrease in the proportion of any one segment of the population, or to a positive or negative change in the behavior or treatment of that group, rather than to more generalized forces. Through this analytical process, we find little change over the past thirty years in the gap between African American and white workers. Among women, the black/white gap was virtually nonexistent in the late 1970s, and rose to 4 percent by 2001. Among men, the gap was 14 percent in 1975, and rose to about 20 percent in the early 1980s before coming back down to 15 percent by 2001. The most striking change in across-group inequality over this period involves gender: while males' wages fell during the late 1970s and 1980s, and recovered modestly in the 1990s, average wages of females rose by about one-fifth over that span of time. Even when wages are regression-adjusted to control for education and experience, we find a dramatic reduction in the gender gap, from 47 percent in 1975 to 27 percent in 1993. (Since 1993, however, it has remained unchanged, hovering at around 25 percent.) This all suggests that no single demographic segment of the population suffered enough of an economic reversal to account for the economywide increases in inequality that have marked the past two and a half decades.

If higher wage and income inequality were counterbalanced by an increased potential for economic mobility, then greater inequality would not require that some stay at the bottom (or at the top). That would be especially true if inequality were the result of a new influx of immigrants. Unfortunately, the evidence shows that the dream of widespread mobility no longer reflects the economic reality of America. In the 1970s, 50.7 percent of families who began the decade in the bottom quintile and 49.1 percent of families who began the decade in the second bottom quintile moved into a higher quintile over the decade. In the 1990s, only 46.8 percent of families who began the decade in the second quintile managed to move into a higher quintile.

The sons of fathers from the bottom three-quarters of the socioeconomic scale (defined by income, education, and occupation) were less likely to move up in the 1990s than in the 1960s. By 1998, only 10 percent of sons of fathers in the bottom quarter had moved into the top quarter; in 1973, by comparison, 23 percent of lower-class sons had moved up to the top. The evidence shows that there is today a smaller chance than in the past that someone from a low-income family will move up the income ladder.

THE APPLE AND THE TREE
Where Those Born into the Poorest 20
Percent of the Population End Up as Adults

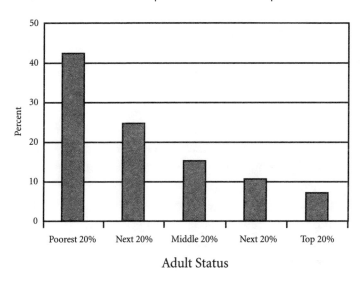

Adult Status

Source: Thomas Hertz, "Rags, Riches and Race: The Intergenerational Economic Mobility of Black and White Families in the United States," in *Unequal Chances: Family Background and Economic Success,* ed. Samuel Bowles, Herbert Gintis, and Melissa Osborn (Princeton, NJ: Princeton University Press, 2005), table 10.

It is particularly sobering to note that, based on international comparisons, the "American Dream" of upward mobility may have become less of a reality in the United States than in many other countries. Recent research indicates that economic mobility in the United States is probably lower than in Finland, Sweden, Canada, and Germany. Having slipped behind many of our western European counterparts in terms of income inequality, it appears that we are headed in the same direction on the economic-mobility front as well.

When you add up rising inequality and lack of upward mobility, what emerges is a large disparity in wealth and living standards. In fact, wealth, which is determined by income trends over time, is distributed much more unevenly than income. In 2001, the richest 5 percent of American households controlled about 59 percent of the country's wealth, while the bottom 40 percent held just 0.3 percent. As with the income statistics, the increase of wealth inequality over the past two decades is striking: while the top 1 percent had on average more than 1,500 times the wealth of the bottom 40 percent in 1983, they had almost 4,400 times the wealth of the bottom 40 percent in 2001. Many of the poorest Americans, in fact, have negative wealth—that is, their debts outweigh the value of everything they own.

Statistics on homeownership, the key component of many families' wealth, at first glance present a more hopeful sign. Homeownership rates rose from 1989 to 2003 across the demographic spectrum—today more than two-thirds of American households own their home—and rates increased faster for groups that began with lower homeownership rates. However, large disparities persist. Homeownership among minorities, for instance, remains below 50 percent, and the gains in homeownership rates from 1989 to 2003 failed to substantially close that gap. Homeownership rates increased across all income levels, but there is no indication that lower-income groups are making any

UNCOMMON WEALTH
Ratio of Wealth Holdings, Top 1 Percent to Middle 20 Percent, 1962–2001

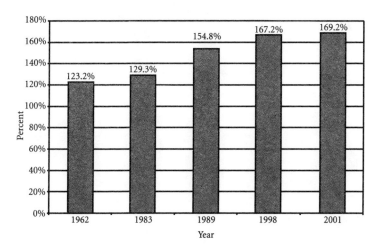

Source: Lawrence Mishel, Jared Bernstein, and Sylvia Allegretto, *The State of Working America, 2004/2005* (Ithaca, NY: Cornell University Press, 2005), and authors' calculations.

inroads into shrinking a large homeownership gap. High-income households had a homeownership rate that was 82 percent greater than that of low-income households in 1989 and still 73 percent higher in 2001. Home values for those who have homes have risen; on the other hand, so has mortgage debt. For some pockets of families—the elderly, for instance—mortgage debt has increased much more quickly than home values.

Other components of household wealth that are not as wide-

AMERICA IN PROFILE

Distribution of Wealth in the U.S., 2001

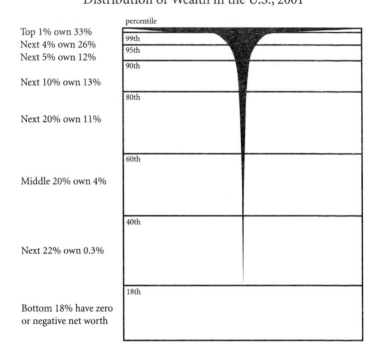

Top 1% own 33%
Next 4% own 26%
Next 5% own 12%

Next 10% own 13%

Next 20% own 11%

Middle 20% own 4%

Next 22% own 0.3%

Bottom 18% have zero
or negative net worth

percentile

99th
95th
90th
80th
60th
40th
18th

Source: Edward N. Wolff, "Changes in Household Wealth in the 1980s and 1990s in the U.S." (April 27, 2004, draft), in *International Perspectives on Household Wealth,* ed. Edward N. Wolff (Cheltenham, UK: Edward Elgar Publishing Ltd., forthcoming).

	PERCENT OF POPULATION	SHARE OF INCOME	SHARE OF WEALTH
Top quintile	20	47.7	84.4
2nd	20	22.9	11.3
3rd	20	15.4	3.9
4th	20	9.7	0.7
5th	20	4.2	0

Source: Mishel, Bernstein, and Allegretto, *State of Working America 2004/2005*, tables 1.12 and 4.3.

spread as homeownership, such as stock holdings, are even more skewed toward the upper end of the economic distribution. Despite claims in the 1990s that Wall Street had become as familiar to Americans as Main Street, equity investing is still primarily the domain of the well-to-do. In 2001, the first year in which the share of households with any stock holdings exceeded 50 percent (a figure that can include the indirect ownership of stock in a company pension or 401(k)-plan), stock ownership remained very unevenly distributed. Only 12.4 percent of households in the bottom income quintile had any stock holdings at all, compared to just under 90 percent of households in the top quintile. The actual amount of holdings is heavily concentrated among the wealthiest Americans: in 2001, the top 10 percent controlled 77 percent of all stock market holdings.

Since wealth is the result of accumulated savings over time, rising wealth inequality reflects the low incomes and lack of upward mobility of many Americans. Low earners are, by necessity, so focused on meeting their immediate needs and expenses that they cannot save to create the wealth that might be invested in their families' futures. Many families fall into generational cycles of poverty that are increasingly difficult to escape—the very opposite of the American Dream.

The numbers tell a clear and consistent story. Inequality has risen to heights not seen in recent memory—some suspect not since the Gilded Age of the late 1800s. Higher inequality has not been accompanied by higher mobility; in fact, the reverse appears to be true, which helps explain the increased concentration of wealth as well as income. If many of us—experts and nonexperts—continue to downplay the meaning and magnitude of the inequality trend, maybe it is not because of shaky evidence, but because the evidence is telling us something about America that we are not eager to hear.

EARTH TO WAL-MARS
Barbara Ehrenreich

WEALTHY PEOPLE have a habit of equating lack of money with lack of character. Words like *lowlife, riffraff, bum,* and *good-for-nothing* used to be spoken with some discretion, however. It is only in recent decades that the old put-downs have been translated into the language of social science, elevated to the status of an "analysis" of poverty, and shared unashamedly with the world at large. In fact, at our tonier think tanks, you can now earn quite a nice living giving lectures and writing articles that trace the origins of poverty to the moral defects of the poor.

When I hear this sort of thing, I am transported back to my experiences in the land of low-wage work. Between 1998 and 2000, I spent a cumulative three months as a waitress, a housecleaner, and a Wal-Mart sales "associate" while researching a *Harper's* magazine piece that became the book *Nickel and Dimed*. The jobs were hardly glorified. Nevertheless, in almost every case I was required to pass a drug test and a personality test, and the questions suggested a rigorous standard of personal morality. Before being permitted to pick undergarments off the floor of a Wal-Mart in suburban Minneapolis, for example, I had to respond on a scale of 1 to 5 (1 for "totally agree," 5 for "totally disagree") to the statement "All rules must be followed to the letter at all times." No irony was intended, I can assure you. After some deliberation, I decided to agree "strongly" rather than "totally," so I wouldn't come across as a suck-up. A needless concern, it turned out. After the test, the personnel manager disappeared into another room to grade my personality on a computer. "You got this one wrong," she said brightly when she returned. "The correct answer is 'totally agree.' "

And total agreement is just what is required in a great many of today's workplaces. People are expected to work hard, follow the rules, and be grateful for the privilege—and many are. Among my fellow "associates," who were making $7 to $8 an hour on the sales floor, there was hardly a whisper of talk about Wal-Mart's CEO, H. Lee Scott, who, according to one news account, was pulling down $60 million per annum. I remember calculating that I would have to put in another five thousand years of work in order to earn what Mr. Scott got in one year. (You may be wondering whether I factored in a promotion for myself after a millennium or so. No. But I was only trying to be realistic, for this was a year or so before a class-action lawsuit raised the company's gender-equity consciousness ever so slightly. A woman being entrusted with a position of responsibility is still a special event at Wal-Mart. Back then, it was almost unheard of.)

My time at Wal-Mart coincided with a run of stories about crime in the suites. The CEO of Tyco Corporation was indicted on a charge of stealing $600 million; his company responded by offering him another $45 million in severance money. Meanwhile, my co-workers and I were treated to a grisly educational video on employee theft. It showed a guy at a cash register furtively stuffing bills into his pocket, followed by drumbeats, the cops rushing in to carry him away, and a portentous voice-over: *"He stole $400 and he got four years in prison."*

Steal $400—you get four years in prison. Steal $600 million—you get a platinum parachute. America is not only an economically polarized society, but also a morally polarized society, as the neoconservatives are wont to observe. But not always in the way they mean.

Inspired by the success of *Nickel and Dimed*, I have been floating the idea of a sequel. For an eight-figure advance, I am prepared to go undercover among the rich, hanging out at charity balls and spas. Since I have yet to find a publisher for this book, I cannot speak from firsthand knowledge about why CEOs and Wall Street muckamucks earn the money they do these days. Some authorities say it has to do with the shift from an industrial to an information age making our economic well-being increasingly dependent on the brainpower of a small cadre of movers and shakers. I can't bring any personal knowledge to bear on that hypothesis. But I believe I can offer some insight into why wages have been stagnating or declining for so many on the lower rungs of the economic ladder.

The experts tell us that technology has made the work more routine and undemanding. That wasn't my experience at all. In addition to my job at Wal-Mart, I was a waitress and a hotel housekeeper in South Florida, a dietary aide at a nursing home, and a maid with a housecleaning service in Portland, Maine. These jobs were hard—physically hard, as I had expected, and also mentally hard, which came as a surprise. When Wal-Mart told me I would be in ladies' wear, my first thought was, "What fun—I'll be dispensing fashion advice to the women of Minnesota." It turned out that the women of Minnesota had not come to Wal-Mart seeking my fashion advice, and I would not have had time to dispense it, in any case. My job—a discouraging proportion of my job—was to pick up the things that people had tossed on the floor, left in the changing rooms, or hidden under the clothes racks. This meant memorizing where hundreds of different items went in a maze of shelves and racks.

And the locations were always changing. Renowned for its computer tracking of customer activity, Wal-Mart is continually rotating items from one place to another, hoping to attract the shoppers' attention. (Not that the management ever shared its insights with us ground-level operatives. As far as I could tell, the only reason for all that rotating was to convince me I had Alzheimer's.) There is an important lesson here. We think of low-wage work and unskilled work as almost identical. But take a moment to look at who these people really are and what they are doing. We're talking about nurse's aides, home health aides, child-care workers, teacher's assistants, call-center operators, bank tellers, meat processors, and data-entry clerks. All these jobs take effort, intelligence, and concentration. I have taken a vow: I will never use the word *unskilled* again.

I should add that low-wage jobs are often unnecessarily hard because of the atmosphere of distrust and intimidation that so many companies seem determined to create. In some of these workplaces, I was prohibited from talking to my fellow employees. Of course, that was partly to ensure that workers couldn't get together and organize. Wal-Mart does not believe in unions, and nowadays our government does not believe in them either. While it is perfectly legal for an employer to ban employee conversation or assembly, it is also legal to require employees to attend anti-union lectures, where they may be warned that a prounion vote is likely to lead to a company decision to shut down the facility. I am not speaking hypothetically: in February 2000, workers who cut and packaged meat at the Wal-Mart supercenter in Jacksonville, Texas, voted to join the United Food and Commercial Workers Local 540. Less than a month later, as another store's employees geared up for a vote on unionization, Wal-Mart announced a plan to shift to all prepackaged meat in some stores. It took the employees three years to obtain a court order calling on Wal-Mart to bargain with the union, and even that decision is still being appealed.

In important ways, America's low-wage workplaces have begun to resemble Third World sweatshops. Take the matter of bathroom breaks. If you are a white-collar professional, you go to the bathroom, you come back to your desk, and you don't give it a thought. Bathroom breaks are not an issue—they're not even a *concept*. But they can be a very big deal for pink-collar and blue-collar workers. For the details, I refer you to the definitive study, *Void Where Prohibited*, by Marc Linder and Ingrid Nygaard. In this massively researched volume, the authors tell tales of women wearing adult diapers to work lest they feel the bodily need at a time the company deems inappropriate. They describe an elementary-school teacher who takes her entire class to the bathroom with her. Employers, it should be said, are required by law to provide toilets for their workers. The only wrinkle is that they are not absolutely required to give workers an opportunity to use them. In some of my jobs, the bathroom breaks were so infrequent that I started feeling nostalgic for that drug test. At least I got a chance to pee.

Overtime pay is another widespread grievance, and, as with so many areas of labor-law abuse in today's America, Wal-Mart has been conspicuous by its presence. It has been sued in at least thirty states for failing to pay overtime. By that, I do not mean failing to pay time and a half; I mean failing to pay *anything.* "Go punch out and come back to the floor," the manager says. "I've got a lot for you to do." That's Wal-Mart's way of informing you that you are about to make a free donation of your time.

I survived Wal-Mart, as I survived my other jobs. I am proud of myself for not screwing up so badly that I got fired. On the other hand, I never even came close to fulfilling my original mission. The point had been to see if I could stay alive not just physically but financially—if I could *support myself.*

Needless to say, I did not undertake my experiment in New York City or San Francisco, where it would have been doomed from the start. I chose a series of comparatively affordable communities, and kept my living expenses to a minimum, hardly spending a dime on anything but food, rent, and transportation. What undid me completely was rent, though I tried to keep my housing aspirations under control. In the Twin Cities, after a brief and obviously hopeless exploration of the mainstream rental market, I shifted my attention to the trailer parks. My objective was a room with a microwave and fridge for $400 a month or less. I found nothing for under $800. Eventually, I discovered residential motels. These places are costly, but they don't ask for a first month's rent or security deposit, and many low-wage people appreciate that. You can have a roof over your head almost immediately—an unaffordable roof, but a roof just the same. My particular motel, which I will call the Clearview Inn, was an unsettling place; in fact, it was downright creepy. Sitting in my ground-floor room without a window shade, I got to feeling pretty sorry for myself—until I looked at my neighbors. Compared to them, I was living in luxury, because I had *my own room*. Many of the rooms around me were occupied by families— couples or single mothers with children.

My mission was partly an attempt to explore the consequences of the Personal Responsibility Act of 1994. This was the measure designed, in President Clinton's proud words, to "end welfare as we know it" by pushing millions of women into jobs paying sub-subsistence wages. Welfare reform was widely regarded as a triumph. After all, people were punching time cards, learning trades, developing self-discipline, and, by and large, not dying of starvation.

On the strength of that last fact, low-income workers are presumed to possess secret strategies for making $7 an hour stretch further than the rest of us, with our school-taught arithmetic, can grasp. One of my tasks was to find out just what those secret strategies are. And I did find out. But they aren't nearly as secret as they are cracked up to be. Or as effective. One strategy is to juggle multiple jobs. Even when I worked two jobs at a time, I found it impossible to cover basic living expenses; and I had serious advantages over most people who are in the low-wage workforce for real. No small children, for starters. I have two children who are not small. Both firmly resisted the opportunity to participate in what they judged to be a weird journalistic frolic with Mom. Frankly, I have no idea how anybody would attempt this with small children. Do the math: a full-time job at $8 an hour—that's roughly $1,200 a month after taxes. Rent consumes $500, optimistically; child care takes another $500. So you've hit the $1,000 mark before you've spent a penny on food, gas, toiletries, or medical care. True, there is federally subsidized child-care assistance for some low-wage people. But like so many safety-net programs today, it's more of a gesture than a serious source of relief. About one out of seven eligible families get the subsidies. That leaves 86 percent who don't.

Strategy number two is to split the rent with a spouse, a boyfriend, or a roommate. This works for some people, as long as their relationships hold together. But there's no margin of safety in these setups. If you haven't fallen off the edge, you're standing right at it. In many cases, the only strategy is to redefine a necessity as a luxury, and go without. I worked alongside women most of us would consider homeless; that's not how they viewed themselves, however, because if you're a low-wage worker with a vehicle to sleep in, you tell yourself that at least you are not on the street. These distinctions are important in America today. Quite a few of my co-workers were on diets—or such was my quaint middle-class assumption when I saw people skipping lunch. In fact, they were simply trying not to spend money they didn't have.

Looking back, I am struck by the absurdity of the way we define poverty today. Officially, about 12 percent of Americans fall below the poverty line. That threshold, however makes no allowance for the soaring cost of housing and child care. When you add those in, estimates of the number of people living in poverty soar. The Economic Policy Institute calculated, in 2001, that some 27.6 percent of Americans living with children under twelve were not earning enough to make ends meet.

Although rent was my undoing, it could have been medical care, if I had needed any. Wal-Mart provides health insurance to employees who work at least thirty-four hours per week, but even full-timers have to wait six months before becoming eligible; the waiting period for part-timers (one-third of the company's labor force) is two years, and even then the coverage does not include dependents. Employees who opt in must pay between $228 and $472 per month (depending on the particular plan)—an unaffordable bite out of the roughly $1,000-a-month pretax earnings of a typical Wal-Mart associate. As a result, fewer than half of all employees are actually covered by the company's health plan.

The company well understands the difficulty this poses for many employees: at some Wal-Mart stores, employee orientation is partly about applying for food stamps and welfare benefits. In Georgia alone, where around 42,000 people worked for Wal-Mart in 2002, 10,261 children of Wal-Mart employees were enrolled in the state's PeachCare for Kids health insurance program, covering kids whose parents cannot afford health insurance. You see this sort of thing in other states too, and it's a point overlooked by critics when they're toting up the billions in public subsidies that Wal-Mart has snared. They're talking about roads and utility lines and tax abatements—not about the large government expenditures required to keep Wal-Mart associates alive. A

House committee estimated that a 200-employee Wal-Mart store may cost federal taxpayers $420,750 annually—about $2,103 per employee—in subsidies for free and reduced-price school lunches, Section 8 housing assistance, federal tax credits and deductions for low-income families, state health insurance programs, and energy assistance, among others.

It would be nice to think of Wal-Mart as an aberration in today's economy. It would be more accurate to think of it as a company on the way to becoming typical of today's economy. Measured by sales, Wal-Mart is already the biggest private business in the world, with 2004 revenues of $285 billion—about the same as the combined GDPs of Israel and Ireland. Roughly 140 million Americans—over half the population—shop at Wal-Mart in an average week. Their visits account for nearly a third of all the toothpaste, shampoo, and other household staples sold in the country.

Wal-Mart has come a long way from the variety store that the iconic Sam Walton opened in Rogers, Arkansas, in 1962. Today, the Walton kids and grandkids and their hirelings administer an empire of more than 3,600 stores in the United States plus more than 1,570 in eight other countries, with plans to open at least 280 new U.S. stores in fiscal 2005. The Wal-Mart workforce numbers about 1.6 million worldwide, and almost 600,000 Americans make an appearance on the payroll every year at the current 44 percent turnover rate. My back-of-the-envelope math indicates that by 4004 or so, every square inch of the United States will be covered by Wal-Mart supercenters. The only place for new supercenters at that point will be on top of existing ones.

That is, unless some recent stirrings prove to be more than a passing spasm of discontent. Sales have leveled off, and Wall Street has lost some of its enthusiasm for Wal-Mart. More ominously, the company has had to deal with a run of bad press. (Others might call it good, if belated, journalism.) Wal-Mart has long been criticized for driving independent stores out of business and sucking the juice out of America's downtowns. Lately, though, Wal-Mart watchers have shifted their attention to the company's labor practices, and to its role in spurring a corporate race to the bottom that has swelled the ranks of the thirty million Americans—nearly one worker in four—who work full-time for less than a poverty-level wage.

Wal-Mart has drawn the attention of law enforcement as well. In October 2003, federal immigration officials raided sixty-one stores in twenty-one states in the course of an investigation of charges that Wal-Mart had knowingly used illegal immigrants to do some of its store cleaning. In June 2001 six current and former Wal-Mart and Sam's Club employees filed a class-action lawsuit in federal district court in San Francisco, alleging systematic discrimination—paying women less than men performing the same work and denying them promotions and raises on the basis of gender. The suit is backed by data showing that while two-thirds of Wal-Mart employees are women, only one-third of store-management and less than 15 percent of store-manager jobs are held by women.

In June 2004 the court certified the class, which now includes all women who have worked for Wal-Mart since December 26, 1998—over 1.5 million in all. Wal-Mart has fought back, requesting a change of venue from California to Arkansas (which was denied) and appealing the court's decision to certify the class. There have been other lawsuits, too, over zoning violations and allegations of employees being locked into stores overnight, unable to get help even in medical emergencies.

Management is worried—you know it must be when the company suddenly shows up as an underwriter of National Public Radio and *The Tavis Smiley Show*. On NPR, frequent announcements now portray Wal-Mart as a source of "jobs and opportunities for millions of Americans of all ages and all walks of life." Wal-Mart spokespeople have even gone so far as to acknowledge the truthfulness of some of the recent charges. Management portrays them, however, largely as the slipups of success: the company has been growing so fast, we are told, that top executives failed to monitor things as closely as they should have. Wal-Mart promises to keep a closer watch from here on out.

That is, of course, a familiar line of defense when imperial rulers are forced to explain unsavory conditions in the provinces. We didn't know. We were too trusting. Those responsible will be called to account. But if there is a vast distance between the corporate headquarters and the sales floor, I'm not sure it's by accident. When bosses are out of touch with reality, sometimes it's because they like it that way. It's harder to exploit people when you have to look them in the face. Maybe the problem with Wal-Mart is not that the company is everywhere, but that, like one of those alien species in the old-time flying-saucer movies, it still hasn't fully decided to come down to Earth. I like to think of these people as visitors from another planet—the Wal-Martians from Wal-Mars—who have yet to learn the biological requirements for human life. We could ask them to go back home, and see how they respond to *that* message. Or we could thank them for their interest in our planet and species, and offer to show them around. Let's start, we could say, with this little thing called *rent*. . . .

THE RETURN OF "SEPARATE BUT EQUAL"
Richard D. Kahlenberg

"SEGREGATION TODAY, segregation tomorrow, segregation for-ever," George Wallace declared, to a thunderous ovation from a crowd of Alabamans who had gathered to see him sworn in as governor in 1963. More than forty years later, it is hard to imagine any group of Americans applauding those words. Yet the every-day reality lived by millions of schoolchildren is not too far from Wallace's defiant vision.

No longer segregated in name, the nation's schools are once again largely segregated in fact—by race and ethnicity, and, in-creasingly, by class. The new segregation enjoys the backing of a new Supreme Court. In 1954, William Rehnquist was a young Court clerk, and the author of a memo of opposition to the his-toric ruling—in *Brown v. Board of Education*—that made integra-tion the law of the land; Rehnquist went on to become chief justice for almost two decades. Thurgood Marshall, elevated to the Court after brilliantly arguing the *Brown* case for the plain-tiffs, was replaced by Clarence Thomas, who, like a number of his colleagues, seems to have no problem with school segregation, unless it is required by law.

In a series of early 1990s decisions, the Court ruled that desegregation plans were meant to be temporary, no matter how much de facto segregation remained. Across the country, school districts from Buffalo, New York, to Charlotte, North Carolina, were released from court orders, and the mighty process that was to be executed with "all deliberate speed" ground to a halt. Even voluntary integration efforts have been found unconstitutional where they used race in deciding which students would attend which school.

With the law in retreat, geography takes command. "Housing policy is school policy," former Albuquerque mayor David Rusk succinctly observes. In some places, geography has helped bring black and white students together, with schools becoming more integrated as neighborhoods do. But while America in general has become less segregated by race, the trend has been less pronounced among families with children. White families in particular have decamped to farther-flung suburbs and exurbs; by contrast, the whites moving in the opposite direction tend to be singles and couples without children.

Racially, the nation's schools became substantially less segregated in the three decades following *Brown*. Since the early 1980s, though, some of the gains have been lost. More than 70 percent of black children now attend mostly minority schools, up from 63 percent in the 1980–81 school year, according to the Harvard Civil Rights Project. The educational experience of Latinos, now the largest minority group in the United States, is even more isolating: about 76 percent of them attend mostly minority schools.

Rusk, who has studied these patterns as closely as anyone, foresees increased economic school segregation in all but six states by 2025.

Economically, segregation has increased in housing and schools alike. Two-thirds of the nation's public-school students are middle-class (as defined by their ineligibility for subsidized lunches). Nevertheless, one-quarter of the schools have a majority of students from low-income households. Poor people of color are especially likely to wind up in schools filled with others like them. That's because while low-income whites often live in middle-class neighborhoods, low-income blacks and Latinos rarely do.

Brown was the culmination of two decades of strategizing and litigating. From the early 1930s to the late 1940s, the NAACP Legal Defense and Education Fund gathered a mountain of evidence of the harm done to black children in the segregated schools of the South. Separation by race was highly insulting and damaging in itself; in addition, the NAACP legal team showed, black schools were getting the short end of the stick materially, financially, and every other way.

Since the early 1990s, lawyers representing parents in poorly funded school districts across the land have been engaged in a similar quest. In forty states and counting, they have called on the courts to outlaw the funding mechanisms (generally based on local property taxes) that cause poorer schools to be saddled with larger class sizes, less qualified teachers drawing lower salaries, and inferior and insufficient equipment and supplies. The equity campaigners point out that although low-income students need considerably more spent on their education than middle-class students do, the balance, nationally, goes the other way: affluent districts, on average, spend a cost-adjusted $7,731 per pupil, compared to $6,383 in high-poverty districts—a difference of $1,348. In some places, the gap is even more striking: Illinois, Minnesota, and New York, for example, all spend at least $2,000 more per student in the wealthiest areas.

The aim of the new litigation, like that of the lawsuits that led to *Brown*, has been to move resources, not children. But while the dollar comparisons help dramatize the problem, they do not define it. Like their forebears of half a century ago, the equity campaigners have found, in their pursuit of resources, that resources are not enough. To put it another way, classmates are a resource, too—in fact, a more crucial one than books, pencils, and laptops.

Although the *Brown* decision focused on race, America learned through its implementation that class was the crucial variable. In places like Boston, where desegregation mingled working-class whites and working-class blacks, achievement gains were insignificant. But in communities where low-income blacks attended school with more affluent whites— Hartford, Wilmington, Charlotte, St. Louis, Nashville, Louisville, and others—African American achievement did rise. This was the lesson of the seminal report authored by the sociologist James Coleman in 1966: the beneficial effect of a student body with a high proportion of white students, Coleman found, came not from their race but from their stronger educational preparation and higher educational aspirations. Subsequent experience has confirmed Coleman time and again. The fact that poor kids of all races do better in a middle-class environment is, according to Harvard's Gary Orfield, "one of the most consistent findings in research on education."

Classmates provide "a hidden curriculum," as the psychiatrist Charles Pinderhughes put it. "What the pupils are learning from one another," he explained, "is probably just as important as what they are learning from the teachers." While students of all economic backgrounds add value to schools, more-affluent classmates bring more academic knowledge, which they share with others every day, on the playground as well as in the classroom. A middle-class child has a vocabulary that is, on average, four times as big as a low-income child's, and words are infectious. On the other hand, a fourth-grade child who attends a poor urban school is likely to be surrounded by peers who "can't read [or] understand a simple children's book," according to a 1998 *Education Week* analysis. Middle-class students are far less likely to act out or engage in disruptive behavior, because their life experience has given them reason to believe that education will pay off.

Yet from the right, the left, and the center, America's thinking about education has taken on a strangely pre-*Brown* quality. There exists today a solid consensus among researchers that school segregation perpetuates failure, and an equally durable consensus among politicians and policymakers that nothing much can be done about it. The equity campaigners avoid the subject, regardless of their personal convictions. Others, whether they call for more resources, more choice, or higher standards—the three great school-reform mantras of the age—are also trying to make "separate but equal" work in the face of overwhelming evidence that it does not.

The past twenty years have seen an explosion of educational policy debate, in which the conservative message has rung very loud. While liberals, loosely speaking, tend to emphasize equity and resources, conservatives have rallied behind the concept of "choice," by which they generally mean the ability of parents to transfer children from public to private schools, taking tax money with them. Talk of choice—the kind that involves vouchers, charter schools, and privatization—is everywhere.

Meanwhile, with far less notice, a handful of cities and metropolitan areas have been trying out a different form of choice—one that operates inside the world of public schools and points explicitly toward economic integration. The results are worthy of far more attention than they have received.

During the 1990s, Wake County, North Carolina, instituted a magnet-school-based racial-integration program. In response to a U.S. Fourth Circuit Court decision striking down the use of race in student assignment in Virginia and Maryland, the Wake County School Board voted in January 2000 to drop a set of explicit racial goals in favor of a system that seeks to balance student populations by socioeconomic status and student achievement. While Wake County's racial and economic integration efforts have not erased achievement gaps between economic and racial groups, integration appears to have improved the achievement of low-income and minority students. Nearly 90 percent of students performed at or above grade level on a recent set of state tests. Wake County's system has been far more successful than that of neighboring Durham, where city schools remain poverty-concentrated and are considered low-performing. La Crosse, Wisconsin, which has the nation's longest-running economic school-integration plan, has also seen rising test scores and a low dropout rate.

Despite innumerable experiments and extensive research designed to identify the keys to educational success, no other variable can compare in importance to the economic-class composition of the student body. Peers are teachers in their own right, and economic integration, in addition to its direct benefits, helps drive a variety of other school improvements. If life were fair, the best-qualified teachers would be found in the most disadvantaged schools. In real life, the best teachers are drawn to the schools with the highest socioeconomic levels. Teachers in middle-class schools are more likely to teach in their field of expertise, more likely to have higher teacher test scores, and more likely to be experienced. Their expectations are higher. The curricula they use are richer and more demanding.

Teacher quality can have a profound effect on student achievement. Recognizing that fact, some jurisdictions have used bonuses to lure talented teachers to high-poverty schools. Not very many teachers have taken the bait, though, because of all the difficulties associated with teaching in such schools. It may well be that the *only* way for large numbers of low-income students to have consistent access to high-quality teachers is to bring them into majority middle-class schools.

When parents volunteer in the classroom and participate in school activities, student achievement improves. For example, a 1996 study using National Educational Longitudinal Study data reports that "a child's academic achievement did not depend so much on whether his or her own parents participated, but on the average level of participation of all parents at the school." And socioeconomic status has been found to be the "primary predictor" of parental involvement. Low-income parents often don't have the flexibility to take time off from work, and they are more likely to feel intimidated by educators, which makes them reluctant to get involved in school activities to begin with. Middle-class parents are four times more likely to join PTAs. They have the political savvy and pull to demand high standards and adequate resources, and the wherewithal to supplement public funds with private donations.

Schools with a core of middle-class families are marked by higher expectations, higher-quality teachers, more-motivated students, more financial resources, and greater parental involvement. In short, virtually all of the conditions that educators identify as markers of good schools are more likely to be found in middle-class than in high-poverty schools.

Conservatives often use the language of equity to justify their call for choice. The wealthy, they note, can always get their children into high-quality schools; they do so either by purchasing a home in an area with top-ranked public schools or by sending their children to private school. With unexpected egalitarian passion, the champions of vouchers and educational privatization argue that poor families should have the same right. (Of course, this represents an enormous shift from the days of racial desegregation, when conservatives stood as the defenders of the "neighborhood school" above all else. Now they are the first to point out that a neighborhood school may not be such a great deal for children stuck in a poor neighborhood.)

That emphasis is largely tactical, however. The choice crusaders know that their best chance to make headway is by forming alliances with minority parents and launching programs that make special provision for the poorest of the poor. Give them a chance to speak their minds, however, and few define their hopes so narrowly. What they are after is unlimited choice for all. No matter how these plans are promoted or constructed, in any case, experience shows that the poorest families are the least likely to take advantage of them. In any population given the liberty to choose, it is the comparatively well off who will do so; everyone else will stick with the neighborhood school. Thus the conservative brand of choice leaves schools more segregated than ever.

That is also a danger of the model of reform (associated with the Bush administration's No Child Left Behind Act) that stresses testing and accountability. No Child Left Behind was promoted in the name of equity, as a way to rescue poor children from the "soft bigotry" of social promotion and low expectations. Through rigorous testing and accountability, schools in disadvantaged neighborhoods would be forced to live up to the same standards as other schools, reducing the achievement gaps among students of differing races and incomes. In return for federal funding, states would be required to test students in reading and math for grades 3–8. If a school failed to make mandated "adequate yearly progress" for a period of consecutive years, the students in that school would be free to transfer to higher-performing schools and gain access to supplemental educational services such as private tutoring. If a school missed the mark for four consecutive years, the district would be forced to take corrective action, which could include adopting a new curriculum or replacing staff.

No Child Left Behind was passed with broad bipartisan support because, on paper, it was about resources and equity as well as testing. The Bush administration promised that if a failed school went on failing, not only would parents be empowered to move their children elsewhere, but, in the most dire cases, the school itself would be overhauled. But very few student transfers have occurred. And very few schools have been overhauled. Thus, in practice, the law has largely boiled down to a program of testing and publicizing test scores—practices that can unintentionally accelerate segregation. Parents look at the scores when they decide which school districts to live in. Since the scores reflect the socioeconomic status of a district's families rather than the value that schools are adding, people with options may increasingly gravitate toward the most affluent districts.

Even without making allowances for No Child Left Behind or the adoption of vouchers, American schools are becoming more segregated. The overwhelming weight of evidence suggests that this will be bad for kids, and bad for the ideal of equal opportunity. In some high-poverty schools today, the dropout rate—which nationally has plummeted—exceeds two-thirds. Among families in the lowest 20 percent by household income, children are more than six times as likely to drop out of high school as children from families in the highest 20 percent. Few students graduating from high-poverty inner-city high schools go on to college: nationally, the figure is just 15 percent. Among high school graduates in 1996, 78 percent of high-income students but only 49 percent of their low-income cohort enrolled in college the following fall.

Education reformers have a habit of railing against "the system." In truth, America does not have an education system. It has, to oversimplify slightly, one system for middle-class students, which is working fairly well, and one for low-income and minority students, which is working very badly. Minority twelfth-graders read at about the same level as more affluent and white eighth-graders. Students in well-off suburban jurisdictions such as Naperville, Illinois, and Montgomery County, Maryland, score near the top in international math and science exams, while students in low-income, urban districts such as Chicago and Rochester, New York, test at the level of students in developing countries such as Iran.

Although the United States may have less progressive public policies than other Western industrialized countries when it comes to housing, welfare, and health care, American schools have historically been more egalitarian. Indeed, America's high tolerance for unequal outcomes rests partly on faith in the public schools as a source of equal opportunity. The *Brown* decision represented an important national acknowledgment of the degree to which the reality fell short of the ideal. *Brown* opened the door to meaningful progress in educational experience, and, perhaps just as important, to a deeper understanding of what was needed. Race was not the answer. But integration was. Today's school reformers seem determined to forget that lesson. While they talk endlessly about fixing failed schools and doing right by the victims, they preside over a set of arrangements that make American education, far too often, an instrument of inequality rather than an answer to it.

THE SNOWBALL AND THE TREADMILL
Meizhu Lui

MY INTEREST IN ECONOMIC INEQUALITY goes back to 1974, when the problem came up and hit me on the side of the head. I was living in Fall River, Massachusetts, a suddenly single mother who needed a job in a city that didn't have many to offer. After pounding the pavement for a few months, I found myself face-to-face with the manager of a Dunkin' Donuts. "You Chinese are good workers, aren't you?" he said to me, like the spider to the fly. And I said, "Ah so, velly good," which tells you how desperate I was.

But that's when the lightbulb went off in my head. Suddenly, I understood my place in the economic hierarchy: as an Asian, I would be expected to work harder, for less pay, than the white "counter girls" beside me. As a woman, I would not even be in the running for the higher-paying job of doughnut mixer, because that was a male preserve. (It was hard for us not to wonder: What sort of special doughnut-making equipment could it be that men have, and women don't have. . . ?)

Six months into the job, the cash register came up $24 short. Four of us had been on duty, and the manager's solution was to dock us $6 each. That clinched it for me. I did some research, found out he had broken the law, and took him to the labor board, winning my $6 back. Beyond the $6, I gained the satisfaction of knowing I had disabused at least one male executive of the belief that women—Asian women in particular—were ripe for exploitation.

I didn't just get angry, I got even, and that made me realize how American I had become. My dad, who started out as a research biochemist at the University of Michigan during World War II, saw white men pass him by in salary and rank year after year. He thought he had stepped onto the escalator to success but found himself stuck on the mezzanine. He did not fight back. Pay, status, career—these things were unimportant, he told us, because the Chinese were culturally superior; we had two thousand years of civilization to fall back on. That argument didn't cut it with me. I was born in America. I wanted my equality in the here and now.

My Dunkin' Donuts experience taught me that life in the United States operates according to rules that are made by people. My path to justice had been paved by trade unionists and working women and men bucking the odds to organize and secure rights not just for themselves but for generations of workers to come—unionized and nonunionized. (My favorite bumper sticker is one that says: "The labor movement—the people who brought you the weekend.") I was also a beneficiary of the civil rights movement and the antidiscrimination legislation that it produced. Eventually, a group of female Dunkin' Donuts employees filed a class-action suit and gained the right to be doughnut mixers as well as sellers.

Unfortunately, the quest for equality in America has lost momentum in recent decades. In 2005, white America had a per capita income of $28,946. Asians stood next, with a per capita income of $26,421; then blacks, with $16,629, followed by Latinos, with $14,483. (Per capita income reveals more than household income because some subpopulations, including Asians, have more members per household.) To be sure, many individual members of these groups have done well. But overall racial economic equality remains a distant prospect. In 1968, the year of Martin Luther King's assassination, African Americans earned, on average, 55¢ for every $1 of white income. By 2005, they were getting 58¢ on the white man's dollar—a gain of 3¢. If things keep on going at that pace, blacks can expect to reach parity in another 437 years!

In one sense, the burden borne by people of color has grown heavier: their problems are no longer widely seen as a problem for America as a whole. In the late 1950s and 1960s, white racism was often in the news, a story reinforced by vivid images of bombings and beatings and children being taunted and cursed on the way to school. After the victories of the civil rights movement, it became easy to think of racial discrimination as a thing of the past. People began to shift the blame: they told themselves that if minorities hadn't caught up despite affirmative action and the other advantages they had been handed, it must be their own fault—maybe they just don't have what it takes.

This great shift in national attitude did not happen by chance. Over the past thirty years, a well-funded and well-orchestrated effort to roll back the gains of the labor and civil rights movements has turned public opinion around 180 degrees. Rob Stein, an independent Washington researcher, has followed the money flow. Since the early 1970s, he estimates, at least $2.5 billion in funding has gone to the forty-three major activist organizations that represent the core of the right-wing political machine. We're talking about an enormous investment, and the payback extends beyond legislation and executive orders into the realm of everyday thinking. In the 1960s, Americans regarded poverty as a national shame, and society was seen as having a responsibility to do something about it. Now poverty is an individual shame, and it is your personal responsibility to do something about it. Even the Clinton administration called its welfare reform proposal the Personal Responsibility Act. It might just as well have been called the Social Irresponsibility Act.

In marketing their view of the world, the pundits and policy wonks of the radical right have both exploited and aggravated fears to do with race. Although whites have always been a majority of the poor in America, the poverty debate has focused relentlessly on African Americans, Latinos, and immigrants from the developing world, who are routinely portrayed as freeloaders. The slurs have left their mark. Many Americans will tell you, for example, that immigrants lack the skills for any but the most menial jobs. In fact, immigrants are often overqualified for the jobs we allow them to do. As an organizer for a group called Health Care for All Massachusetts, I worked with immigrants from around the world. One of them, Habib Herzi, was an eye surgeon trained in Italy. He spoke four languages. Because of the civil war in Somalia, Dr. Habib had landed in a refugee camp in Kenya before making his way to the United States. In our globalized economy, corporations can go abroad, present their credentials, and set up shop without much difficulty. Skilled workers often can't. Dr. Habib's credentials did not transfer. He finally found a job as a community health outreach worker at close to the minimum wage.

Immigrants and people of color don't just earn less; they own less. Much less. The typical white family had a net worth (including homes and cars) of $121,000 in 2001; the net worth of the typical black household was $19,000. To put it another way, while white median family income was almost one-third more than black income, whites had more than *eleven times* the wealth of blacks. Nearly one out of every three black families, moreover, had zero or negative wealth—that is, nothing at all to fall back on. The comparable figure for whites was 13 percent. Four out of five African American families and three out of four Latino families had savings that would run out in three months or less; that was true of only 38 percent of white families.

Why this yawning chasm in wealth? If income is a snapshot, wealth is a movie. Wealth is what's left over after daily expenses are met. It's what allows economic security to be passed down from generation to generation, and wealth itself is shaped by the advantages and disadvantages that accrue to individuals and groups of people over many years.

In the United States, wealth and whiteness go way back together. One of the many things that Europeans brought to this continent was the concept of land as private wealth. Among Native Americans, land was regarded as something that could not be owned, any more than the water or the sky could be. From the mid-1700s to the late 1800s, white settlers and soldiers waged a series of brutal wars that reduced the Native populations to a small fraction of their original numbers and confined most of the survivors to areas deemed to have little value as real estate. As the

Native Americans were defeated, the land they had once used freely was expropriated by whites: the Homestead Act of 1862 was a massive transfer of land wealth from Native to white hands.

One of the first official uses of the word *white* can be found in the Naturalization Act of 1790, which reserved citizenship for white immigrants. At the time, it was far from obvious who fit the description. Asian immigrants were especially puzzled: what color were they? Since their adopted country had made its preferences clear, one Asian nationality after another went into court claiming the right to be white. Immigrants from India won some of their early cases because they were classified as belonging, like Europeans, to the Caucasian race. It was not until the 1920s that the Supreme Court firmly decided their place in the hierarchy, ruling that though Indians might be Caucasian, they were still not "white" in terms of "common understanding." In other words, reckless eyeballing became the way whiteness was defined by our highest court.

The Chinese never even got that far. My family came to the United States in the 1840s, for the same basic reason as the Irish immigrants of the day: famine at home, jobs and riches across the ocean. If it had not been for the Naturalization Act of 1790, Chinese Americans might be close to Irish Americans in numbers, social status, wealth, and political power.

African Americans were at a unique disadvantage in the competition for wealth: they *were* wealth, tallied up in the same financial ledgers as horses and farm implements. The French and British, interestingly, had two different transatlantic shipment strategies for their slaves: the French packed them loosely, in order to minimize the number of deaths en route, while the

British crammed in as many slaves as a ship would hold, tolerating a larger number of deaths in the hope of arriving with a higher absolute number of survivors. But neither country's merchants viewed the slaves as anything but a commercial commodity; they had simply reached different conclusions about how to achieve the best business result.

At the time of the Civil War, there was frank discussion of the link between wealth and freedom. Because you cannot be free if you own nothing, some people argued, true emancipation would have to involve something more than a change of legal status. That was the thinking that led General William T. Sherman, as he marched through Georgia, to issue his legendary "forty acres and a mule" edict. For a few years, the Freedmen's Bureau continued to give out parcels of land, as Sherman had done; but after the war, in a political sellout, the bureau was closed down, and much of the property in black hands was cheated away or forcibly taken back by former Confederates.

The asset story of Latinos was shaped by "manifest destiny"—America's assertion of a divine right to expand from sea to shining sea. After provoking and winning a war with Mexico in 1848, the United States seized not only Texas, the territory supposedly in dispute, but also the lands now known as Arizona, New Mexico, Utah, Nevada, California, and western Colorado. Mexico was reduced to half its former size in the process. While the Treaty of Guadalupe Hidalgo theoretically allowed individual Mexicans to retain their land holdings, many were never informed of that detail. In practice, most of their property was finagled away through legal transactions and documents executed in a language they could not read.

The landmark social legislation of the twentieth century was race neutral on its face but contained a secret color code between the lines. Social Security is often cited as the model of a universal program, establishing a financial cushion for all. In fact, the framers of the act were careful to omit the two occupations in which African Americans and Latinos were most heavily concentrated: domestic and agricultural work. The GI Bill is remembered for opening the doors to higher education and homeownership, and helping create the great postwar middle class. In complexion, though, the postwar middle class wasn't so different from the prewar middle class—and that, too, was built into the legislative design. The housing and education benefits of the bill were theoretically available to all veterans, and some returning soldiers of color were, in fact, able to use them. But many others were excluded: to attend a college, they discovered, you had to be accepted by one. The few black colleges were inundated with applicants. The great majority of American colleges either excluded people of color altogether or admitted a symbolic handful, and the GI Bill did nothing to alter that. Nor did it tell banks and realtors to end the discriminatory lending practices that kept many blacks from buying homes.

An enormous heritage of rules, laws, and practices—many long since eliminated—continues to shape the economic conditions of Americans today. Like snowballs rolling down a hill, many of the families and communities of white America have been gathering wealth from generation to generation. Disadvantages also accumulate. People of color, lacking inheritances that enable them to go to college or buy a home, are stuck on an intergenerational economic treadmill, constantly struggling to make ends meet.

Homeownership patterns tell you a lot about the distribution of wealth. Between 1989 and 2003 the rate of homeownership rose across the demographic spectrum, and in fact rose faster for groups with lower homeownership rates to begin with. While the white homeownership rate increased 2.7 percent (from 69.4 to 72.1 percent), African American homeownership increased 5.3 percent (from 42.9 to 48.1 percent), and Latino homeownership 6.4 percent (from 40.3 to 46.7 percent). Still, even with a slower growth rate, more than 75 percent of whites owned homes in 2003; fewer than 60 percent of Asians and Native Americans and fewer than 50 percent of African American and Latinos did.

One explanation for these gaping disparities is continued discrimination by the financial services and real estate industries. In the Boston area, Nancy McArdle of the Harvard Civil Rights Project found in 2004 that high-income African Americans were more likely than low-income whites to be steered toward so-called subprime loans, which charge higher interest rates and mortgage costs. Loan sharks and predatory lenders also tend to swim in low-income communities of color, where they cheat unwary homeowners out of their hard-earned homes. (These practices produce an unusual amount of homeownership "churning," which the aggregate statistics do not reveal.)

Housing wealth depends partly on whether a family owns a home, and partly on how much the home is worth. In 2000 (the most recent year for which we have data), the median home value for white households was $123,400; for African Americans, it was $80,600; for Latinos, $105,600. To be sure, incomes are lower, on average, in neighborhoods of color, but that fact accounts for only some of the difference in home value. Regardless of income, if you live in a white community, the value of your house will tend to go up; if you live in a community that becomes majority black, the value of your house will tend to go down. One big reason is that most whites do not want to live in black neighborhoods. With the housing marketplace largely limited to black buyers, lack of competition drives prices down.

Almost without trying, a great many middle- and upper-middle-class American families have made killings in the real-estate market. The trick, UCLA sociologist Walter Allen explains, was to pay something like $23,000 in the 1950s or 1960s for a home that is worth $1 million or more today. But, as Allen notes, "Blacks weren't allowed to buy those $23,000 houses." Even with all this disparity, homeownership, sadly, is the realm of wealth in which people of color have made the greatest strides.

In *The Hidden Cost of Being African-American,* Brandeis University sociologist Thomas Shapiro looks at black and white families with comparable incomes and finds enormous economic differences driven by wealth. Black families, according to Shapiro, are much more likely to be carrying a heavy load of college debt and to have no significant inheritance or retirement income, and much less likely to own stock. While young white Americans often have parents who can pay their college tuition or give them a down payment on a house, African Americans in the same age range are frequently called on to provide financial support for elderly parents.

An optimist might conclude that despite the continuing white advantages, America has at least dismantled some of the most important barriers and stopped creating new ones. But that, too, is a delusion. Today's government policies continue to widen the wealth gap. The current Bush administration, for example, has given money back to those who own stock, in the form of a tax reduction on dividend income. In 2001, 25 percent of whites owned stock, compared to 11 percent of people of color. Moreover, the mean value of white stock holdings was $51,932; for blacks, it was $3,940; for Latinos, only $3,243. Tax policy thus enables already wealthier whites to pull even farther ahead.

The role of wealth is not simply to fill in for those times when the income stream is interrupted, although it comes in mighty handy when you're faced with a layoff or a health emergency. Wealth can also be used to generate new income, to leverage more dollars, and to give your children a head start. It serves this function not only for the rich but also for individuals and families with more modest assets, when they invest in college tuition or in a car to drive to work, start a small business, or contribute to a retirement fund. "Lack of income means you don't get by," Ray Boshara of the New American Foundation likes to say. "Lack of assets means you don't get ahead."

What's to be done? America needs government-funded asset-building programs on the scale of the GI Bill. We need tax incentives that will allow the poor to accumulate wealth. And to build support for initiatives of this kind, the myth of the "self-made" man or woman badly needs to be debunked. Throughout our history, the government has been a powerful force in the creation of individual wealth. If it takes a village to raise a child, it just as surely takes one to raise a billionaire. When we call on government to reduce the inequality of wealth, then, we are asking government to address a problem that it helped bring about. We can be confident, moreover, that by making the rules fairer we will end up with a better economy and a stronger democracy.

The racial economic gap and the role of government in creating that gap were on the mind of Martin Luther King when he addressed the March on Washington in 1963. "When the architects of our republic wrote the magnificent words of the Constitution and the Declaration of Independence, they were signing a promissory note to which every American was to fall heir," King declared. "The note was a promise that all men would be guaranteed the inalienable rights of life, liberty, and the pursuit of happiness." America, he went on, "has defaulted on this promissory note insofar as her citizens of color are concerned. Instead of honoring this sacred obligation, America has given the Negro people a bad check which has come back marked 'insufficient funds.' But we refuse to believe that the bank of justice is bankrupt. We refuse to believe that there are insufficient funds in the great vaults of opportunity of this nation."

That speech is widely remembered for the lines in which King evoked a vision of true equality. America has dubbed it the "I Have a Dream" speech; but in the process, we have taken the sting out of King's message, giving us a version of his story that fits nicely with any number of Hollywood movies about the triumph of faith, dedication, and, indeed, "personal responsibility." King did not go to Washington to tell America about a dream. He was talking about social responsibility first and foremost. He was there to cash a promissory note—to ask for the money that it would take to bring Americans of color up to the starting line. Half a century later, his plea remains unanswered.

SHREDDING THE RETIREMENT CONTRACT
David A. Smith and Heather McGhee

ONE OF AMERICA'S PROUDEST ACHIEVEMENTS during the second half of the twentieth century was a steady reduction in poverty among older citizens. Since the end of the Second World War, each retiring cohort has done better than the previous one, culminating in the "golden years" retirees of the Greatest Generation. Altogether, the poverty rate for people over the age of sixty-five declined from 35 percent in 1959 to just over 10 percent in 2003. This remarkable success story was the result of a three-legged system of retirement security, involving individuals, government, and private employers. But as our country heads into the twenty-first century, the system has begun to come undone.

Social Security "reform" is not the problem—not yet. For all the consternation surrounding the Bush administration's proposals, they remain (as we write in the spring of 2005) a speculative concern. In fact, government's contribution to the retirement contract has, up to now, remained strong: 40 percent of the elderly were kept out of poverty in 1999 by Social Security, and almost 50 percent of their medical bills were paid by Medicare (government's other main role in the retirement equation). Nor have retirees been badly damaged, in the aggregate, by our much-maligned lack of personal savings, since savings have never amounted to much for the median U.S. household. If savings are a more important factor than they used to be, it's only because they are now needed to replace what is already, for many retirees and prospective retirees, the missing piece of the retirement puzzle: a private pension with a guaranteed payout. Between the 1940s and the 1980s, these "defined-benefit" pensions, as they were known, became a standard part of worker compensation for millions of middle-income American workers. Today, less than half of households nearing retirement include someone earning a traditional, employer-provided defined-benefit pension—down from almost two-thirds in 1983. The decline is even more pronounced among younger workers.

Defined-benefit pensions have been replaced by an array of retirement devices—401(k)s, IRAs, Keoghs, and the like—that rely on worker contributions and individual stock market choices, rather than on employer contributions and pooled investments. The Employee Benefit Research Institute estimates that so-called defined-contributions plans are now utilized by 40 percent of American households. Workers' contributions and participation continue to grow with the transition from defined-benefit plans, yet there is little reason to believe that these accounts will reach levels allowing average households to replace the income that their forebears received from the employer-provided pensions. In 2002, the average 401(k) balance was a little more than $33,000, and the share of households making the maximum allowed contribution was only 6 percent.

All of this makes the current proposals to weaken and individuate the strongest remaining segment of the retirement contract, Social Security, particularly troubling. Social Security currently provides 90 percent or more of total income to over one-third of all elderly households. These are the seniors who have not benefited from employer pensions, and who were unable to save sufficiently from modest earnings during their working lives. As pension coverage continues to decline and the economy puts more pressure on household balance sheets, retirees' reliance on Social Security will only grow.

It is becoming increasingly apparent that Americans' future retirement years—if they have them—are poised to mirror the anxiety, insecurity, and inequality of their working lives. It should come as little surprise, given the nation's growing wealth inequality (documented by Heather Boushey and Christian Weller elsewhere in this volume) that a greater reliance on the individual's retirement contribution will create more income inequality among elderly households in the decades to come. Important work by the economist Edward Wolff explores this phenomenon. Wolff tells us that while average household wealth soared by 44 percent for older households between 1983 and 2001, so much of that growth was concentrated among the very richest households that at the median, wealth actually fell during that period. Unequal savings translate directly into unequal retirement incomes. That inequality will no longer be buffered by pension income for most households. The median value of defined-contribution accounts for households in the middle of the income distribution is only $5,000, and only $20,000 for those closest to retirement—a troublingly insufficient replacement for the traditional pension.

There are reasons why the defined-benefit pension, with its guarantee of security, has been incompatible with the inequality economy of the last twenty-five years. Defined-benefit pension coverage peaked in the early 1980s and quickly fell with deindustrialization in that decade. At the same time, there was a drastic reduction in the share of the economy made up by unionized firms. Without a voice at work, employees could count on little security from their employers in the here and now, much less in retirement. The quickly expanding service sector that took the place of manufacturing for the working class was for the most part without unions, family-supporting wages, tenure tracks, employer-paid benefits, or job security.

Such industrial changes made it impossible to broadly deliver benefits through the increasingly tenuous employment relationship. Nevertheless, it is crucial to recognize that the result—forty-six million uninsured by 2005, retirement insecurity on the rise—was not inevitable. There was also a political failure to recognize that America's unique hybrid system of public-private benefit delivery would fail the majority of workers in the new economy. The social contours of this political failure must also be taken into account. Compared to industrial manufacturing, the newly dominant service sector is made up of more people who are underrepresented in our political hierarchy: women, immigrants, young families, and people of color.

Changes in family formation are often blamed for the rising inequality of the past quarter century. More out-of-wedlock births, late childbearing, divorces, and more individuals living alone in the baby boom generation, the logic goes, have moved us away from the most successful household model. That successful model—two parents, one breadwinner—was, after all, the norm for the golden retirees of the previous generation. But the family-formation understanding of inequality serves to normalize a problem while denying its political dynamic. The previous generation's retirement security was hard-won, through collectively bargained defined-benefit pensions and the legislative triumphs of Social Security and Medicare. The typical household entered retirement with a degree of financial security afforded not intrinsically by a family model of single breadwinner, but socially, by a political environment and policies that supported such a model. Today's society, on the other hand, systematically fails to support contemporary families, instead throwing roadblocks in their path to secure retirement.

American workers are now essentially required to fund their own retirement out of household wealth. Those resources, while never abundant in the past, have been further reduced by rising costs for the new essentials of family life: child care, education, housing, and health care. The toll on the savings of the typical family nearing retirement today has been acute, as data from the Survey of Consumer Finances reveals. An important yet often overlooked starting point for this analysis is everyday household savings. Since managed investment vehicles have never been equitably distributed among households, bank accounts where average families can or can't afford to put money aside from each paycheck are a critical measure. The percentage of households headed by a fifty-five- to sixty-four-year-old (those nearing retirement) holding transaction accounts—checking, savings, and money market—has stayed high and steady at over 80 percent since 1983. In 1983, the typical preretiree household had $17,750 at its disposal in such accounts (in 2001 dollars). By 2001, that number had dropped significantly, to only $5,500. A step up on the savings ladder, interest-bearing savings bonds and certificates of deposit (CDs), shows a decline among preretirees as well. The median dollar amount declined less sharply (from $23,115 in 1983 to $21,500 in 2001), but far fewer preretiree households now hold these safe assets—from 30 percent to 15 percent for CDs and from 21 percent to 14 percent for savings bonds.

Is the story that today's families, perhaps less risk-averse than previous generations, are forgoing the security of everyday and low-interest savings for bigger returns from the stock market? While median stock and bond values held by this age cohort nearly tripled between 1983 and 2001, the wealth gain failed to reach much more of the preretiree population. The share of fifty-five- to sixty-four-year-olds holding these assets grew exactly one percentage point—from 5 to 6 percent for bonds, and from 25 to 26 percent for stocks—in nearly three decades. Among the general population, stock ownership is extremely concentrated, with the richest 1 percent of stockholders owning 37 percent of all shares of stock and the richest 5 percent holding 65 percent. Mutual funds are now held by 21 percent of fifty-five- to sixty-four-year-old households, up from less than 5 percent in 1983. The median value of mutual funds, like individual stocks and bonds, has risen for those who hold them—from $31,117 in 1983 to $60,000 in 2001. (It should be noted that these figures were collected in May–December 2001, before large stock losses and the revelation of widespread accounting fraud in mutual funds.) The fifth of preretiree households with mutual funds have made up for the lost share in more secure savings vehicles. But with a base of only $20,000 in median defined-contribution pension wealth, their savings are being called on to do much more for retirement than their predecessors'.

Why aren't Americans saving? The same economic and political changes that have made personal savings more important than ever to retirement security have made it harder for the average worker to save. Simply put, in order to save money, families must have stable incomes that are higher than their costs. That scenario has now become the exception, not the rule. Stagnant or declining real incomes for the bottom 60 percent of the income distribution have dogged the working years of families nearing retirement now. Meanwhile, high job-displacement rates and the growth in contingent labor have meant less regular paychecks for millions of workers. In any three-year period over the last two decades, 8 to 12 percent of workers suffered at least one job loss. More frequent unemployment has become longer and meaner, too. By the most conservative measure, between 1976 and 1998, the amount of time unemployed workers could expect to be without work rose by 17 percent, or the equivalent of two weeks. And losing a job now sentences workers to lower wages (average wage loss of 14 percent) and fewer benefits (nearly one out of three moves to a job entirely devoid of health benefits).

Unemployment benefits have failed to modernize to reflect the new modes of work. At the end of the 1975 recession, three-quarters of the nation's unemployed workers received benefits; by 2001, that number had declined to less than half. At just $262 a week, the average unemployment insurance benefit leaves families to cope with job loss by draining savings—if they have them—or by going into debt. Among families with children, 72 percent of bankruptcies are now precipitated by a loss of employment.

A failure to restructure economic supports for the new family model, which includes working women, has resulted in families spending more of their volatile incomes on basic needs. As Elizabeth Warren and Amelia Tyagi Warren calculate, the average two-income, two-child family today makes 75 percent more in inflation–adjusted dollars, but has less money to spend than one-income families did thirty years ago. They spend 21 percent less on clothing, 22 percent less on food, and 44 percent less on appliances compared to one-income families a generation ago. But they spend 69 percent more in inflation-adjusted dollars on their home mortgage and 61 percent more on health insurance. They spend nearly $10,000—almost a quarter of their after-tax income—annually on child care, a new and necessary expense. Seventy-five percent of boomer women are employed, and nine million households are headed by single women with children. Yet the economic priorities of working women and their families—health coverage, community development, child care, and education—have not become public policy priorities in America as they have in other nations.

Perhaps no other measurement more dramatically reflects the damage wrought by the inequality economy on family economic security than debt. Revolving consumer debt, which includes outstanding balances on credit cards, has increased by an astounding 1,101 percent since 1983, to over $800 billion. In this time, pricing regulations on consumer credit have been eviscerated, dramatically altering the availability, marketing, and cost of credit. Abundant and expensive credit has come along at a time when the three most substantial costs for working families—housing, child care, and health care—have all grown because of disinvestment from employers and the public sector. Credit cards, payday loans, home equity loans, and jumbo mortgages have become a private safety net—but one that ensnares millions of families with mounting interest and fees, rather than stabilizing them financially. The dramatic rise in household debt has a direct effect on the ability of families to save. In 1981, the average family saved 11 percent of income and held 4 percent in credit card debt. In 2000, the average family held 12 percent of income in credit card debt and saved –1 percent.

Not surprisingly, the same survey that recorded the drop in personal savings among preretirees from 1983 to 2001 reveals a startling rise in indebtedness. In constant dollars, the typical preretiree household's outstanding mortgage debt more than doubled, from $21,515 in 1983 to $55,000 in 2001. Outstanding consumer debt, which includes credit card, installment, and other consumer loans, rose from an average of $3,022 to $36,400 in 2001. These debts are carrying over into retirement for millions of families, and senior citizens are now the fastest-growing age group in the bankruptcy courts. Demos's *Retiring in the Red* reveals that average balances among seniors over sixty-five shot up by 149 percent between 1989 and 2001. On fixed incomes, debt service is an increasing burden: one out of every five middle- to low-income seniors is now in a state of debt hardship, spending over 40¢ of every dollar in income on debt payments.

How has the government responded to the savings crisis? Government policies should compensate for workplace inequalities to ensure a common good, and yet the tax code is failing to serve the average citizen when it comes to retirement savings. While our national savings rate has bottomed out, the federal budget carves out $335 billion a year to "encourage savings" through tax-advantaged investment vehicles and incentives. The federal government now spends more money on tax breaks for savings than Americans actually save. The Bush administration raised the limits on these tax breaks in 2001, providing an even greater advantage to the well-off who make up the mere 6 percent of savers who contribute the maximum to their 401(k)-type plans. If encouraging more Americans to save (as opposed to enabling a few Americans to save more) were the true policy goal of the government's $335 billion annual expenditure, tax incentives would be credits, refundable for the average worker. For previous generations, pensions acted as a social leveler by rewarding lifetime investments of work, not wealth, with security in retirement. As these pensions have disappeared, workers are being required to buy into a complex system of tax shelters that have the effect of rewarding existing wealth with more wealth.

Unlike in every other developed economy, Americans must now provide for their retirement during their working years. The mechanisms that were designed to help them do that have been sharply compromised in recent decades, giving rise to two troubling possibilities—no retirement at all, or growing inequality among the retired. As we have argued above, changes in workplace provision of secure retirement benefits, combined with two decades of wage stagnation for most households, have made the Social Security leg of the retirement stool even more important. Yet some would reduce Social Security benefits and replace them with yet another scheme that depends on individual contributions. We believe that providing more of what does not work well and reducing the strongest part of our retirement mechanism is exactly backward. Social Security's long-run stability can be secured with a few modest changes. For instance, removing the current cap on taxable wages could, depending on phase-in and design details, close all or most of the seventy-five-year actuarial deficit now foreseen by Social Security's trustees. Importantly, this could be accomplished without compromising current income replacement rates or the system's progressive benefit structure.

But even a fully secured Social Security system would not make up for the growing gap in retirement income that looms. We must develop an additional universal mechanism that responds to the continuing decline in the availability of defined-benefit pensions. Even with a sharp increase in union membership, it is unlikely that these benefits will ever return to the levels reached in the early 1980s. It is even less likely that the defined-contribution plans that have been offered as a replacement can ever fill the void. A new retirement benefit should be portable, require an employer contribution, and use public funds—perhaps using resources from the repeal of the recent tax cuts—to make additional contributions on behalf of lower-income workers. Current fiscal policies make large public contributions unlikely in the short run, but there is no reason not to begin with required employer and means-tested employee contributions.

Much of the problem we have recounted has its roots in stagnant incomes and reduced supports for working families. Retirement income must be earned during a worker's years on the job—otherwise there can be no retirement at all. Elsewhere in this book our colleagues recount the increasing burdens that working families face to pay for education, housing, and the child care required by many in an economy where the two-worker household is the norm. As those costs have risen—and public and employer support to help meet them has diminished or failed to appear—incomes have not. Not surprisingly, American families have been forced to reduce today's savings—or tomorrow's retirement wealth—to try to make ends meet. Stronger unions and an increase in the minimum wage would be a good place to start, but we also need widely available and affordable child care and a return to the broad support for higher-education costs promised by the Higher Education Act of 1965. Filling those gaps would help today's families to save more.

These three steps—a secure Social Security system, new universal retirement savings mechanisms, and making work pay—are necessary if we are to avoid turning the retirement clock back to the America of the first half of the twentieth century, when over a third of all elderly households lived below the poverty line.

THE GROWING COLLEGE GAP
Tamara Draut

"THE FIRST IN HER FAMILY to graduate from college." How many times have we heard that phrase, or one like it, used to describe a successful American with a modest background? In today's United States, a four-year degree has become the all-but-official ticket to middle-class security. But if your parents don't have much money or higher education in their own right, the road to college—and beyond—looks increasingly treacherous. Despite a sharp increase in the proportion of high school graduates going on to some form of postsecondary education, socioeconomic status continues to exert a powerful influence on college admission and completion; in fact, gaps in enrollment by class and race, after declining in the 1960s and 1970s, are once again as wide as they were thirty years ago, and getting wider, even as college has become far more crucial to lifetime fortunes.

Since the seventies, income differences between workers with high school diplomas and those with bachelor's degrees have grown steadily. A young person with some college can now expect to earn, on average, about $1.5 million over the course of a lifetime; an associate-degree holder will make slightly more: $1.6 million. By contrast, a young adult with a bachelor's degree can look forward to average lifetime earnings of $2.1 million— roughly a one-third advantage over those who don't finish college, and a twofold advantage over those who never get past high school. The wage premium goes up further for holders of advanced and professional degrees. A master's degree yields about $2.5 million; a professional degree (the kind associated with lawyers and doctors) is worth about $4.4 million.

Dollars tell only part of the story. Back in the seventies, a professional with a college degree and a blue-collar worker with a high school degree could live in the same community, own similar cars, eat at the same restaurants, and send their kids to a good public school. But as the incomes of high school and college grads have diverged, so too has their quality of life. The college-haves and college-have-nots increasingly live in separate worlds, largely defined by enormous differences in earning power.

About 70 percent of today's high school graduates attend college. But that impressive-sounding figure glides over the increasingly hierarchical structure of American higher education. African American, Latino, and lower-income students are more likely to be enrolled in two-year community-college programs, while wealthier students are battling it out for seats at a handful of elite private institutions. The increasing demand by employers for graduate degrees is perpetuating further class inequality in a spiraling credential craze.

The paradox facing young adults today is meeting the demand for more credentials in a context of declining financial-aid support and skyrocketing tuition. The more diplomas you earn, the better your chances of getting into the middle class and staying there. Unfortunately, as the postindustrial transition gained steam and the college-haves took a greater and greater share of the spoils, elected officials began changing the focus of financial aid in ways that would perpetuate inequities in access to higher education. Over the last two decades, this country has steadily retreated from both the spirit and the policies that did so much to open doors of opportunity during the long postwar expansion.

In 1944, Congress passed the GI Bill, which was intended to provide millions of returning veterans with the education, skills, and money to readjust successfully to civilian life. The GI Bill offered grants to help cover the cost of tuition, books, and health insurance. It included a monthly stipend for living expenses. Over its seven years, the legislation cost the government about $91 billion in today's dollars. About 8 million veterans took advantage of its various provisions; 2.3 million attended colleges and universities. By 1960, half the members of Congress had gone to college on the GI Bill.

A generation after the GI Bill, Congress enacted the Higher Education Act of 1965 (HEA), which established the system of college grants and student loans on which today's system is largely based. While the GI Bill had focused on veterans, the HEA was meant to ensure access to college for all. Upon signing the bill, President Lyndon Johnson summarized its key goals: "The Higher Education Act of 1965 means that a high school senior anywhere in this great land of ours can apply to any college or any university in any of the 50 states and not be turned away because his family is poor."

As a result of this landmark legislation, the number of low-income students in American colleges and universities nearly doubled between 1965 and 1971. In 1972, grant aid was further expanded through the creation of Pell Grants. Throughout the seventies, low-income students continued to close the enrollment gap between them and their wealthier classmates. Unfortunately, progress has stalled since the late 1970s.

During the 1980s, as the haves were quickly pulling away from the have-nots, our nation began a steady and prolonged retreat from the goal of making college affordable. Grant aid declined on a per student basis, loan aid outpaced grant aid, and need-based aid fell out of fashion as more states and institutions started giving away financial aid dollars based on grades or test scores. In the 1990s, President Bill Clinton further exacerbated the shift away from need-based aid at the federal level. The HOPE Scholarship and Lifetime Learning tax credits initiated during the Clinton administration now account for about 8 percent of federal financial aid. Despite claims that the tax credits would help families pay for college, they've done little to stem the tide of student borrowing, which has risen steadily. In addition, the benefits of the HOPE credit overwhelmingly go to middle- and upper-income individuals. And in the new century, states have consistently slashed their support for state and community colleges as a way to deal with their budget deficits—ushering in rapidly rising tuition costs.

The federal aid system has failed to address two major trends in higher education: more students going to college and rising tuition costs. Tuition has more than doubled since 1980 in inflation-adjusted dollars, rising much faster than the average family's income. In the 2003 school year alone, the price rose as much as 24 percent at some state schools. While the federal government is spending more than ever before on student aid, over $70 billion to be exact, funding has not kept pace with enrollments or tuition prices. That means that aid is spread more thinly across a greater number of students.

The anemia of the federal financial aid program becomes clear when we examine the purchasing power of the Pell Grant, our country's primary way of making college affordable for low-income students. In 1976–1977, Pell Grants covered 72 percent of the average price of a four-year college. Today, the average Pell Grant covers 34 percent of the costs at a four-year college. In order for the maximum Pell award to cover the same share of costs at a public four-year institution as it did in 1977, it would have to rise from $3,750 to around $7,000.

It wasn't only federal policy changes that contributed to the affordability crisis hitting families today. Over the last decade, both state governments and colleges themselves have shifted their aid dollars toward merit-based awards, rather than need-based. This shift happened rather quickly and it coincided with rising enrollments and rising tuition costs. Between 1991 and 2001, spending by the states on need-based scholarships for undergraduates increased 7.7 percent annually, while spending on merit programs increased by 18.3 percent annually. The proportion of state grants awarded based on merit, rather than need, rose from 11 percent to 24 percent during this period.

When student aid is focused on merit rather than need, it tends to go to students from families who can already afford college tuition. A merit award typically doesn't change behavior—these students would have gone to college without the scholarship. The same can't be said for need-based aid. The availability of grant aid has a big influence on whether lower-income students will enroll in college at all.

Given the extraordinary shift in financial aid, it's not surprising that college-enrollment gaps between poor and wealthy students are as high as they were three decades ago. The difference in college enrollment rates among white, black, and Hispanic students has actually widened over the last thirty years: in 2000, the enrollment gap between white and black students was 11 percentage points, up from only 5 percentage points in 1972. The enrollment gap between white and Hispanic students was 13 percentage points in 2000, up from a 5 percentage-point gap in 1972.

As grant aid has dwindled and tuitions at public colleges have skyrocketed, students from low- and moderate-income households often find that even after grant and loan aid, they're thousands of dollars short of the money needed to pay for college. According to the Advisory Committee on Student Financial Assistance—a body that was created in 1986 by Congress to advise on student aid—in 2001 alone, unmet need forced 410,000 *college-qualified* students from households with incomes less than $50,000 to enroll in community college instead of going to a four-year college or university. Another 168,000 *college-qualified* students don't enroll in any college at all. Unmet need has forced low- and moderate-income students to abandon the most successful recipe for obtaining a college degree: full-time on-campus study.

As a result of declining federal aid and increased demand for postsecondary education, enrollments at community colleges have soared. Today, community colleges enroll 44 percent of all undergraduates attending colleges. For many young adults, community colleges are their only choice for postsecondary education, either because they're not academically prepared for university-level study or because they're seeking specific skills training. But increasingly, students who can't afford the cost of a four-year college are turning to community colleges. Forty percent of young adults report that they either delayed going to school or went to a less expensive school because of student loans. Nearly six out of ten African American and Hispanic college students, and four out of ten white students, report that they would have chosen a different school if money were not an issue.

The inequity in college choice that is driven by dwindling grant aid and soaring tuition costs means many young people aren't receiving the amount of education they desire or could accomplish. Of all college entrants, half of low-income students attend community colleges, compared to just one in ten high-income students. As the cost of four-year colleges has risen, more students are choosing to start down the bachelor's degree path at a community college. The research is mixed on the success of this strategy. Only about 40 percent of community college students who enroll with the intention of transferring end up doing so, according to one study. Other studies find that bachelor's-seeking students who enroll in community colleges with the intention of transferring to a four-year college are much less likely to earn their degree. One of the main reasons why persistence may be lower at community colleges is that unlike students at four-year colleges, eighteen- to twenty-two-year-olds at community colleges are more likely to work full-time and attend school on a part-time basis. Even among students who enroll in community college specifically to get an associate's degree, many don't complete their schooling. Five years after entering community college, only about one in five students who enrolled with the intention of getting an associate's degree had accomplished that goal. In the struggle between doing classwork and paid work, it is usually the classwork that ends up being dropped.

For low-income students who are able to attend four-year colleges, the likelihood of them dropping out is much higher. Students from low-income families complete degrees at a much lower rate than their wealthy counterparts: within five years of entering college, 40 percent of students from the top socioeconomic quartile will earn a four-year degree, compared to only 6 percent of students from the lowest quartile.

The inequity in higher education isn't limited to disparities by race and class in who goes to four-year colleges and who goes to community colleges. At the undergraduate level, there is now an enormous quality gap too. Nearly three-quarters of students at the nation's top 146 colleges come from families in the top quarter of the socioeconomic status (SES) scale. Only 3 percent are from the lowest SES quartile, and only 10 percent are culled from the entire bottom half of the SES distribution. These 146 colleges represent the top two tiers in *Barron's Profiles of American Colleges 2005,* constituting the most selective 10 percent of the 1,400 four-year institutions in the nation. There is actually greater underrepresentation on these elite college campuses by class than there is by race, though blacks and Hispanics are still underrepresented. Black and Hispanic students make up only 6 percent of the freshman classes at these selective institutions, even though they make up 15 percent and 13 percent, respectively, of the eighteen-year-old population.

The benefits of attending the nation's best are multiple. Students in selective colleges are more likely to graduate and more likely to get into top-notch graduate schools. There is also a wage premium enjoyed by graduates of top schools, though its magnitude is not as significant as many believe. The same study finds, however, that students from lower SES backgrounds gain more of a wage premium than their higher SES counterparts from attending elite colleges. Why would the gain be greater for students from lower-income backgrounds? It's likely because attending an elite college gives these students access to a social and professional network that they otherwise wouldn't have access to.

The class cleavage that has developed at the country's best colleges has been facilitated by fierce competition among undergraduate colleges to compete for the best students. Over the last decade, middle-class and first-generation students have struggled to afford a decent education from public universities. But as they've been borrowing and working their way through public colleges, their upper-income counterparts have been engaged in a battle of a whole different nature. They are competing for slots at the nation's most elite schools, fearing that getting into anything less than a name-brand school will result in a life of mediocrity, or complete failure. Fueling this race to the top is a profound sense of the reality that being one of the "winners" today is the only sure way to the good life. As the spoils of our economy are increasingly spread among only a small group of top performers, getting into the winner's circle from the outset is imperative. And there is a burgeoning, profitable industry of tutors and consultants at the ready to help students boost test scores, sharpen essays, and nail an interview.

Run-of-the-mill prep courses from places like Kaplan or the *Princeton Review* cost $800, with individual tutoring available for $1,900 to $4,199, depending on the number of hours. Test preparers are just some among the cadre of professionals for hire to help students get into the best schools. An admissions consultant typically charges about $150 an hour or offers packages that may run from $1,500 to $3,000. These consultants help students find the right college for their abilities and aspirations; they coach them on interviews with admission officers; and they can help add sparkle and shine to a lackluster college essay. There are still other ways to boost a high school résumé and beef up a college application. There are intellectual boot camps that allow high school students to take college courses and get a feel for the campus environment. Getting a sneak peak at the college experience doesn't come cheap; these trial runs cost from $4,000 to $6,000.

There are also special tours that allow students to tour different campuses with a group of other ambitious students. One package includes all the tony East Coast schools—Georgetown, Columbia, Yale, Harvard, and others—for just over $2,000. With airfare and meals factored in, the total cost could exceed $3,000.

While the news media make it seem as if test preparation and consultants have become ubiquitous, the reality is that the high cost of these services makes them out of reach of the average family. According to the trade association for professional education consultants, only 6 percent of high school graduates get help from professionals. But that's up from 1 percent in 1990. Compare that to the amount of free college guidance offered at public high schools, which is essentially zero. The average high school guidance counselor has a caseload of nearly five hundred students a year.

The vast and growing disparities in who gets into college and completes bachelor's degrees is becoming even more troubling as four years of college are increasingly viewed as only the first rung on the credential ladder. In many ways, a bachelor's degree has become equivalent to what a high school degree used to be: the bare minimum for competing in the economy. As a result, a master's degree is becoming the new bachelor's degree. The growing demand for advanced degrees is being fueled by a credential craze among America's professional class. Occupations that used to require only bachelor's degrees have steadily been upgrading their educational requirements. To get to the management level in any business field now requires an MBA. Even social workers, librarians, and teachers are expected to earn a master's degree. The demand for advanced degrees began growing in the late 1970s as the society transitioned from an industrialized to a knowledge-based economy. And not coincidentally, over the same period the economy was becoming a winner-take-all system in which the rewards were increasingly concentrated at the top among CEOs, shareholders, and top executives. Judith Glazer, a scholar who studies trends in higher education, points to several related factors behind the proliferation of advanced degrees: individuals wanting job advancement and mobility, a demand from employers for more highly trained practitioners, and an eagerness in many professions to enhance their status by upgrading the degree requirement for entry to the occupation. This credential craze stands in stark contrast to the purpose and pursuit of advanced degrees a generation ago. Prior to the mid-1970s, most master's degrees were in nonprofessional fields, stressing theory over practice. The motivation for graduate study wasn't a better job or better money, but pure intellectual pursuit. Not anymore. Today about 85 percent of all master's degrees are practice-oriented, as opposed to theoretical. Business and education are the major dominators in the master's degree craze, with each representing about 25 percent of all advanced degrees.

The demand for graduate degrees is generating more inequality in access to higher education. The number of students earning graduate degrees rose 58 percent between 1986 and 1999, to just under 500,000, but the number of bachelor's degrees rose by only 25 percent, to just over 1.2 million. Just as the rich have gotten richer over the last two decades, the well-educated have gotten supereducated.

Even though graduate enrollments are growing among women and students of color, holders of advanced degrees are still a very select group. Numerous studies have found that among students who wish to pursue an advanced degree, those with high levels of undergraduate debt are less likely to pursue additional study. College students who graduate with debt are more likely to have parents without college degrees, come from low-income backgrounds, or be students of color. The surging demand for advanced degrees by employers has put many first-generation holders of bachelors degrees at a disadvantage.

The current inequities in access to higher education will become even more acute as the largest generation since the baby boomers begins to age out of high school. The traditional college-age population is projected to grow by 16 percent between 2000 and 2015. This generation will be more ethnically diverse, better prepared for college, and more likely to have financial need for college. By 2015, 43 percent of the college-age population will be nonwhite, with students from low-income families representing an increasing proportion of high school students.

Without major new efforts by the federal and state governments and our nation's colleges to widen access to higher education, a new social inequality will emerge. We'll have a well-educated minority that is mostly white, and a swelling, undereducated majority that is mostly African American and Latino. As the college-age population grows swiftly, our nation's financial aid system will leave millions of college-ready students without the means to fulfill their dreams. The Advisory Committee on Student Financial Assistance projects that if current enrollment trends persist, over the next decade 4.4 million students from households with incomes below $50,000 will not attend a four-year college, and 2 million students will not attend college at all. And those are conservative estimates. Who knows how many scientists, nurses, teachers, and doctors we will lose as a result?

The loss to both individuals and society is just too large to allow such social cleavages to develop.

COLD TRUTHS ABOUT CLASS, RACE, AND HEALTH

David R. Williams and James Lardner

SUPPOSE YOU WERE PLAYING A GAME of word association, and someone said "health." If you answered "doctor" or "medicine" or "hospital," you would be thinking the way most Americans think. It is the way we have been taught to think. The job of the health reporter on TV, after all, is to cover the latest miracle drug or surgical procedure. A government agency with *health* in its name is one that sets the rules or pays the bills for medical treatment. In the world of charitable organizations, *health* generally means the search for a cure to a dreaded disease.

Medicine has worked wonders in the past two centuries. But medicine has not been the driving force in the progress of human health. Most of the gains in overcoming illness and extending life, researchers largely agree, can be traced to improvements in hygiene and nutrition and rising standards of living, not to health care per se. During the 1853–54 cholera epidemic in London, John Snow drew a map of cholera cases and noticed a cluster around a water pump on Broad Street. By removing the pump handle, he controlled the outbreak—three decades before Robert

Koch discovered the bacterium that causes that disease. In Britain overall, the death rate from tuberculosis fell from four thousand per million in 1828 to four hundred per million in 1948, which is roughly when streptomycin and other treatments began to be applied on a wide scale. In the United States as well, the use of vaccinations, drugs, and surgical remedies typically came decades after a marked decrease in mortality from the conditions they were designed to address.

"It is one of the great and sobering truths of our profession that modern health care probably has less impact on the population than economic status, education, housing, nutrition and sanitation," Theodore Cooper, assistant secretary for health while Gerald Ford was president, observed in 1976. "The notion of high-quality medicine as the answer to illness," Cooper said, is "a fiction, a hoax."

Sadly, there is no better proof of this than the health record of the United States itself. In 2001 we had a higher per capita gross domestic product than any other country except Luxembourg, and devoted the highest proportion of our GDP to health care—13.9 percent, or nearly $4,900 per person. Our closest competitor, Switzerland, spent only 68 percent of that. The 293 million people who call themselves Americans now account for roughly half the money that goes for doctors, drugs, and other health expenses on a planet of nearly 6.4 billion human inhabitants. Line up the nations in order of longevity or infant mortality, however, and the United States does not even make the top twenty. The places we trail, in addition to the usual suspects—Sweden, Norway, Switzerland, and Canada—include Greece, Hong Kong, and Martinique.

No country spends more money on health, or more time talking about it. Yet, you could listen to the media coverage or the political debate for hundreds of hours on end, and remain blissfully
unaware of the gulfs between the United States and other developed nations—or, for that matter, between one U.S. population
group and another.

Part of the reason we don't get the same results as other countries is the steeply skewed distribution of our health care dollars
by class and race or ethnicity. In 2000, the World Health Organization rated the performance of the United States health care system thirty-seventh among all nations, largely because of these
inequalities. Even if everyone had access to needed health care,
however, that would allow for a better response to the consequences of disease, but it would have little effect on the conditions that make people sick in the first place. Class and race, and
their influence on the way we live, would remain powerful deter-
minants of health.

The relationship between class, or socioeconomic status, and
health has been the subject of an enormous amount of research
in the last decade. In 1996, George Davey-Smith and his colleagues reviewed mortality rates (annual deaths from all causes
per 1,000, 10,000, or 100,000 persons) for American men. Deaths
for those in the lowest income category, they found, were nearly
twice as high as they were for those with the highest incomes.
With almost every step up the economic ladder, Davey-Smith de-
tected a corresponding improvement in health. In fact, low-
income adults turn out to experience illnesses in their thirties
and forties that are not commonly seen in others before sixty-five
or seventy-five. Americans who haven't graduated from high

school have an overall mortality rate two or three times that of college graduates.

Class and race are inextricably linked: racial and ethnic minorities tend to have greater health problems than whites in part because, proportionally, more of them are poor or near poor. But race also has its own effect on health, above and beyond that of class. On average, white Americans live 5.5 years longer than black Americans do. Blacks die from stroke 41 percent more often than whites; from heart disease, 30 percent more often; from cancer, 25 percent more often. Asians, Pacific Islanders, and Hispanics all have lower heart disease rates than whites.

During the 1980s federal government researchers came up with a new way to measure these disparities: "excess deaths." Those are deaths that would not have occurred if a minority population's mortality rate had been the same as the white population's. By that standard, there were sixty-six thousand excess deaths of African Americans in 1940, and roughly one hundred thousand in 1999. That's the equivalent of one plane crash—with no survivors—occurring every day of the year.

It is important to note that we are discussing a span of years in which the health of all major population groups improved. But despite overall reductions in deaths from most causes, there is evidence that socioeconomic disparities in death rates have increased since 1960. Nor have most racial disparities narrowed in that time, and in some areas, notably infant mortality, they, too, have widened. In 1950 a black infant was 1.6 times more likely to die before his or her first birthday than a white infant. In 2002 a black infant was 2.4 times more likely to die before his or her first birthday. The same pattern—of black-white ratios that are larger today than they were in the 1950s—holds for overall mortality, heart disease, and cancer.

This summary record masks short-term shifts with interesting historical parallels. For example, the Council of Economic Advisers documented economic gains for blacks relative to whites during the 1960s and early 1970s, during and after the civil rights movement and the advent of expansionist government programs. Between 1968 and 1978, health indicators for blacks improved relative to whites. Economic progress stalled in the mid-1970s, and by the 1980s, health improvements for blacks also slowed.

While the press has largely ignored the issue of health disparities, sociologists, epidemiologists, public health experts, and demographers have been hunting for an explanation. In fact, the puzzle has begun to resemble one of those Agatha Christie–type whodunits in which the cloud of guilt keeps shifting from one suspect to another.

SUSPECT NO. 1: HEREDITY AND BIOLOGY

When race enters the picture, can a genetic explanation be far behind? Between groups of people who look different, could there be differences in physical characteristics that predispose them to the diseases they suffer more frequently? It seems logical, but the research tells a very different story. For example, rates of hypertension among people of West African ancestry vary sharply, depending on where they live. Blacks in West Africa are not especially prone to hypertension. (In fact, whites in the United States have higher blood pressure, on average, than West African blacks.) Hypertension levels were highest among blacks in the United States and intermediate among three black Caribbean groups.

High blood pressure is only one of a number of health conditions that tend to develop in the second or third generation of immigrant populations, but are rarely found among immigrants themselves. In Latinos, the problems that follow this pattern— their frequency increasing with the length of stay in the United States—include infant mortality and low birth weight.

Genetics obviously can't explain this. In fact, genetics can't explain much of anything to do with race, which is a socially constructed rather than a biologically based concept to begin with. The fact that you and I know what race we belong to tells us more about the society we live in than about our physical makeup. Some white people are more similar genetically to black people than they are to other white people. Race is truly a pigment of our imagination.

SUSPECT NO. 2: ACCESS TO CARE

People without health insurance are far less likely to seek care, and less likely to get it if they seek it. About forty-five million Americans, or nearly 18 percent of the nonelderly population, were uninsured in 2003—up from forty million in 2000. Most of the increase is due to erosion of employer-based insurance, which covered sixty-six million people in 2000 and sixty-two million in 2003. Of the uninsured, twenty-six million were full-time workers and 56 percent of those were poor or near poor. The lower you go down the income ladder, the higher the rate of uninsurance. In 2003, 36 percent of those under the poverty line and another 30 percent of those with less than double a poverty level of income had no coverage. While the uninsurance rate for whites was 13 percent, the rate for Asians was 20 percent; for blacks, it was 21 percent; and for Latinos, 34 percent.

Because poor people and people of color are more likely to lack insurance, they are also more likely to lack regular care. That, in turn, means that health problems often go undetected when they would be most amenable to successful treatment. Children may be especially vulnerable to these effects: among poor children under age six, 21 percent of those without insurance lack a regular source of care, compared with only 4 percent of those with insurance.

But insurance isn't the only determinant of access. Some communities, particularly those in isolated rural areas and inner-city neighborhoods, have too few providers generally or too few who will care for low-income people with or without insurance. For these reasons, an estimated thirty-six million Americans lack access to a primary care provider. Proximity to transportation, hours of service (including evenings and weekends for those who work), waiting times, and availability of translation/interpretation also affect access. Perhaps the most blatant inequalities are found where residential segregation by both income and race fosters multiproblem areas with unsafe housing, low-performing schools, high crime, and an absence not just of health care but of other civic services. Health-status measures in such areas can be as poor as, or poorer than, those in Third World countries.

Even when the availability of care is removed from the equation, though, the link between socioeconomic status and health remains powerful. In fact, we owe much of our knowledge of this relationship to a body of research—the Whitehall Studies—in which health care was virtually a nonissue because the subjects all enjoyed access to Britain's no-questions-asked national health insurance. Since 1967, a team of researchers based at University College London has been engaged in a massive effort to track the health of more than eighteen thousand civil servants. Even among this fairly elite group—people with high job security, and the means to feed and house themselves decently—health outcomes turn out to follow income and rank closely.

SUSPECT NO. 3: QUALITY OF CARE

Obviously, not all health care is equal. In fact, in the United States today, it is shamefully unequal. At one extreme stand the emergency rooms and old-style outpatient clinics where patients wait on hard benches for hours to see a different provider each time they come, with little continuity or acknowledgment of barriers to communication, and a high chance of being used as "teaching material" for untrained students. At the other extreme are the new luxury wings of hospitals where the nurses and aides wear hotel livery, the latest films are shown, and gourmet meals are delivered. The differences are not just in ambience or bedside manner; lower-income patients may receive lower-quality treatment and die as a result. Imagine two car accidents, identical in all respects but one: Victim A has insurance, Victim B does not. Somewhere between the crash site and the intensive-care room, the health care system starts treating the two cases differently. The end result is a 37 percent better chance of survival for Victim A.

Here, too, class is compounded by race. Consciously in a few cases, unconsciously in many more, doctors and administrators make decisions that lead to substantially worse results for people of color. While African Americans suffer strokes as much as 35 percent more often than whites, they are less likely to receive major diagnostic and therapeutic interventions, be screened and treated for cardiac risk factors, given appropriate cardiac medications, or undergo bypass surgery. With or without insurance, minorities are less often screened for cancer (where they have a 30 percent higher death rate), placed on waiting lists for kidney transplants, or given state-of the-art treatment for HIV.

But as important as differences in quality of care are, they still don't explain all of the class or race differential in health status. So the search continues.

SUSPECT NO. 4: LIFESTYLE

If doctors aren't responsible, how about patients? To what extent can lower-income and minority people be said to bring their health troubles on themselves? In the 1970s, when Jimmy Carter was president, the government set forth an ambitious program known as Healthy People to establish goals and track improvements, with campaigns to promote healthy lifestyles as a major component. Commenting on the results of these efforts two decades later, the Department of Health and Human Services noted that "only the higher socioeconomic groups have achieved or are close to achieving the target, while lower socioeconomic groups lag further behind." This was true for major causes of death as well as for such behaviors as smoking and receipt of preventive care. You don't need a huge research grant to figure out that the people running laps in the park at dawn are more prosperous, on the whole, than the people eating French fries at McDonald's. In fact, America is well on the way to transforming obesity from a disease of affluence to a disease of poverty.

If low-income Americans are less healthy, maybe it's because they pay less attention to the proselytizing. But we might do better to ask why. Not surprisingly, the reasons tie back to socioeconomic status. If the U.S. Department of Agriculture dietary guidelines are tough for middle- or upper-class people who shop in supermarkets and specialty stores well stocked with produce and fresh meat and fish, and who have the time and money to plan their meals, how much harder must they be for people who live in neighborhoods where most of the commercially available food comes from fast-food restaurants and high-priced delis and convenience stores? Many of those same neighborhoods, and the people who live in them, have more liquor stores and more smoking and alcohol ads targeted at them. And how realistic is it to recommend sixty minutes of daily exercise to someone who comes home exhausted from working two low-wage jobs, who once home has to care for children or elderly relatives, and who has no safe place to walk or run because crime in her neighborhood is uncontrolled?

"When you have eliminated the impossible," Sherlock Holmes liked to say, "whatever remains, *however improbable,* must be the truth." If we can't blame the problem on heredity or insurance or doctors or ourselves, what is it about socioeconomic status itself that damages people's health? The British epidemiologist Richard Wilkinson (whose ideas are most recently articulated in *The Impact of Inequality: How to Make Sick Societies Healthier*) sees the problem as one of inequality translated into social structure—the sense of standing low on a tall ladder.

Among the developed nations, as Wilkinson points out, the least healthy tend to be the most unequal. Once a society achieves a basic threshold of prosperity, he argues, its overall health appears to depend less on national or per capita income than on the way income is apportioned. Thus, Greece, where GDP per capita is less than half that of the United States, outdoes us in longevity. By the same token, Costa Rica, a relatively egalitarian nation, has managed to achieve an average life expectancy of 77.3 years despite a per capita GDP less than a fifth of that in the United States.

Scholars have taken issue with some of Wilkinson's data, and, as he acknowledges, there are no global rules for collecting income and wealth statistics or measuring inequality. Since Wilkinson first advanced his theory, however, a number of other researchers have arrived at similar conclusions by different paths. Research teams in the United States have found correlations between inequality and health at the state and city levels. The 25 percent of metropolitan areas with the least income inequality have mortality rates significantly below the rates of the 25 percent with the greatest inequality. Inequality and poverty together, according to George Kaplan of the University of Michigan and his colleagues, appear to impose a statistical "burden of mortality" greater than that of lung cancer, AIDS, diabetes, suicide, homicide, and automobile accidents combined. While the reasons may be debatable, many health researchers see inequality as a source of stress, which can weaken arteries and immune systems, making people more vulnerable to all manner of sickness.

Some view Wilkinson's focus on inequality as a distraction from what they see as the clearer and less sensitive question of poverty. But the poverty-versus-inequality debate itself can draw attention away from a point on which both camps now agree: in today's America, the economic givens of early childhood are frighteningly good predictors not only of access to health care, but of lifelong health as well. Using the Green Line of Washington's Metro system to illustrate, the epidemiologist Michael Marmot points out that in a forty-five-minute ride from Southeast DC to suburban Maryland, you can cover a fifteen-year gap in life expectancy "between poor blacks at one end of the journey and rich whites at the other."

Poverty, low social status, racial/ethnic disparities, and economic inequality are the Axis of Evil of health in today's affluent societies. Because their influence is deeper and more powerful than medicine or biological science can fully comprehend, we must look beyond medicine and biology for answers. To reduce health disparities, we need to incorporate questions of economic and social policy into our conception of health policy. Spending more on health care overall is obviously not sufficient; we already spend more than other nations, and more each year than the year before. Reducing disparities in access to care and quality of care would be more to the point; but reducing economic inequality (by investing more in education, child development, and the improvement of living standards, working conditions, and neighborhood environments) might make more of a health difference than anything we can do within the health care arena itself. To put the proposition another way, as Americans learn to tolerate higher levels of economic inequality, we are not simply deciding to live with steep material differences. We are making our peace with the idea of large, and growing, gaps in health between economic winners and losers.

OF THE FEW, BY THE FEW, FOR THE FEW
Charles Lewis

IMAGINE A COUNTRY whose leader's brother commands multi-million-dollar fees for advising companies on technical matters about which, by his own admission, he has no knowledge. The leader's father, an ex-leader in his own right, earns money helping client companies land government contracts in a region where the country is at war. The leader's second-in-command used to head a company that is the largest recipient of those contracts. A chief political ally of the leader left government to do business in the war zone. There is no standardized voting system in place throughout the country, around half of its citizens never bother to vote, and the reelection rate for its legislature is well over 90 percent.

A cronyism-infested banana republic? A corrupt Middle East monarchy? Alas, we are talking about the United States of America under the presidency of George W. Bush—and about a set of underlying conditions that would be much the same if any other likely candidate held the office.

There is a one-word explanation for why America's political

class has become so small and insular, why our politicians are more interested in pleasing corporations than constituents, why some people can get a one-on-one breakfast with their senator while others are fortunate to get the senator's photo signed by an autopen. The word is *money*. The connections between concentrated wealth and the political process are now so well established as to seem almost natural. But they are, in their way, as great a threat to our democracy as war and terrorism.

The cost of running for office is higher today than it has ever been. In 2004 the average cost of winning a Senate seat was a little under $8 million. The average House seat cost just over $1 million. As stunning as those numbers are, they pale beside the expense of competing for the presidency. The Bush and Kerry campaigns together spent more than $650 million. Add in the expenditures of the other candidates, the parties, and the "527"s and other independent groups, and the total cost of the campaign came to well over $1 billion. It was by far the most expensive election in American history—indeed, in world history.

Some of the money that courses through our political system is used to register voters and get them to the polls. Some enables candidates and aides to meet the electorate and pay for mailings, Web sites, and office maintenance. There are dollar costs associated with developing a message—today the stuff not of passionate, articulate candidates but of consultants, pollsters, and focus groups. By far the greatest portion of all the money, however, goes into television advertising. The typical fifteen- or thirty-second sound bite may be useless as a means of conveying information of any substance. But as national and especially local news organizations devote a shrinking amount of time to covering political campaigns and issues, candidates find that the only way to get their names and proposals before voters is to buy their way onto TV.

Even before the first primary vote gets cast, and months before the first commercial is aired, money is how the political and media elites keep score. To be seen as a serious contender by the media and party leaders, a potential candidate has to demonstrate his "organizational" prowess by raising a respectable amount of cash—$30 million to $40 million for a would-be president. Political reporters who couldn't find the Federal Election Commission if their life depended on it spend months of the preprimary season reading FEC reports, not because they care about the insidious influence of those who buy access but only as a way of guessing who's ahead in the horse race.

This "wealth primary" is so crucial that, except for a handful of mega-millionaires who financed their own campaigns, the candidates raising the most money in the year before a presidential election have ultimately emerged as their parties' nominees in every presidential contest from 1976 through 2000. (Howard Dean, whose collapse in the 2004 primaries ended this streak, was an odd case in other ways: with little corporate support, Dean achieved his wealth-primary victory by using the Internet to galvanize more than 330,000 individual donors.) In Congress, incumbents spend their terms accumulating huge campaign "war chests" to scare off possible challengers. The fact that it is impossible for a candidate with no money to beat an incumbent, but impossible to raise money if you're not an incumbent, is the catch-22 that keeps the congressional reelection rate safely above 90 percent. Or as former senator and presidential candidate Bob

Dole put it, "You've got so much money in politics now that the incumbent almost has to fall out of a ten-story building with somebody else's wife to be defeated."

Where does all the money come from? Not from backyard barbecues and bake sales. At today's prices, only two kinds of people can run for federal office: millionaires and those able to tap the fortunes of millionaires. Some of the strongest candidates belong to both groups. In fact, 40 percent of U.S. senators are millionaires (one of them, Jon Corzine of New Jersey, spent over $60 million dollars for his seat), even though millionaires make up less than 1 percent of the total population.

For the most part, though, the money used to run political campaigns is drawn not from the pockets of candidates but from the bank accounts of wealthy contributors. America's political donors represent a tiny segment of America's population: by some estimates no more than 4 percent of Americans give any money at all to candidates at the federal, state, or local level. Those who give significant sums are an even smaller fraction: about 0.25 percent of Americans contributed $200 or more to congressional candidates in 2002. A check for the maximum an individual can contribute, now $2,000, comes from less than 0.1 percent. Not surprisingly, this political donor class is highly unrepresentative of the population as a whole. Only 12 percent of Americans earn more than $100,000 per year, but 95 percent of substantial political contributors come from this well-to-do segment. America's financial elite and its political elite are one and the same.

It is not only the amount of money that big contributors give but the brazen ways that they give it that raises skepticism about the nobleness of their intentions. For almost a century, corporations have been prohibited by law from contributing directly to candidates for federal office. However, executives, partners, and employees of corporations, often along with their spouses and children, have a tendency to all contribute the maximum individual amount permitted, all on the same day. You might think that corporations would strive to conceal the fact that they are dancing so close to the line of federal law; instead, they have established a system (called "bundling," in which checks are meticulously coded with "tracking numbers") designed to make sure that their efforts are recognized and remembered.

George W. Bush's greatest strength as a presidential candidate wasn't a bold policy vision or smooth communication, but fundraising. His 2000 campaign established a network of so-called Pioneers who each pledged in writing to raise at least $100,000 in bundled contributions. (In the 2004 race, the Pioneers were one-upped by a group of $200,000-pledging "Rangers.") But making big contributors feel appreciated has become a bipartisan enterprise: President Clinton infamously boarded some of his biggest donors in the Lincoln Bedroom. Ten-thousand-dollar-a-plate political fund-raisers are nearly nightly events on the Washington social calendar. The always-quotable Bob Dole describes the process candidly, and unflatteringly: "There's something about it that's so demeaning. To get on the phone and say, you know, 'This is Bob Dole—you know, the majority leader. And I know you've been thinking about my campaign, and I know you want to make a good contribution, don't you?' . . . But it's pretty obvious what you are doing. It's a shakedown."

The consequences of having a political system almost wholly

funded by America's wealthiest citizens are not hard to imagine. A special report by some of America's leading political scientists puts it dramatically but aptly: "Citizens with lower or moderate incomes speak with a whisper that is lost on the ears of inattentive government officials, while the advantaged roar with a clarity and consistency that policy-makers readily hear and routinely follow." This task force report cites numerous academic studies finding that the wealthy have much more influence on legislators' votes than do average constituents.

The scholarly research merely confirms what anyone who follows the connections between money and politics has long known: that contributors aren't simply public-spirited citizens wishing to enhance vigorous political debate, but are looking for more tangible rewards for their generosity. If they were seriously disappointed, the contributions would cease. "People don't just give money away for no reason," Harry Truman observed.

The 2004 presidential race offered several illuminating examples. Senator John Kerry asked the FCC to delay a spectrum auction, benefiting his brother's law firm, which represents the telecommunications industry and has given the senator more than $222,000. As a member of Congress, Richard Gephardt pushed to lower alcohol taxes five times over the years, much to the pleasure of his largest career patron, Anheuser-Busch, which gave him more than $517,000. Senator Joseph Lieberman, a beneficiary of hundreds of thousands of dollars in campaign contributions from biotechnology companies, hired the industry's top lobbyist for his staff and went on to introduce and co-sponsor bills on which this sector lobbied. Even Howard Dean, the self-styled insurgent running against the Washington establishment, had pushed as governor of Vermont for utility contract provisions that saved power companies millions of dollars—while costing Vermont families commensurate millions in higher rates. Vermont's largest energy provider also provided large contributions to Dean's political action committee.

On the other side of the ballot, the list of favors and benefits bestowed on President Bush's donors is long indeed. Before the Enron Corporation collapsed in a flurry of fraud and incompetence, it gave more to George W. Bush than to any other politician in America. In the first year of Bush's presidency, Vice President Cheney (then the chair of the administration's energy policy task force) or his aides met with Enron officials six times; one such meeting was followed by the insertion of a provision favorable to the company into the task force's final report. Today, Bush's top patrons include financial giants such as Morgan Stanley, Merrill Lynch, PricewaterhouseCoopers, MBNA, and other companies that stand to benefit from the president's push for cutting capital gains and dividend taxes, tightening the bankruptcy laws, and privatizing Social Security. Average Americans will see little benefit from these measures—in many cases they may be deeply harmed by them—but the president's big contributors stand to gain millions.

The contracting process in the rebuilding of postwar Iraq and Afghanistan offers still more examples of big favors to big donors. A subsidiary of Halliburton (Vice President Cheney's former company), Kellogg, Brown and Root, had been a generous campaign contributor over the years, particularly to Republicans: the company gave nearly $2.4 million in political contributions between 1990 and 2002, almost all of it to the GOP.

When the time came to hand out contracts for reconstruction in the Bush administration's two war zones, KBR wasn't forgotten: it has so far been awarded over $11 billion in government contracts, many of which were not competitively bid. The company is already the subject of numerous investigations, at least one with the possibility of criminal charges, for overcharging the government for services. Still, KBR is one of the world's largest and most experienced engineering and construction companies; even more appalling are the many cases in which companies with thin or no credentials landed major multimillion-dollar contracts. An Afghanistan contractor in Nebraska bluntly stated that efficiency and quality are secondary to politics in the contracting process: "It depends on who knows who in the Administration, USAID and the State Department."

The influence of big money is felt not only in the favors politicians grant and the things government does or considers doing, but also in the things it doesn't do and doesn't consider—in what's not on the table. The Internal Revenue Service calculates, for example, that up to $200 billion in taxes is evaded every year; nevertheless, politicians carefully bypass opportunities to crack down on tax evaders, especially those who have shifted their holdings to offshore tax havens. To understand the investigative reporter's motto—"Watch what they do, not what they say"—we have only to recall the speeches in which President Bush has called for the closing of the so-called Bermuda loophole, and then to note his steadfast refusal to support any of the bills that might actually accomplish that aim.

As David Cay Johnston documents elsewhere in this volume,

middle-class Americans are the ones left holding the bag for the massive taxes going unpaid by the well-to-do. That's because the middle class doesn't have so many friends in Washington.

But it is not just our wallets that are threatened by politicians looking out for the interests of their wealthy sponsors: our health and safety are imperiled as well. Nearly every month brings news of another widely prescribed drug being pulled from the market because of safety concerns, even as the FDA continues on its course of cutting testing and approval times for new drugs and allowing drug manufacturers to market their wares directly to consumers. The pharmaceutical industry has given more than $100 million to politicians since 1989. Regulations and legislation on food safety, gun safety, and airline safety (even after September 11) are all weaker because of the effectiveness of these industries' lobbying and contribution strategies.

As outrageous as these stories are—as clear a picture as they paint of our government's support of the wealthy and the powerful at the expense of average Americans—it is important to take a step back from the individual cases to consider the overall effect that this convergence of money and influence has on our democracy. The American Political Science Association Task Force cites sobering statistics regarding how unresponsive citizens believe government is to their concerns. Over the past several decades, Americans' trust that government will "do the right thing" has diminished drastically. More than three-quarters of Americans now agree that "the government is run by a few big interests looking out only for themselves," and two-thirds say that "public officials don't care about what people think." As our trust in government and in our democratic ability to influence government erodes, it is little wonder that voter turnout barely tops 50 percent.

For many Americans, unfortunately, this isn't cynicism, but realism. Even more unfortunately, it creates a vicious cycle: people don't participate in the process because politicians ignore their concerns, and politicians feel free to ignore their concerns because they don't participate in the process. The people who have been most fully abandoned by the political system are the very ones most in need of government protection: the economically disadvantaged. As the task force report also shows, affluent Americans are more likely than the poor to engage in the full range of political activity: voting, writing a representative, joining a political organization, working for a campaign—even protesting! With a political system as beholden to money as ours is, economic inequality leads inevitably to political inequality.

The path of reform is not easy to make out beneath the overgrowth. After a decade of prodigious effort, the McCain-Feingold Act—the most significant piece of campaign finance law since Watergate—was finally enacted in 2002. It was a very modest first step. While McCain-Feingold closed the "soft money" loophole that used to allow individuals to write seven-figure checks to political parties, direct contributions to candidates flow in faster than ever (with the limit now raised to $2,000 each). Much of the soft money that went to the parties is, in any case, now diverted to so-called 527s—independent or pseudo-independent organizations that are permitted to raise unlimited sums and spend it with few restrictions or scruples, as the 527-financed "Swift Boat Veterans for Truth" so memorably demonstrated.

The passage of McCain-Feingold set off a small panic among the influence peddlers and their clients. But it was short-lived. On the whole, the big-money interests have no great cause for concern. Politicians who enjoy 90-plus percent reelection rates have little incentive to change things—in fact, they have now mastered high-tech redistricting techniques to make their jobs even more secure. Wealthy individuals and corporations have little incentive to change things—they get what they want much more than they would in a truly representative democracy. Even the media have little incentive to change things—television stations benefit by selling all of the advertising that those big contributions pay for.

For more than two hundred years, the United States has been an ongoing experiment in democratic government, a system in which each person has a theoretically equal say in collective decisions, the workings of government are transparent for all to see, and the will of the majority prevails over narrow factional interests. Today we appear to be launching a new experiment—one in which access to power is rationed by money, politicians can choose to reveal only what will benefit them, and each industry and special interest sets its own rules. Such a system can be called many things, but democratic isn't one of them.

Part Two

DYNAMICS OF INEQUALITY

WHY DO SO MANY JOBS PAY SO BADLY?
Christopher Jencks

THE AMERICAN ECONOMY turned out $7.6 trillion worth of consumer goods and services in 2004—enough to provide every man, woman, and child with almost $26,000 worth of food, housing, transportation, medical care, and other things. If all that stuff had been divided equally, the typical household, which now has three members, would have gotten about $78,000 worth. Yet as an abundance of recent research confirms—and as all can plainly see—many Americans had to scrape by on far less than that. About one American worker in six reported having been paid less than $8 an hour in 2003. That works out to less than $17,000 a year even for someone employed full-time. And many low-wage workers earned far less than $17,000 because they were unemployed part of the year, worked fewer than forty hours a week, or earned under $8 an hour.

Some of those low-wage workers were teenagers who didn't have to pay most of their own expenses, much less support anyone else. For them, $8 an hour was a pretty good wage. But many of America's low-wage workers were single mothers trying to support a family. Others were married men whose wives stayed home with their children. These workers are eligible for the Earned Income Tax Credit, but most of them still find making ends meet a constant challenge. Most Americans think these workers deserve a better deal and tell pollsters that the minimum wage (currently $5.15 an hour) should be raised. But a market economy is not designed to ensure that workers get paid what other people think they deserve. The logic of a market economy is that we should all be paid the smallest amount that will ensure that our work gets done, and that is what low-wage workers generally receive.

American economists and business leaders have long argued that the best way to improve low-income families' standards of living is to make the economy more productive. At times economic growth truly has benefited almost everyone. When World War II dragged the United States out of the Great Depression, unskilled workers and their families gained proportionately more than most other Americans. Even after the war ended, the rich and the poor enjoyed roughly similar percentage gains in income until the early 1970s. So when John F. Kennedy said that "a rising tide lifts all boats," he was describing the experience of his generation. Since 1973, however, things have been very different. Productivity and national income have increased but wages have diverged.

Measuring changes in purchasing power is complicated and contentious, but the best historical measure is probably what the Commerce Department's Bureau of Economic Analysis calls the chain price index for personal consumption expenditure. Using this measure, the nation's output of consumer goods per worker rose 58 percent between 1973 and 2003. Yet if we use the same price index to measure the mean hourly earnings of nonsupervisory workers, we find that they rose only 6 percent.

Among men without any college education, real wages have actually fallen since 1973. Immigrants now do many of the jobs that native-born high school graduates would once have done, and this competition has driven down wages. As a result, male high school graduates and dropouts are having more trouble supporting a family. Meanwhile, more women have entered the labor force, and their tolerance for men who cannot pay the bills has diminished, especially if these men are also hard to live with, as they often are. Marriage rates have fallen, and divorce rates exceed 50 percent among couples with below-average earning power. More than half of all mothers without college degrees now spend some time as a single parent. Most married couples now feel that they need two breadwinners rather than one. Partly for that reason, the number of workers has grown more than the adult population while the number of children has grown less than the adult population.

The net result of all these changes is that while the economy grew dramatically between 1973 and 2004, most of the benefits went to those who needed them least: affluent, college-educated couples. The best trend data on household income now comes from the Congressional Budget Office (CBO), which pools data collected by the Census Bureau with data on similar individuals collected by the Internal Revenue Service. These figures, which are available from 1979 through 2000, allow the CBO to calculate households' total income, including capital gains and noncash benefits like food stamps, and also to subtract taxes. Mean household income rose 40 percent between 1979 and 2000. But in sharp contrast to the situation between 1940 and 1973, more than a third of the total increase since 1979 has gone to the richest 1 percent of all households, and another third has gone to the next richest 19 percent. That hasn't left much for the bottom 80 percent. While the incomes of the top 1 percent tripled between 1979 and 2000, the income of the median household rose only 15 percent, and the incomes of those in the bottom quintile rose only 9 percent. The gains at the bottom almost all came between 1994 and 2000.

The moral of this story seems clear: while economic growth is almost always a necessary condition for improving the lives of those in the bottom half of the income distribution, America's experience over the past generation shows that growth alone is not sufficient. So what makes the difference? Why are the benefits of growth sometimes widely shared and sometimes not? If you ask economists and business leaders why households in the bottom half of the distribution have benefited so little from economic growth since 1973, they tend to talk about impersonal forces like globalization, computers, and skill deficits. But if these explanations were sufficient, we would see the same pattern in every rich country, and we don't.

The Luxembourg Income Study (LIS) now provides roughly comparable measures of how household income is distributed in most wealthy democracies. Data on Britain, Canada, France, Germany, Sweden, and the United States is available back to the 1970s. Even then the United States was the most unequal of the six nations. Sweden was the most equal. But at that time, Canada, Britain, France, and Germany all looked more like the United

States than like Sweden. Since then the distribution of household income has grown substantially more unequal in both Britain and the United States, while hardly changing at all in Canada, France, Germany, or Sweden. The LIS has data going back to the 1980s on a number of other rich democracies. This body of evidence also tells a mixed story. Household income inequality increased somewhat in Australia, Austria, Belgium, Finland, and Norway, but it has hardly changed in Denmark, Ireland, or the Netherlands. Today the United States is by far the most unequal rich democracy in the world.

Impersonal forces like globalization, computerization, and skill deficits are not promising explanations for these differences. Most of the countries with stable income distributions are even more dependent than the United States on the global economy. Computer use and sales spread faster in the United States than in most other countries, but by the end of the 1990s, computers had permeated every affluent society. Thus, if the skills required to use computers or interpret their output were in short supply, and if this explained the run-up in inequality, we should now see the same pattern in every technically advanced society. The International Adult Literacy Survey does suggest that workers' reading and math skills are somewhat more unequal in the United States than in the other wealthy countries, but because the correlation between these skills and workers' earnings is quite modest, the distribution of such skills cannot explain why inequality is greater in the United States. A somewhat more credible story points to faster growth in postsecondary school enrollment in Europe than in the United States, which could have kept the price of skilled labor lower in Europe. But European workers still have less schooling than their American counterparts, and educational change cannot easily explain why European workers' pay is more equal than ours.

So why do ordinary American workers get to keep less of what they produce than ordinary workers in other rich countries? And why is this form of American exceptionalism becoming more pronounced? The answer turns out be pretty simple: "It's politics, stupid." Political scientists have been churning out papers on this question for more than a decade, and while the details differ, they mostly tell a broadly similar story. At least in rich democracies, differences in income distribution seem to be traceable to differences in constitutional arrangements, electoral systems, and economic institutions. Those differences in turn affect the political balance between left and right, the level of spending on the welfare state, and a wide range of economic policies.

Economic inequality is less pronounced in countries where the constitutional system has few veto points, allowing the government of the day to make fundamental changes. Rules that favor a multiparty system rather than a two-party system also produce more equal economic outcomes. So does proportional representation. Such arrangements apparently make it more likely that a ruling coalition will seek to protect labor unions, raise the minimum wage, and centralize wage negotiations, all of which tend to reduce wage inequality. Such coalitions also tend to expand the welfare state.

If you think all of this sounds very different from the United States, you are right. The men who drafted the U.S. Constitution were property holders. Most of them worried about the possibility that democratic governments might be tempted to appropriate their property, or at least impose very high taxes in order to provide benefits to less affluent voters. The founders wanted a system of government that would make such populism easy to resist, and to a large extent they got what they wanted. Despite the subsequent spread of cultural egalitarianism, both federal and state legislators have remained remarkably solicitous of property holders' rights. Legislators have also shown a persistent preference for relying on private markets rather than public institutions to make economic decisions.

These legislative priorities enjoy broad popular support. Americans are less likely than Europeans to tell pollsters that income differences are too large. Americans are also more suspicious of government than Europeans, which means that Americans are less likely to endorse policies for reducing wage inequality that involve government "meddling" in the marketplace. But these attitudes are not built into Americans' DNA, nor are they an inescapable legacy of our history. In part, of course, they reflect the public's tendency to endorse the institutional status quo, which most Americans think has served the nation well. The pro-market consensus also reflects the influence of journalists and political pundits, most of whom seem to be even more skeptical about government than about private enterprise or the current influence of the business elite. This consensus owes something to the absence of a political party that questions it. The absence of such a party derives both from rules that make third parties extremely difficult to organize and from a system of campaign finance that makes every party dependent on rich contributors.

But none of these obstacles to redistribution are insuperable. Americans are not as unhappy as Europeans about economic inequality, but most Americans still say that income differences are too large and, by a sizable majority, favor increasing the minimum wage. While there are certainly institutional obstacles to redistribution, most of those obstacles also existed between 1940 and 1970, when the distribution of income became more equal.

Low-wage America is a mosaic of occupations and industries. Many tightfisted employers face relentless competitive pressure to cut costs, and many are operating in fields where logistical considerations and other factors make it particularly easy to knock down wages domestically or ship work overseas. In almost every line of business, though, executives turn out to have a good deal of discretion about how they structure and reward work. Some take the low road and squeeze their frontline workers, driving down wages and working people harder. Others take the high road, adopting new technologies that keep their operations competitive, upgrading workers' skills, and reorganizing the way work gets done.

You can find instances of both in the same sector of the economy. In retailing, for example, Wal-Mart has been a Wall Street darling, in part because of its low wages and stingy benefits, which analysts and investors associate with high profits. But Costco, whose warehouse sales outlets directly compete with Wal-Mart's Sam's Club stores, has achieved similarly impressive results while paying its workers about 40 percent more in wages (an average of $15.97 an hour in 2004, compared to Wal-Mart's $11.52) and providing much more generous and inclusive (and costly) health insurance. In return, Costco gets a remarkably productive and loyal workforce; only 6 percent of its employees leave after the first year, compared with 21 percent at Sam's. "I'm not a social engineer," says Costco CEO James D. Sinegal. "Paying good wages is simply good business."

You can find plenty of success stories along the high road. Indeed, it defies common sense as well as economic logic to believe that a poorly skilled and badly paid American workforce could, in anything but the *very* short run, be the key to global competitiveness (never mind an attractive society). Which road a firm chooses depends on the social context in which its managers operate. They are more likely to take the high road if they are connected to institutions, public and private, that promote such alternatives. The U.S. system for connecting highly skilled work to advanced technology, unfortunately, is rudimentary and fragmented. Managers are also more likely to choose the high road if they face a strong progressive union that can make abusing workers costly while simultaneously making collaborative efforts between workers and managers easier. But American business is almost uniquely hostile to unions. The experience of other countries suggests that managers will also be more inclined to choose the high road if they have to pay a high minimum wage, forcing them to think more inventively about how to keep a firm competitive. Perhaps most important, managers will be more likely to take the high road if they are honored and rewarded for doing so. Too often, sadly, the honor and the rewards go to those who drive wages down instead of up.

HOW THE MIDDLE CLASS IS INJURED
BY GAINS AT THE TOP

Robert H. Frank

SUPPOSE YOU HAD TO CHOOSE between two worlds: World A, where you earn $110,000 a year and everyone else earns $200,000, and World B, where you earn $100,000 and everyone else earns $85,000.

Most neoclassical economists would have an easy time deciding. Neoclassical economics, long the dominant wing of the profession, tends to equate personal well-being with absolute income, or purchasing power. By that standard, World A wins hands down: even as the low earner on the totem pole, you would be doing 10 percent better there than in World B. In other words, you could have 10 percent more food, clothes, housing, airplane travel, or whatever else you wanted.

And yet, when the choice is put to American survey respondents, many seem torn, and most actually end up opting for World B. Is this just an amusing example of human irrationality? Are people so preoccupied with status and rank that they lose sight of objective reality? Or could it be the neoclassical economists who have missed something?

For a glimpse of the possible downside of World A, it may help to consider Wendy Williams, a lanky, soft-spoken adolescent living in a trailer park in an upscale Illinois community during the boom years of the late 1990s. Every morning, according to reporter Dirk Johnson's account in the *New York Times,* Wendy shares a school bus ride with a group of more affluent classmates, who "strut past in designer clothes" while she sits silently, "wearing a cheap belt and rummage-sale slacks." She is known as Rabbit because of a slight overbite—"a humiliation she once begged her mother and father to avoid by sending her to an orthodontist."

Most children have been counseled not to measure their financial circumstances against the circumstances of others. That advice can sometimes be easier to dispense than to follow, however. Wendy Williams makes a game effort to bridge the socioeconomic gap. "That's a really awesome shirt," she tells one of the other girls on the bus. "Where did you get it?"

But teenagers can be cruel. "Why would you want to know?" the other girl replies with a laugh.

It is odd that economists who call themselves disciples of Adam Smith should be so reluctant to introduce the psychological costs of inequality into their discussions. Smith himself recognized such concerns as a basic component of human nature. Writing more than two centuries ago, he introduced the important idea that local consumption standards influence the goods and services that people consider essential—the "necessaries," as Smith called them:

> By necessaries I understand not only the commodities which are indispensably necessary for the support of life, but whatever the

custom of the country renders it indecent for creditable people, even of the lowest order, to be without. A linen shirt, for example, is, strictly speaking, not a necessary of life. The Greeks and Romans lived, I suppose, very comfortably though they had no linen. But in the present times, through the greater part of Europe, a creditable day-labourer would be ashamed to appear in public without a linen shirt, the want of which would be supposed to denote that disgraceful degree of poverty which, it is presumed, nobody can well fall into without extreme bad conduct. Custom, in the same manner, has rendered leather shoes a necessary of life in England. The poorest creditable person of either sex would be ashamed to appear in public without them.

The absolute standard of living in the United States today is of course vastly higher than it was in Adam Smith's eighteenth-century Scotland. And higher living standards create a whole new set of necessaries. For a teenager in an affluent suburb, it is no stretch to imagine that these might include straight teeth. Looking good is an irreducibly relative concept; but it is one, we all know, that sometimes has objective consequences. No one would accuse you of foolish vanity if you went to a job interview with IBM wearing your best suit and tie rather than a tank top and jeans. Impressions count.

And impressions are not the only reason to be conscious of other people's choices. Think about buying a car. Thirty years ago, a middle-class family with kids might have been content with a four-door sedan of modest size. Imagine the grown-up child of that family, with children of her own, facing the same decision. She might be tempted to say, "A 2,500-pound sedan was good enough for my mom, so it's good enough for me." But on today's roads, surrounded by 6,000-pound Lincoln Navigators and 7,500-pound Ford Excursions, a 2,500-pound Honda Civic doesn't simply look a lot smaller and frailer than it did in 1975. It's objectively more dangerous. The odds of being killed in a collision rise roughly fivefold if you're driving such a vehicle and the other party sits at the helm of a Ford Excursion. In sheer self-defense, you might want a bulkier—and costlier—car than Mom's.

In the housing market, as in the automobile market, you don't have to be a spendthrift to feel pressured into overspending. Imagine a young couple who buy a house in a prosperous suburb, taking on mortgage payments that commit them to working nights and weekends and leave them with no margin of safety in the event of a health or professional setback. We might consider them reckless if they assumed these burdens just to get a few hundred extra square feet of floor space, a Jacuzzi, and the bragging rights that go with an address in Pinnacle Heights. But if, in addition to spacious houses, Pinnacle Heights offered an outstanding school system for their children, we would probably judge them less harshly.

The housing and car markets present two possible instances of what I have termed a "spending cascade," in which top earners—the people who have fared the best in the current economy—initiate a process that leads to increased expenditures on down the line, even among those whose incomes have not risen. Logic suggests that growing inequality of income and wealth might encourage additional spending in this way. Empirical evidence suggests it, too.

Two small midwestern cities, Danville, Indiana, and Mount

Vernon, Illinois, make the case pretty clearly. The median income in Mount Vernon was more than $10,000 higher than it was in Danville in the year 2000, but Danville's incomes were much more unequally distributed. In Danville, a family at the ninety-fifth percentile mark earned more than $141,000, while the equivalent family in Mount Vernon earned just over $83,000. Despite its much smaller median income, Danville's median house price was almost $131,000—more than double the Mount Vernon median. It turns out that Danville and Mount Vernon follow the pattern of other American communities: median house prices depend not only on median incomes, but also on income inequality.

The Danville–Mount Vernon story illustrates how the huge income gains accruing to top earners in the United States in recent decades have imposed costs on those in the middle. Of course, nobody is *forced* to buy an expensive house or car. But inequality may be creating an increasing number of situations in which we are forced to choose between unpleasant alternatives. And through a series of decisions that make good sense for us individually, we appear to be moving in a direction that makes little sense for us as a society.

The family that overspends on housing at the cost of heavy debt, long working hours, financial anxiety, and a scarcity of family time is not just a familiar anecdote, but also a fair description of where middle-class America as a whole has been going. The median size of a newly constructed house in the United States was 1,600 square feet in 1980. By 2001, it was more than 2,100 square feet. Meanwhile, commutes were getting longer and roads more congested, savings rates were plummeting, personal bankruptcy filings were climbing to an all-time high, and there was at least a widespread perception of a sharp decline in employment security and autonomy.

Happiness is not as easy to measure as house size. Nevertheless, there is evidence that house size doesn't do much for it. If you move from a 2,000- to a 3,000-square-foot house, you may be pleased, even excited, at first. In time, however, you are likely to adapt and simply consider the larger house the norm—especially if other houses have been growing, too. Yet the sacrifices we make in order to pay for bigger houses often take a lasting toll.

One strategy of cash-strapped families is to limit their mortgage payments by commuting from longer distances. Your adaptation to a long trip from home to work through heavy traffic will probably not be as complete as your adaptation to a bigger house. Even after a long period, most people experience long commutes as stressful. In this respect, the effect is similar to that of exposure to noise and other irritants. A large increase in background noise at a constant, steady level seems less intrusive as time passes; nonetheless, prolonged exposure produces lasting elevations in blood pressure. If the noise is not only loud but intermittent, people remain conscious of their heightened irritability even after extended periods, and their symptoms of central nervous system distress become more pronounced. This pattern has been seen, for example, in a study of people living next to a newly opened highway. Interviewed four months after the highway opened, 21 percent of the residents said they were not annoyed by the noise; that figure dropped to 16 percent when the same residents were interviewed a year later.

The prolonged experience of commuting stress is also known

to suppress immune function and shorten longevity. Even daily spells in traffic as brief as fifteen minutes have been linked to significant elevations of blood glucose and cholesterol, and to declines in blood coagulation time—factors that are positively associated with cardiovascular disease. Commuting by automobile is also linked with the incidence of various cancers, especially cancer of the lung (possibly because of heavier exposure to exhaust fumes). The incidence of these and other illnesses rises with the length of commute, and is significantly lower among those who commute by bus or rail, and lower still among noncommuters. Finally, the risk of death and injury from accidents varies positively with the length of commute and is higher for those who commute by car than for those who use public transport.

Among rush-hour travelers, the amount of time wasted in stalled traffic increased from 16 hours to 62 hours per year between 1982 and 2000; the daily window of time during which travelers might experience congestion increased from 4.5 hours to 7 hours; and the volume of roadways where travel is congested grew from 34 percent to 58 percent. The Federal Highway Administration predicts that the extra time spent driving because of delays will rise from 2.7 billion vehicle hours in 1985 to 11.9 billion in 2005.

If long commutes are so hazardous, why do people put up with them? It may be because they have unconsciously allowed their spending decisions to lean toward conspicuous consumption (in the form of larger houses) and away from what, for want of a better term, I call "inconspicuous consumption"—freedom from traffic congestion, time with family and friends, vacation time, and a variety of favorable job characteristics.

Can we attribute this to rising inequality? Although there is no simple way to prove or disprove the hypothesis, it is consistent with a substantial body of research. In a 2005 study, for example, Bjornulf Ostvik-White, Adam Levine, and I found that areas with higher inequality—specifically, with higher ratios between the income of households in the ninety-fifth and fiftieth percentiles—had significantly higher personal bankruptcy rates, divorce rates, and average commute times. Analyzing international data over time, Samuel Bowles and Yongjin Park found that total hours worked were positively associated with higher inequality.

The wealthy are spending more now simply because they have more money. But their spending has led others to spend more as well, including middle-income families. If the real incomes of middle-class families have grown only slightly, how have they financed this additional consumption? In part by working longer hours, but mainly by saving less and borrowing more. American families carry an average of more than $9,000 in credit card debt, and personal bankruptcy filings are occurring at seven times the 1980 rate. Medical expenses account for a significant share of that debt. Some forty-five million Americans have no health insurance—five million more than when Bill Clinton took office. The national personal savings rate was negative in several recent years, including a few of the peak years of the 1990s economic boom. Millions of Americans now face the prospect of retirement at sharply reduced living standards. Increased spending by top earners may not be the sole cause of financial distress among middle-income families. But it has clearly been an important contributor.

Spending cascades are also an indirect cause of the median voter's growing reluctance to support expenditures for what were once considered essential public goods and services. Nationwide, more than 50 percent of our major roads and highways are in "backlog," which means they will cost from two to five times as much to repair as those that are maintained on time. We face an $84 billion backlog in the repair and replacement of the nation's bridges. Between blown tires, damaged wheels and axles, bent frames, misaligned front ends, destroyed mufflers, twisted suspension systems, and other problems, potholes on American roads cause an average of $120 worth of damage per vehicle each year, and untold numbers of deaths and injuries.

Americans spend less than we once did to assure the safety of the food we eat. Despite growing instances of contamination from E. coli 0157, listeria, and other highly toxic bacteria, the Food and Drug Administration had resources sufficient to conduct only five thousand inspections of meat-processing plants in 1997, down from twenty-one thousand in 1981. And although food imports have doubled since the 1980s, FDA inspections of imports have fallen by half. Exposure to E. coli alone causes an estimated twenty thousand infections a year, and between two hundred and five hundred deaths.

We have been woefully slow to upgrade our municipal water-supply systems. The century-old pipes in many systems are typically cast-iron fittings joined by lead solder. As these conduits age and rust, lead, manganese, and other toxic metals leach into our drinking water. According to one estimate, some forty-five million of us are currently served by water systems that deliver potentially dangerous levels of toxic metals, pesticides, and parasites.

We have grown reluctant to invest in cleaner air. The Environmental Protection Agency recently proposed a tightening of standards for concentrations of ozone and particulate matter that would prevent more than 140,000 cases of acute respiratory distress each year and save more than fifteen thousand lives. The EPA proposal drew intense and immediate political fire, and bills were introduced in both houses of Congress to repeal the new standards, which have yet to be implemented.

Although spending on public education has not declined relative to historical norms, here, too, important inputs have not kept pace. For example, the national average starting salary for primary- and secondary-school teachers fell from 118 percent of the average salary of college graduates in 1963 to only 97 percent in 1994, a period that saw a significant decline in the average SAT scores of people who chose public-school teaching as a profession. And although we know that children learn more effectively in small classes than in large ones, we have offered fiscal distress as the reason for allowing class sizes to grow steadily larger during that same period.

We have slashed funding not only for services that benefit middle- and upper-income families, but also for the Head Start program, the school lunch program, homeless shelters, inner-city hospitals, and a host of other low-overhead programs that make life more bearable for the poor. We cut these programs not because they did not work, not because they destroyed incentives, but because the median voter decided that he couldn't afford them. And that perception was, in large part, a consequence of the growing income gap.

When we choose between conspicuous and inconspicuous consumption, we confront a conflict between individual and social welfare that is structurally identical to that of a military arms race. We become like the superpowers during the heyday of the Cold War, robotically obedient to the doctrine of mutually assured destruction (with its memorable acronym MAD). The person who stays at the office two hours longer each day to afford a house in a better school district has no conscious intention of making it more difficult for others to achieve the same goal. But that is an inescapable consequence of her action. The best response available to others may be to work longer hours as well, thereby preserving their current positions. Yet the ineluctable mathematical logic of musical chairs assures that only 10 percent of all children can occupy top-decile school seats, no matter how many hours their parents work.

A family can choose how much of its own money to spend, but it cannot choose how much others spend. Buying a smaller-than-average vehicle means a greater risk of dying in an accident. Spending less on an interview suit means a greater risk of not landing the best job. Spending less than others on a house means a greater risk of sending your children to inferior schools. Yet when all spend more on heavier cars, more finely tailored suits, and larger houses, the results tend to be mutually offsetting, just as when all nations spend more on missiles and bombs. Spending less frees up money for other pressing uses, but only if everyone does it.

If it is hard for nations to unwind from such a spiral, it is surely no easier for individuals. But the first steps are probably the same: We need to look at ourselves. We need to think about our actions in relation to their consequences. We need to talk.

THE VANISHING COMMONS
Jonathan Rowe

SOUTHERN PLANTERS faced a major dilemma in the years after the Civil War. Not only had they lost their investment in slaves; now many of the former slaves refused to work on the terms the planters offered. The freedmen had become too independent, it was said, and a big part of that newfound independence involved access to the commons.

The term *commons* suggests images of sheep pastures in Olde England. Yet the concept was a central part of life in the young America. In the South, it took the form of law and custom allowing people to hunt, fish, and even graze their cattle on land they did not own, so long as the owner had not put a fence around it. (Such fence laws were common throughout the United States. They survive today in the requirement that landowners "post" their land to keep hunters off.) Private property rights yielded to the needs of subsistence—to common rights. The commons supported slaves during their long bondage, and after the war, it gave a measure of independence to former slaves and poor whites alike. Which is why, of course, it had to go. Across the South in those years, planters did what their counterparts in England had done already: they closed the commons and declared private land off-limits, fenced or unfenced, and regardless of whether the owner was putting it to any use.

In England, the enclosures had driven many former commoners into cities, where they became a desperate labor force for the Satanic mills. In the American South, the effect was to help force the former slaves back into submission, as sharecroppers or low-wage help. "Believing black dependency to be the handmaiden of work discipline," Steven Hahn observed in *The Roots of Southern Populism*, "the planters moved to circumscribe the freedmen's mobility and access to the means of production and subsistence."

The means of production and subsistence—today we associate these mainly with the market, and we think about equality almost entirely in terms of money and financial wealth. But that sets the frame too narrowly. There is more to life—more to an economy—than the market; more to life, for that matter, than the market and the state. The processes that support us extend beyond the realm of commercial transactions and dollar bills. We will never bridge the wealth gap in real—as opposed to statistical—terms until we begin to address the enclosure of the commons that has continued from the postbellum years to the present, at an accelerating pace.

By *commons* I do not mean government or the "public sector." I mean the wealth of nature and society that precedes both the market and the state. The rivers, oceans, and atmosphere; the sidewalks and public spaces; the vast array of languages and species; the processes of democracy; the accumulated store of knowledge—these and more make up the foundation of human well-being and, indeed, of life itself. No person created them, and no one should be able to monopolize them or their fruits. Properly conceived, the commons can provide tangible forms of sustenance even in our urban market society. It can be a source of financial assets for meeting individual and social needs. If the commons belong to all of us, which it does, then the financial returns should come to all of us as well.

Almost from the moment the Pilgrims landed on Cape Cod, the commons were central to both material sufficiency and equity in this—to Europeans—new land. The first settlers built their towns around what they actually called a commons, which was a shared pasture for livestock. In North and South alike, private woodlands customarily were open for hunting or cutting wood, unless the owner fenced them. The Massachusetts Colonial Ordinance of 1641–47 declared that "any man . . . may pass and repass on foot through any man's property" to fish or fowl at common ponds.

Such provisions were typical of a spirit that pervaded daily life. The concept of property that the early settlers brought with them was not the walled fortress of today's ideologues. It was a permeable membrane that sought to reconcile the parts and the whole. (Politicians who invoke the piety of our forebears generally ignore the economic arrangements to which those convictions led.) Residues of this thinking lingered in the minds of the founders, especially when they thought about the future—which is to say, about invention and ideas.

America itself was an idea, the first nation so conceived, and so the founders' views on this point are especially telling. Jefferson and Madison considered the mind to be the mother lode of freedom, and they would brook no restrictions—governmental or private—on its operations and fruits. The copyright and patent clause of the Constitution was not the corporate money spigot it has since become. The government-bestowed monopoly in literary works was limited to a term of fourteen years; then they were to go back into the commons (the public domain) that had spawned them. Here they would be available to all, just as the woods and waterways were available to all.

Patents, too, were tightly limited in scope. Benjamin Franklin had a sharp eye for a dollar. But he drew the line when it came to patenting inventions that advanced practical knowledge. "As we enjoy great advantages from the inventions of others," Franklin wrote, "we should be glad to serve others by any invention of ours." (Franklin also founded the nation's first public lending library, to much the same purpose.)

That was not an extraordinary sentiment in the atmosphere in which this nation was founded. Today it prompts a double take (Franklin said *what?*) that should awaken us to the distance between his time and ours. Over the century that followed, mountainous fortunes were made by enclosing the commons. Some monopolized the gifts of nature (e.g., the Standard Oil Trust), while others expropriated the public domain (the railroads receiving gifts of public land and financing). The patent system became a petri dish of greed. Thomas Edison, America's trademark inventor, was almost equally ingenious in his conniving over patents. As one of his biographers, Robert Conot, put it, Edison's view was that "ethics was alien to business."

Edison, Rockefeller, and the rest deserved their due as innovators and builders. But deserving also were the commoners whose joint wealth was, in today's parlance, a central part of every great industrialist's business plan. (Not to mention the many competitors and even colleagues they cheated along the way. "Edison is really a collective noun and means the work of many men," a former colleague said.) This was very much on the minds of the reformers of the era, including the framers of the original income tax in 1913.

Those legislators had no intention of taxing the earnings of ordinary working people. Rather, they focused on gains that were unearned and, in their minds, not wholly deserved. Representative Dan V. Stephens of Nebraska spoke for many when he said that new revenues should come from the "surplus wealth of the nation that has already been collected into private hands in abnormal proportions." The income tax they enacted in 1913 didn't halt the rise of great fortunes, as moneyed interests have contended; but, along with the estate tax, it was a balancing force, maintaining a crucial distinction between constructive economic activity and sponging off the common wealth.

As decades passed, this ideal eroded too. The reform mind gravitated to technocratic liberalism. An agenda of government programs displaced the Progressives' concern with the nature and origins of wealth. Liberals, in fact, became the primers of the economic pump, the bold stokers of the growth machine—a role the right has happily co-opted in more recent years. The nature of the growth promoted, and the enclosure it entailed, became nonissues.

Today, the expropriation of the commons for private gain has reached an epidemic level. New technologies, and the relentless appetite of the market, have resulted in a grab for every last inch of natural and social space. The physical atmosphere has become a toxic waste dump. Psychological space is saturated with corporate come-ons. Broadcast air has become the private preserve of media conglomerates, which use it without compensation to us owners. When the city of Philadelphia—Ben Franklin's home—proposed to make Wi-Fi available to local residents, allowing them to use their own air to connect to the Internet and one another, the telecom industry prevailed upon Pennsylvania governor Ed Rendell to stop other localities from following suit.

What has happened to the atmosphere has happened also to practically everything that occurs within it. The social commons of the traditional Main Street has been decimated by big-box stores; university research labs have been turned into patent factories for corporations; public schools have become marketing free-fire zones. Corporations have even begun to stake out claims on the genetic substratum of life itself.

Most of us could add to the list. But we don't always remember that these are (in the legal parlance of property-rights zealots) takings—that is, seizures of wealth with the help of government and without compensation. It is not coincidental that, as the process of privatization has accelerated, so too has the gap between the very rich and everyone else. Turn a public school into a free-fire zone for junk-food advertisers, or transform sneakers and jeans into branded goods that sells for $150 or more, and who gets richer and who poorer? Who gains, exactly, when media conglomerates control the airwaves and university research is driven by corporate patent agendas rather than by the common good?

These are missing questions in our political debate. But those who doubt the impact on our democracy and our lives might listen to Norberto Ferretti, chairman of the Ferretti Group, which builds yachts for the superrich. Ferretti was explaining to a *Wall Street Journal* reporter why his customers like the privacy of yachts. "Rich people can go to a beautiful hotel and pay $3,000 a night for a suite," he said. "The trouble is, when you go down the elevator, you are in the lobby with people who paid twenty times less. My clients don't like that."

That is an apt summation of the economic dynamic at work in the nation today. When the commons gets enclosed, the problem is not just that the assets we own together get siphoned off by the very rich. No less important, the social glue begins to crack. The commons is the part of life that engages the "we" side of human nature. The fact that rich and poor can stroll together in Boston's Common or New York's Central Park is significant both literally and metaphorically. Eradicate the parts of life that so engage us, and the society devolves into a black hole of "me." Declare everything private, and you summon the linguistic root of that word—the Latin *privare,* which means "to deprive."

The "Me Generation" has come back with a right-wing face. Reviving the commons is not just a matter of social justice. More, it is a question of whether there will be a society at all.

The commons is not inherent in the molecular structure of things. Like the market, it is a way of looking at things—a mode of consciousness that is reinforced, or consigned to oblivion, by the pathways of daily life. To resurrect the commons as a source of equity and well-being, it helps to start with things that are part of daily life.

Activists are quick to note when oil or timber corporations undermine a subsistence commons in the Third World. We need a similar vigilance with regard to commons closer to home. Take fishing. Some thirty-five million Americans fish, and a fair number of them live in cities. A visit to Hains Point on the Potomac River in Washington, DC, or to the Oakland, California, waterfront would illustrate the point: most cities are built on water, and they would be good fishing sites if the water were not so foul.

But the federal government does not look at individual fishing as a source of food. The National Survey of Fishing, Hunting and Wildlife Associated Recreation, compiled by the U.S. Fish and Wildlife Service, divides fishing into two categories: commercial and recreational. The government sees the world as a market, and we get to play one of two market roles: business or consumer. The government touts "recreational" fishing for the $36 billion spent on tackle and the rest. Commons-based production isn't on the map. Thus we tend not to see that the ruin of rivers and bays is comparable to what the southern planters did to the forest commons a century and a half ago, closing off an important avenue of economic self-sufficiency.

Community gardens, for example, are commons-based production, for use rather than gain, on land the gardeners themselves do not own. There are some six thousand such gardens in thirty-eight U.S. cities, according to the American Community Gardening Association. That name might call to mind urban dilettantes with Smith & Hawken hoes; in fact, community gardens represent real production meeting real needs. The Food Project in Boston raises over 120,000 pounds of fresh vegetables on twenty-one acres, including 1,200 pounds on two city lots less than two miles from downtown. Most of the produce goes to people who need it.

But the needs of far more people could be served. There are some seventy thousand parcels of vacant land in Chicago, and thirty-one thousand in Philadelphia. Vacant lots occupy 18 percent of Trenton, New Jersey. This land could become a prolific urban commons that, like the woods of early America, helps ordinary people subsist. In 1943, in the midst of World War II, Americans raised half the national supply of fresh vegetables in Victory Gardens, as they were known.

Fishing and community gardens cannot replace food stamps, the WIC program, and subsidized school lunches. But a productive commons is necessary too. In an "ownership" society especially, we should think about what we own in common, not just what we keep apart. In Philadelphia, urban gardeners save (by their own reckoning) some $700 a year on food bills, and get satisfaction from growing their own. For many immigrants, community gardens provide a connection to rural life in another land. For everyone, they can be the start of a genuine sense of neighborliness and community.

The commons could change the way we think about health as well as nutrition. Much is made, and rightly so, of the gross inequities in medical care in the United States today. Yet the treatment gap is a symptom of something larger—a gap in access to the means of healthful living. The epidemic of asthma among poor children is, for example, in part a result of the bad air they breathe. Childhood obesity and diabetes are marketing-related diseases, promoted by the junk-food propaganda that fills the lives of children nowadays. Marketing affects all kids, of course, but the ones most vulnerable to media images of romanticized consumption are those who yearn the most for what they do not have.

People involved in a community tend to be healthier than those who aren't. Studies have documented this. Historically, most of the advances in human longevity have come not from heroic feats of individual medicine but from improvements in public health or social and community conditions. (See David R. Williams and James Lardner, "Cold Truths About Class, Race, and Health," in this volume.) Individual medicine is finite by definition. There will be only so many doctors and hospital rooms, only so much money for treatment and drugs, no matter what kind of financing structure one conceives. As technology becomes more sophisticated, costs will continue to increase beyond the means of society to pay. A commons-based health policy could be the only way out.

A modern economy is an urban economy, which means a monetary economy. It operates through the transaction of symbols of value as opposed to things of value. To be unhinged in this way from the creation of useful things tends to set loose the greed in human nature. It brings no end of trouble, as Jesus among many others saw. But that is the world we live in, and therefore we must think of the commons as a source of money to meet human needs. In other words, we must think as owners. To be sure, many commons should stay free, in particular where more use enriches the whole. If more people use the Internet, or the English language, or the sidewalks of a city (up to a point, of course), those resources become more valuable for everyone. An intuitive sense of justice suggests that no one should have to pay to breathe clean air or walk down a city street. Water, in quantity sufficient to meet basic human needs, should cost no more than the cost of providing it, if that.

Many uses of the commons, however, tend to degrade it or to exclude others. When one takes, everyone else becomes poorer. Use the air as a dump, and others breathe less freely. Corral the airwaves for media conglomerates, and independent voices become scarce. Extract oil and minerals from the public domain, and they are gone for good—except for the poisons that come back at us at the other end of the pipe. In such cases, there should be payment to us owners, as well as limits on the extent and kind of use.

Peter Barnes, a founder of the long-distance telephone company Working Assets (and my colleague at the Tomales Bay Institute), has developed a prototype for the atmospheric commons, called Sky Trust. It would work much like the Alaska Permanent Fund, which distributes revenues from state oil lands. Every year, each Alaskan gets a check—often for more than $1,000—as compensation for the oil that oil companies take from state lands. (Another portion goes to a fund to support the state when the oil runs out.) This is not "taxation" in the usual sense. It is a return to the rightful owners for the depletion of their commons.

In similar fashion, Sky Trust would auction off space—within strict overall limits—to those who use the atmosphere as a dump. (The auction would involve "upstream" sources, such as oil companies, rather than individual drivers.) The proceeds would come back to us Americans as a clean-air dividend; a portion could be used for common social needs as well. There would be a crucial difference from the Alaska model, however. The Alaska Permanent Fund builds a constituency for oil development because more development means bigger payouts. The Sky Trust, by contrast, would build a constituency for cleaner air. Stricter pollution controls mean less dump space; and less space means higher rents.

A Sky Trust with a cap on carbon emissions equal to the one in the Kyoto Agreement could, in theory, yield several hundred dollars per American, or about $1,200 for a family of four. (That amount could be adjusted to provide more to families with greatest need.) It is possible to apply the same basic principle to other common assets: water, parking space, rush-hour driving lanes, the public airwaves, and minerals and timber on public lands. If broadcast corporations paid for the use of the airwaves, that alone could easily produce several billion dollars of public revenue a year.

Instead, Congress has gone in the other direction. It has lengthened the term of copyright many times over. (The "strict constructionists" on the Supreme Court have somehow construed the constitutional stipulation of "limited times" to mean practically unlimited ones.) Both Congress and the courts have expanded the scope of patent monopolies to a ridiculous degree: the Patent Office granted one not long ago for the idea—the *idea*—of illustrated training manuals. IBM got a patent for a system for keeping track of people waiting to use the bathroom.

Grants of this sort have nothing to do with encouraging

"science and the useful arts," as the Constitution requires. They are a way of gaming the system for profit, pure and simple. Intellectual-property law needs to be brought back into the constitutional frame. Perhaps we commoners should start to get a royalty from the monopolies that we license. The case is especially compelling when we pay as taxpayers for the research that leads to the patent, as often happens in the pharmaceutical world. A small royalty on the most lucrative patents—one that clicked in after research and development costs had been recovered—could yield billions for the meeting of common needs, including the research and training to feed the next round of innovation.

Public lands are another commons that our politicians seem to enjoy giving away. We taxpayers spend more on roads and the like for timber companies operating on public lands than we get back from the companies in fees for the timber they cut there. Under the antiquated Mining Law of 1872, those who mine valuable minerals on public lands pay a pittance for the privilege. The Congressional Budget Office estimates that a mere 8 percent royalty on net revenues (that is, minus the mining costs) would yield $25 million annually. That kind of money could send a lot of deserving kids to college.

Virtually all wealth is a collaboration of individual, society, and nature. The most "self-made" of men and women have silent partners whom they choose not to acknowledge. When they speak the English language or perform mathematical computations, they draw on the vast common pool of knowledge that they themselves did not create. They benefit as well from the schools, the courts, the police—the services that government provides—and from many other supportive influences of the society at large. Warren Buffett, whose candor is in the same league as his wealth, says that society is "responsible for a very significant percentage of what I've earned."

If private wealth is partly common wealth, there are tax implications. The legitimate object of taxation might not be income per se, but rather the portion of income or wealth provided by the commons. Land is a case in point. Nature created it; humans claim ownership of it; and then they ride the escalator of market values that the society creates. If I buy a lot in San Francisco, make no improvements, and sell it for a killing ten years later, who has created that increase? Not me. Who gets it? Me.

That insight has led to proposals to confine the property tax to land alone, and leave out buildings and improvements, which are the fruits of human toil. The same principle informed the original income tax, which was intended to apply only to unearned gains. The income of ordinary working Americans was not taxed at all until World War II, and the intent was not just to raise revenue to defeat Hitler. Equally important, Congress wanted to take money out of the pockets of working people and thus prevent inflation on the home front. After the war, the new broad-based tax stayed, partly for the same purpose, and partly because the revenues were simply too important to give up. In other words, middle- and working-class Americans today are paying a tax that was designed to make sure they had less money to spend. Is it really a surprise that they are less than enamored with such a system? The notorious loopholes at the top have only made the problem worse.

A commons-based approach would put the revenue system back onto a moral basis. It would tax what people take—from the commons—rather than what they make in genuine earnings. It would not so much redistribute wealth as restore wealth to its rightful owners. When Winston Churchill was a young member of Parliament, he put the issue well. "Formerly the only question of the tax gatherer was, 'How much have you got?'" he told his fellow members of Parliament. "Now we also ask, 'How did you get it?'"

When we start to frame the revenue question this way, taxes will seem less an arbitrary imposition and more an outgrowth of basic moral principles. They will no longer be an obstacle to genuine wealth creation but rather will encourage that creation, including the protection and advancement of our common wealth. We cannot go back to the days when the woods and streams sustained daily life. But we can revive the principle that made those woods and streams available for sustaining life, and apply it to the problems that we face today.

THE GREAT TAX SHIFT
David Cay Johnston

ALONG THE WAY to creating what historians have called the world's first democracy, the Athenians of the fifth century B.C. invented another social arrangement that has stood the test of time: the idea of progressive taxation, or taxation based on the ability to pay. The brunt of the tax system inherited from Athens's tyrannical days fell on ordinary citizens, who were compelled to work so hard paying for the functions of government that they had little time or energy left for a role in the decisions of government. When the tax burden shifted to the wealthy, democracy flowered in Athens. That mutually reinforcing relationship has remained a characteristic of democratic government ever since, while tax systems that place the heaviest burden on the less well-off have continued to go hand in hand with feudalism, oligarchy, plutocracy, and other forms of top-down rule.

When the United States adopted the income tax in 1913, only the wealthiest Americans had to pay. The estate tax followed soon after to finance the war effort, with proponents arguing that if young men were going to be conscripted, then so should the wealth they were fighting, and dying, to protect. As a Pennsylvania congressman said at the time, "The luxury of a large standing army and a great navy [should be] supported by those whose interests demand that kind of army and navy." In 1918, 85 percent of American families paid no income tax at all, and even Andrew Mellon, the rich banker who was treasury secretary from 1921 to 1932, accepted that that the wealthy should bear most of the tax burden. "The fairness of taxing more lightly income from wages [and] salaries [than] from investment is beyond question," Mellon wrote.

Today, by contrast, taxes on investment are decried as "antigrowth," the regressive Social Security payroll tax accounts for almost 40 percent of federal revenues, and about 63 percent of Americans pay federal income taxes as well. Two-thirds of Americans pay more in Social Security taxes than in income taxes, an indication of how the tax burden weighs heavily on those with modest incomes. From a tax standpoint, the United States is moving more in the direction of the tyrannical Athens than the democratic one.

On paper, tax rates still rise with income. In practice, the tax code has become so shot through with advantages and loopholes favoring the affluent that when you add up all the elements of the system—payroll taxes, state and local income taxes, sales and excise taxes—and take account of the myriad methods of understating and deferring income, what you get, according to the prominent New York City estate lawyer Sanford J. Schlesinger, is "pretty much a flat tax."

Flat, or, from the perspective of some wealthy citizens, better than flat. Americans who made $100,000 to $200,000 in 2002 paid a greater share of their income in Social Security and income taxes than those making $10 million or more. As one gets closer to the very tip-top of the income distribution, tax rates fall sharply.

Factor in all the unreported income and economic benefits that go to the top 1 percent of earners, and they pay a smaller percentage of their income in taxes than does the middle class, and about the same percentage as the poor. In proportional terms, then, the burden of paying for everything from public schools and highways to police officers and firefighters and homeland security falls more heavily on the poor and middle class than on the rich—just the opposite of taxation based on the ability to pay.

As the tax burden has shifted, so has income distribution. Between 1970 and 2000, economic productivity increased by roughly 70 percent. That overall gain did not translate into sharply higher wages and incomes; instead, wages and incomes for most Americans stayed flat, and a very few at the top harvested most of the benefits.

In 1970, the average American in the bottom 90 percent of income made $27,060 (in 2000 dollars). By 2000, that amount had decreased slightly, to $27,035. By 2002, the last year for which data is available, it had fallen to $25,646, a decline of more than 5 percent.

Meanwhile, the incomes of the top 10 percent rose by an average of 89 percent, but even those gains were concentrated at the very top. The incomes of the top 1 percent more than doubled; and 0.01 percent, the richest 13,400 households, saw their average income balloon from about $3.6 million in 1970 to just under $24 million in 2000—an increase of more than 550 percent. At that elevated plane, the top 0.01 percent of the population collectively make more money than the bottom third; that's twenty-eight thousand of us outearning ninety-six million of us.

And a still smaller elite, the top four hundred income earners, earned an average of $174 million in 2000, more than triple what they earned in 1993. That works out to about a half million dollars per day, or $2.5 million every five days, which is more than most Americans make *in a lifetime.* Imagine that you worked a full fifty years, earning an average of $50,000 a year, which would, in fact, be above-average earnings. Half a century of punching time cards, dealing with bosses and co-workers, putting in overtime, and bouncing between layoffs and promotions would bring you about the same earnings as a week's work would bring one of the high-flying top four hundred.

This thin and superrich slice of Americans have received huge tax cuts. In 1993 they paid 30 percent of their reported income in federal income taxes. By 2000 that was down to 22.2 percent, their tax burden reduced by a fourth. I calculate that with the Bush tax cuts in full effect the top four hundred now pay a bit more than 17 percent. The administration refuses to release the actual figures for 2001 and 2002, however. One official who has seen the data would tell me only that my estimate was on the high side.

The fact that the earnings of the rich have soared while their tax rates have shriveled is hardly coincidental. In the 1980s, a Democratic Congress and the Republican administration of Ronald Reagan collaborated on the first round of what would become a bipartisan, twenty-five-year-long campaign to cut tax rates, particularly on those in the upper brackets. While the incomes of the wealthiest Americans have been going through the roof, the highest tax rates have dropped; they fell from 70 percent in 1980 to 28 percent in 1987, rose in 1991 and 1993, but have now been cut again to 35 percent, half the rate of 1980. The cuts were derided by critics as "trickle-down economics"; proponents said that they would increase incentives for the wealthy to make job-creating investments, which would ultimately benefit workers throughout the economy. But the effect has been just the opposite: not trickle down, but Niagara up! Today, people making as little as $30,000 are taxed more so that the wealthiest can pay less.

The federal tax code—"the most political law in the world," to quote the New York tax lawyer Jonathan Blattmachr—is shaped by elected officials beholden to the corporations and wealthy individuals who make up America's political donor class. Through a swirl of lobbying activities and campaign contributions, they have swept the interests of average working Americans aside while galvanizing support for a series of self-serving changes in the rates and the rules, many of which the politicians do not even understand.

What is commonly referred to as *the* tax code might be better described as two codes: one that forces most Americans to account for every nickel of income they earn, and another that allows the wealthy to reveal or conceal at their discretion. Every April 15, local television news teams set up camp at post offices to film Americans mailing in their last-minute tax returns. For the most part, those taxes have already been reported, paid, and spent by Uncle Sam. If you are a wage earner, your employer reports to the IRS your income down to the penny, withholding from every paycheck the amount due (and usually a bit more) and sending it on to the Treasury. Most wage-earning Americans couldn't significantly cheat on their taxes if they wanted to.

By contrast, people who make their money through ownership of businesses, investments, and property have plentiful opportunities to defer taxes and put money outside the tax
system—and then they have enormous opportunities to under-
state income, invent deductions, and shift their tax burden onto
you. Many of the wealthiest Americans take most of their income
in forms that, unlike wages, are not independently reported to
the Internal Revenue Service, which then has no way of knowing
that billions of dollars of income are improperly left off of tax returns. And the rich employ an army of lawyers and financial advisers who are expert at a certain kind of magic trick: making vast
sums of money appear invisible to the IRS.

The variety of schemes available to those with means is limited only by the imaginations of their tax advisers. In recent years,
wealthy Americans have learned how to construct tax-evading
charitable trusts whose chief beneficiaries are themselves; how to
invest in multilayered partnerships that make income nearly impossible to monitor; how to manipulate stock trades to get credit
for taxes never paid; how to charge lavish employment perks such
as private planes and fancy apartments to shareholders and ultimately to taxpayers. Corporations have set up legal headquarters
overseas, and wealthy Americans have gone so far as to renounce
their citizenship in order to avoid American taxes while enjoying
the benefits of the economic system that those taxes enable because no one enforces the laws limiting how much time they can
spend in the nation they have renounced.

That Congress puts favors for the rich into the law is one
thing. But how about its turning a blind eye to what even IRS
commissioners have warned them is rampant criminal tax eva-

sion? The opportunities for tax evasion have expanded dramatically in recent years as Congress has cut funds for audits and collections, effectively handcuffing the tax police at the IRS, at least when it comes to wealthy tax evaders.

Thanks in large part to political strategists like Frank Luntz, the pollster who taught his Republican clients that the surest way to win votes was to attack the IRS, members of Congress routinely demonize and undermine the very agents they depend on to collect the money that pays for their programs (not to mention their salaries). In a series of hyperbolic hearings in 1997 and 1998, Republican senators accused the IRS of "Gestapo-like tactics" (based on a few trumped-up incidents). Then Congress passed an act that, by creating complex new "oversight" and "taxpayer rights" procedures, allowed the agency to be tied in procedural knots by anyone who had the incentive to challenge collection attempts—in other words, people who owed big on their taxes. Not surprisingly, the IRS's use of standard methods to collect the revenue due from big tax cheats—things like property seizures, garnishments of paychecks, and liens—has plummeted in recent years, making the incentives to cheat greater than ever. IRS claims that the agency has now gone back to enforcement are mostly talk about a few high-profile prosecutions.

Congress has also eroded funding of the IRS to such an extent that a cheater's chance of being caught is remote. The agency's technology is so out-of-date that simple computer techniques for more effectively processing returns and identifying likely tax dodgers are unavailable. The IRS cannot even seem to stop people who file returns claiming zero income and request a refund of all their taxes—refund checks to such crooks are routinely issued, while going after them is rare because it is costly. Staff and budgets for conducting audits have been slashed, and some highly trained revenue agents have been placed on telephone duty to field inquiries from the public about things like the filing deadline. By the year 2000, the audit rate for people making more than $100,000 per year was 1 in 145. (Meanwhile, because of a congressional effort to crack down on low-income people illegitimately claiming the Earned Income Tax Credit, audit rates for the working poor were about 1 in 47.) And the IRS still pours many of its dwindling resources into hunting for detail cheating among wage earners, instead of looking into the much more ample opportunities for evasion by business owners, investors, and landlords. Former IRS commissioner Charles Rossotti borrowed one of my lines when he wrote in his new book that the IRS is like "a police department that was giving out lots of parking tickets while organized crime was running rampant."

But the flaws in our tax code aren't all about cheating, dodging, and lax enforcement. In fact, many of the techniques used by the superrich to avoid their legitimate share of the tax burden are, by the letter of the law, perfectly legal. And the policies that overburden the poor and middle class while letting the wealthy off easily are not accidental, but the result of deliberate decisions by lawmakers.

Take, for example, the payroll tax that funds the Social Security system. Unlike federal income taxes, there is no threshold for the payroll tax—it takes 6.2 percent from your first dollar of income (plus another 6.2 percent from your employer), whether you make $1,000 a year or $10 million. For a poor or middle-class family, a significant chunk of income that could be used to avoid debt or set aside for the future disappears before they ever see it. There is, however, a cap on payroll taxes, which about 90 percent of Americans may not be aware of because they never reach it. But at that cap (currently $90,000), all further earnings are exempt from the payroll tax. The person making $90,000 pays the same amount into Social Security as does Bill Gates or Donald Trump. And a two-income couple at that level pays twice what the pluto-crats pay. What that means is that the wealthy pay a smaller effec-tive payroll tax rate than the poor and middle class, just as in tyrannical Athens. If you make $5,000 or $50,000 per year, your payroll tax remains 6.2 percent from your first dollar to your last. But at $500,000, the effective rate on your total income is about a penny on the dollar. At $5 million, it's about a penny on every $10.

Social Security is also a vivid example of how the middle class pays more to finance tax cuts for the rich. Since the 1980s, the government has been overcharging workers on payroll taxes above what is required to fund the Social Security system. In the-ory, this surplus was to pay off the federal government debt and then establish a trust fund which could be drawn upon when the large baby boom generation retires. But the 1980s were also the period in which huge breaks for the rich became the stated goal of American tax policy, resulting in equally huge revenue shortfalls for the government. So instead of the federal debt being paid off, it has ballooned. And the government spent the money to make up for the taxes that the rich did not have to pay. When the time comes to pay out Social Security benefits for the baby boomers, the only way to pay benefits will be by raising taxes, as Paul H. O'Neill said when he was treasury secretary early in the Bush ad-ministration.

The tax burden for many middle-class families is about to become greater still, again because our elected representatives decided that lowering taxes on the affluent was the first priority. The alternative minimum tax (AMT), or "stealth tax," was first established during the Nixon administration to prevent wealthy Americans from escaping all income taxes by claiming excessive, and often exotic, deductions. It established a parallel calculation of a taxpayer's bill based on the AMT's rates and stricter rules on deductions; the taxpayer then owes whichever calculation (regular or AMT) produces the higher tax bill. But because of small tweaks to the law over the years, and a conscious choice by Congress in the 1980s not to automatically adjust the AMT's tax brackets for inflation, more and more middle-class families are being forced into paying the higher AMT rates. Worse, Congress added to the list of tax breaks ignored by the AMT your exemptions for yourself, your spouse, and your children; your state income and local property tax deduction; and the standard deduction.

And here is what is truly awful: if you or a loved one gets sick or injured and you spend more than 7.5 percent of your income on medical bills, your income taxes go up—and the money is explicitly used to help finance tax cuts for the rich. The amount of money is small, but the symbolism goes to the heart of a heartless Congress that depends on the donations of those among the rich who want a free ride.

The alternative minimum tax was originally written to apply only to people with annual incomes of $1 million or more in today's dollars. By the year 2000, it was collecting over 70 percent of its revenue from people making less than that. By 2010, according to the nonpartisan Tax Policy Center, the AMT will become the de facto income tax system for nearly everyone making between $75,000 and $500,000 per year, thus silently and steadily raising their tax bill. A significant number of people making as little as $30,000 per year will also be affected.

This may come as a surprise to taxpayers, but not to President Bush and the U.S. Congress, who have carefully avoided opportunities to turn back what by the president's own standard is a middle-class tax hike. Much was made of the fact that the majority of the Bush tax cuts in 2001 went to the top 1 percent, but many middle- and upper-middle-class Americans still supported the cuts because they assumed they would get their share as well. But, thanks to the AMT, what the Bush tax cuts giveth they also taketh away. Families making between $100,000 and $500,000 per year will lose on average 71¢ on each $1 of their Bush tax cuts to the AMT. (Those making over $1 million, on the other hand, will lose only 8¢ on the dollar, and most of that will be because of their aggressive use of exotic tax breaks.) In fact, the design of the Bush tax cuts depended on the silent extension of the AMT, at a cost of more than $500 billion over ten years, to hold down the apparent costs of the cuts going to the rich. One more case of huge tax breaks for the rich funded by quiet tax increases on the middle class.

Middle-class Americans often don't realize how skewed the system is against them, and end up supporting tax cuts like these that overwhelmingly benefit the superrich and leave them holding the bag. Sometimes this may be due to simple ignorance, or, more charitably, wishful thinking: surveys have shown that 15 to 20 percent of Americans believe that they are in the top 1 percent income group. But it is also the result of interest groups and politicians who wage elaborate public relations campaigns to sell average Americans on tax cuts for the wealthy.

President Bush came into office promising to end the estate tax. Borrowing his language from the high-priced lobbyists who had been pushing the idea for almost a decade, he called it the "death tax" and described its elimination as a way to preserve small businesses and "keep farms in the family." Neither the White House nor the American Farm Bureau Federation was ever able to come up with a single example of a family that had lost its farm because of the tax. Nevertheless, many middle-class Americans supported its repeal, and in doing so, to embrace higher tax bills for themselves and their children and grandchildren so that a handful of the most affluent Americans could pay less.

Tax cuts in Washington are only one side of the story, because as the federal government reduces its tax rolls, it shifts the responsibility of paying for many essential services to states and localities. If anything, state tax systems are even more unfair to poor and middle-class Americans than the federal system is. But as states are being asked to bear more of the costs of government services, some governors are learning that tax systems that squeeze average workers while letting the rich pay a pittance are no way to fund a government. Even conservative Republican governors such as Mitch Daniels of Indiana and Alabama's Bob Riley have tried to require the wealthy in their states to shoulder more of the tax burden.

As a congressman, Alabama's Governor Riley had been an arch-defender of tax cuts for the rich and saw Ronald Reagan as his political role model. But while campaigning for the statehouse, he came across an article by a University of Alabama law professor arguing that the state's tax code was, from a Judeo-Christian perspective, immoral. For instance, Alabama's income tax applied to families of four making as little as $4,600 a year, the lowest threshold in the nation; its high sales tax applied to necessities such as food, clothing, and over-the-counter medicine; and its property tax structure allowed wealthy landowners to avoid taxes on most of the value of their holdings. Riley, a Southern Baptist, took the professor's article very seriously, adopting its language and moral arguments during his campaign and, after he was elected, in his push for a constitutional amendment to reform the state's tax system.

Ultimately, Riley wasn't able to muster the grassroots support necessary to pass the amendment. The Christian Coalition of Alabama sided with the state's wealthy interests rather than with the scripture-quoting conservative governor who wanted to help the poor. Many of the poor voted against the plan, unable to believe that, after years of favoring tax cuts for the rich, Riley had had a conversion on the road to Montgomery. His proposal went down to a solid defeat by the voters.

Riley's effort at reform is an indication that the heavy burdens placed on those with less are beginning to register with some politicians. Putting taxes in moral terms is as important today as it was in ancient Athens. "For too many years," Riley said in the televised address laying out his reform proposal, "our state has been living on borrowed time and borrowed money—robbing Peter to pay Paul." A better description of America's tax system is Robin Hood in reverse: robbing the poor and middle class to give tax cuts to the rich.

AMERICA DISCONNECTED
Theda Skocpol

THE AMERICAN LEGION is every liberal's least favorite veterans' group—power-happy in foreign affairs, socially conservative, a reliable supporter of the anticommunist witch hunts of the 1950s. It was also the pivotal force behind one of the most generous and inclusive federal social programs ever enacted—the GI Bill. Powerful, broad-based membership organizations like the American Legion have largely vanished from the scene, and we are a poorer country for it. And a more unequal country.

During our first two centuries of independence, Americans came together in trade unions and farmers' associations, fraternal chapters and veterans' organizations, women's groups and public-reform crusades, to create a raucous democracy in which citizens from all walks of life could be leaders and help to shape community life and public agendas. But our civic life has changed fundamentally in recent decades. Popular membership groups have faded while professionally managed groups have proliferated. Ordinary citizens today have fewer opportunities for active civic participation, and big-money donors have gained new sway.

Not coincidentally, public agendas are skewed toward issues and values that matter most to the highly educated and the wealthy.

To understand the changes wrought by this sweeping civic reorganization, it is useful to consider the significant role these membership groups played in American life dating back at least a century. From the 1800s through the mid-1900s, countless churches and voluntary groups of all sizes needed volunteer leaders. Indeed, the country's largest nation-spanning voluntary federations could have as many as seventeen thousand local chapters, each of which might need at least a dozen officers and committee leaders each year. Looking at the twenty largest voluntary federations alone in 1955, my colleagues and I estimate that some 3 percent to 5 percent of the adult population was serving in leadership roles—and that additional recruits would be needed each year.

Voluntary federations taught people how to run meetings, handle money, keep records, and participate in group discussions. Often, they exposed members to the inner workings of representative democracy—from parliamentary procedures and elections to legislative, judicial, and executive functions. And, importantly, these traditional voluntary associations reinforced ideals of good citizenship. They stressed that members in good standing should understand and obey laws, volunteer for military service, engage in public discussions—and, above all, vote. Political scientists Alan Gerber and Don Green show that people are more likely to turn out to vote in response to face-to-face appeals, and America's traditional popular associations routinely provided such appeals.

This exposure to democracy in action wasn't reserved for the elite alone. Many such organizations mixed social classes. There were plenty of opportunities for men and women from blue-collar and lower-level white-collar occupations to participate. And within the world of volunteerism, upward mobility was possible, as local activists got on leadership ladders toward responsibilities at district, state, and national levels.

Like citizens of other advanced industrial democracies, Americans joined occupationally based groups. But they were more likely to belong to what I call fellowship associations—with members from various occupations who saw themselves as joined together in shared moral undertakings. Rooted in dense networks of state and local chapters that gave them a presence in communities across the nation, major fraternal groups, religious groups, civic associations, and organizations of military veterans predominated.

All sorts of large membership associations were involved in public affairs. This is obvious for what's now the AFL-CIO and the American Farm Bureau Federation. Beyond these, to give just a few examples, the PTA and the General Federation of Women's Clubs were active in a variety of legislative campaigns having to do with educational and family issues. The American Legion and the Veterans of Foreign Wars sought benefits for veterans and their families. And the Fraternal Order of Eagles championed Social Security and other federal social programs.

In the 1960s, these old-line membership organizations began to decline, to be replaced by professionally managed advocacy groups and institutions. These new groups arose partly in response to a newly activist national government. We often think of voluntary groups as making demands on government, yet it is also true that government institutions and policies influence group formation. In the late 1950s and the 1960s, the federal government intervened in many new realms of social and economic life—and thousands of new associations formed in response. For example, new advocacy groups speaking for feminists and minorities proliferated, not before, but *after,* the Civil Rights Act of 1964 and the establishment of federal agencies to enforce affirmative-action regulations. As this happened in many policy areas, moreover, newly formed groups could maneuver more effectively if they hired professional staff members—lawyers who could advocate and litigate on behalf of their unique interests, media-relations experts who could spin the national media, and lobbyists who could press the groups' cases before a growing army of congressional aides and executive-branch officials.

At the same time, new technologies and resources allowed the association builders to operate from centralized offices in Washington and New York. Back in the nineteenth century, when Frances Willard was working to build the nationally influential Woman's Christian Temperance Union, she traveled across the country recruiting organizers to found and sustain a nationwide network of local chapters. By contrast, when Marian Wright Edelman was inspired to launch the Children's Defense Fund, she turned to private foundations for grants and then recruited an expert staff of researchers and lobbyists. And the founder of Common Cause, John Gardner, used a few big donations to set up a mailing-list operation.

To be sure, as the Children's Defense Fund illustrates, certain kinds of advocacy groups can enlarge our democracy by speaking on behalf of vulnerable citizens who could not otherwise gain a voice. Nevertheless, in an associational universe dominated by business organizations and professionally managed groups, the mass participatory and educational functions of classic civic America are not reproduced. Because patron grants and computerized mass mailings generate money more readily than modest dues repeatedly collected from millions of members, and because paid experts are more highly valued than volunteer leaders for the public functions of today's public-interest groups, the leaders of these groups have little incentive to engage in mass mobilization and no need to share leadership and organizational control with state and local chapters.

In mailing-list organizations, most adherents are seen as consumers who send money to buy a certain brand of public-interest representation. Repeat adherents, meanwhile, are viewed as potential big-money donors.

This money chase overlaps with America's growing economic inequality to further marginalize those with few resources. America today is full of civic organizations that look upward in the class structure, holding constant rounds of fund-raisers and always on the lookout for wealthy "angels."

Today's advocacy groups are also less likely than traditional membership federations to entice masses of Americans *indirectly* into democratic politics. In the past, ordinary Americans joined voluntary membership federations not only for political reasons but also in search of sociability, recreation, cultural expression, and social assistance. Recruitment occurred through peer networks, and people usually had a mix of reasons for joining. Men and women could be drawn in initially for nonpolitical reasons, yet later end up learning about public issues or picking up skills or contacts that could be relevant to legislative campaigns, electoral politics, or community projects. But today's public-interest associations are much more specialized and explicitly devoted to particular causes—like saving the environment, fighting for affirmative action, opposing high taxes, or promoting "good government." People have to know what they think, and have to have some interest in politics and the particular issue, *before* they send a check.

Three intertwined transformations fundamentally remade American civic life after the mid-1960s. First, business groups lost ground as a wide array of public-interest groups—environmental associations, abortion-rights and antiabortion advocates, good-government groups, and so on—proliferated. In the years between 1960 and 1990, the total number of national associations grew from some six thousand to twenty-three thousand; of those, the share comprising business associations shrank from 42 percent to 18 percent, while groups focused on social welfare and public affairs burgeoned from 6 percent to 17 percent. The balance of organized voices in U.S. public affairs shifted markedly as new public-interest groups spoke for more causes and constituencies than ever before.

Second, once-hefty blue-collar trade unions and fellowship federations went into sharp decline. Mass memberships shrank, and networks of chapters grew much sparser. Tellingly, however, elite professional societies experienced much less decline than popularly rooted membership organizations.

Finally, voluntary groups founded in the 1970s and 1980s adopted new forms of organization. Some—such as public law groups, think tanks, foundations, and political action committees—are not actually membership groups at all. And many others are staff-centered associations that have few, if any, chapters and recruit most supporters individually via the mail or media messages.

No single cause spurred the great civic reorganization. Instead, the Vietnam War coincided with social, political, and technological trends to undercut older groups and encourage new civic ventures. Unlike earlier wars, which brought millions of American men together in veterans' and fraternal groups, the experience in Vietnam broke the tradition of cross-class civic solidarity. Instead, the war drove a wedge between social strata and generations.

The "rights revolutions" of the 1960s and 1970s also transformed civic life. As new ideals of racial and gender integration took hold, young people and educated Americans became reluctant to join associations with histories of racial exclusion and separation of the genders. The mass movement of women into the paid labor force, the increase in female-led families, and related changes in work and family life also presented new obstacles to participation.

Apart from shrinking opportunities for participation, changes in civic life have undercut America's capacity to use government for broad socioeconomic redistribution. The weakening of labor unions helps to explain declining voter participation among less privileged citizens and tilts public debates away from policies helpful to the working class. Similarly, the dwindling of once-huge cross-class membership federations has hurt the prospects of policy making for the majority.

Historically, popular and cross-class voluntary membership

federations championed inclusive social programs. It was the otherwise staunchly conservative American Legion that drafted, lobbied for, and helped to implement the GI Bill of 1944. The Legion had a nationwide network of chapters that could persuade conservative and liberal congressional representatives alike to support generous veterans' benefits—and it was motivated to take this course both to help veterans and by the hope of attracting millions of new dues-paying members from the ranks of the sixteen million Americans who served in the military during World War II.

Ideologically, many traditional voluntary federations trumpeted values of fellowship and community service, so their decline leaves the way clear for alternative modes of public discourse less likely to facilitate broad social programs. Modern advocacy associations are more likely to use "rights talk" and champion highly specialized identities, issues, and causes. Stressing differences among groups and the activation of strong sentiments shared by relatively homogeneous followings, advocacy-group tactics may further artificial polarization and excessive fragmentation in American public life. In the eloquent phrasing of Karen Paget, the proliferation of advocacy groups can add up to "many movements" but "no majority."

Perhaps the most intriguing evidence on the distributive effects of recent civic changes appears in Jeffrey Berry's recent book, *The New Liberalism*. As Berry's longitudinal research shows, professionally run public-interest groups have increasingly made quality-of-life causes such as environmentalism more visible, and they have increasingly prevailed after going head to head with business interests in legislative battles. But Berry also offers some more discouraging conclusions. Recent gains by citizen associations have crowded out advocacy by unions and other groups speaking for the interests and values of blue-collar Americans. Furthermore, Berry shows that liberal-leaning citizen-advocacy groups have become *less* likely over time to ally with traditional liberal groups on behalf of redistributive social programs, instead favoring "issues that appeal to their middle-class supporters."

So what? Does civic reorganization matter for the health of American democracy? Optimists correctly point out that public agendas have been enlarged by expert advocacy groups fighting for social rights and fresh understandings of the public interest. Yet those who look on the upside fail to notice that more voices are not the same thing as increased democratic capacity. And they do not see that gains in racial and gender equality have been accompanied by erosions of cross-class fellowship and democratic participation and representation.

Scholars have established that a combination of resources, motivation, and mobilization explains who participates in public life, how, and at what levels. Individuals from privileged families have advantages of income and education, gain civic skills at work, and also tend to be contacted regularly by civic organizers and election campaigns. Nevertheless, civic disparities can be partially counteracted if popularly rooted political parties, unions, churches, and associations spread skills and mobilize and motivate average citizens.

The bottom line is that variety and voice have been enhanced in the new American civic universe forged by organizing upsurges from the 1960s to the 1990s. But the gains in voice and public leverage have mainly accrued to the top tiers of U.S. society; Americans who are not wealthy or well educated now have fewer associations representing their values and interests, and fewer opportunities for participation.

The shift from mass-membership federations to professional organizations has profoundly affected the political economy of influence. Not surprisingly, research shows that highly educated, upper-middle-class people are the ones most likely to send checks to public-interest advocacy groups. And the same seems to be true of Internet-based movements, the latest twist in civic innovation.

Given that powerful forces have propelled civic reorganization, what can be done? Clearly, it is neither possible nor desirable to go back to the traditional world of American voluntarism. For all of their effectiveness in mobilizing citizens across class lines, traditional fellowship federations were usually racist and gender-exclusive. What's more, they failed to pursue many causes that are vital for Americans today. Yet the recent proliferation of professionally managed civic organizations—from advocacy groups to nonprofit agencies—creates a situation in which the most active Americans tend to be higher-educated and privileged people doing things *for* their fellow citizens, rather than *with* them. On the liberal side of the spectrum, especially, there are too few opportunities for large numbers of Americans to work together for broadly shared values and interests. This leaves our public life impoverished and suggests that those organizing to shape the political future must find innovative ways to re-create the best traditions of American civic life while preserving and extending the gains of recent times.

CORPORATIONS UNBOUND
Joel Bakan

IT WAS SEPTEMBER 11, 2001, and Carlton Brown, a normally unflappable commodities broker, was deeply troubled. As flames shot through the World Trade Center, Brown recalls, "All we were thinking was, 'Let's get those clients out.'"

Out of the gold market, that is. Although no one knew the towers were about to collapse, Brown's instincts told him that gold trading would end early that day, and prices were up. That was "the first thing you thought about" when the airplanes hit, he says. Fortunately, over the next few days "we got them all out . . . everybody doubled their money." September 11 thus turned out to be "a blessing in disguise, devastating, you know, crushing, heart-shattering." But "in devastation there is opportunity. It's all about creating wealth."

The corporation, too, is all about creating wealth. No internal restraints, whether moral, ethical, or legal, limit what or whom corporations can exploit to create wealth for themselves and their owners. To *exploit,* according to the dictionary, is to "use for one's own selfish ends or profit." Over the last century and a half, the corporation has sought and gained rights to exploit most of the world's natural resources and almost all areas of human endeavor. In their 1932 book *The Modern Corporation and Private Property.* Adolf Berle and Gardiner Means predicted "a time when practically all economic activity will be carried on under the corporate form." That time has come.

One large barrier remains, however. The twentieth century saw the emergence of a widespread belief that government should take a share of the responsibility for protecting citizens' social rights and meeting their basic needs. Essential public interests, and social domains believed to be too precious, vulnerable, or morally sacred to subject to corporate exploitation, were placed inside protective boundaries. Human beings could not be owned and children could not be exploited, either as workers or as consumers. Institutions crucial to human health and survival (such as water utilities and health and welfare services), to human progress and development (such as schools, universities, and cultural institutions), or to public safety (such as police, courts, prisons, and firefighters) were deliberately put beyond the corporation's grasp, as were precious natural domains, which became parks and nature reserves.

This public sphere, which exists to greater and lesser degrees in all modern nations, is now under attack. Historically, corporations have been hostile to it as an unwarranted expropriation of potentially profitable domains, and in recent decades they have waged a determined campaign to push back its boundaries. Through a process known as privatization, governments have capitulated, handing for-profit corporations control of a great many institutions once considered inherently "public." No public function has been immune. Water and power utilities, police, fire and emergency services, day care centers, welfare services, Social Security, colleges and universities, research, prisons, airports, health care, genes, broadcasting, the electromagnetic spectrum, public parks, highways, and even some military functions have all, in various jurisdictions, undergone, or been considered for, full or partial privatization.

The privatizers have an ambitious agenda. Their intellectual godfather, economist Milton Friedman, recommends that only 10 to 12 percent of total income—compared to what he estimates as 40 to 50 percent in the United States today—should come from government. Nothing but the most basic functions—the judicial system, the armed forces, and relief of the most extreme cases of poverty—would be within government's control if Friedman had his way, and many other economists and policy makers agree. William Niskanen, the chairman of the Cato Institute, sees "very few functions"—the only one he could think of was the military—that should remain in the public sphere. Michael Walker, who heads the Fraser Institute, Cato's Canadian partner, was asked if he would like to see every square inch of the planet under private control. He responded with an enthusiastic "Absolutely!" Such views may yet prevail. In the not-too-distant future, the public sphere could be reduced to a quaint historical anomaly.

"The classic investment opportunity is where there's a problem," says investment banker Michael Moe. "The larger the problem, the larger the opportunity." And "there is no larger problem today"—and hence no larger investment opportunity—"than how to better educate our populace." Inspired by that belief, Moe helped raise more than half a billion dollars to finance Edison Schools, a for-profit company that operates schools on behalf of local governments and plans eventually to own and run its own schools. Edison Schools is the largest education management organization (EMO) in the United States, with 133 schools and seventy-four thousand students currently under its control. It, along with roughly forty other EMO corporations, reflects a growing trend in the United States toward privatization of kindergarten through twelfth grade (K–12) education. Huge opportunities await corporations such as Edison that manage to infiltrate K–12 education in any significant way. It's "almost unimaginably vast," says Edison chairman Benno Schmidt Jr., of the potential for growth in the industry. "Education is bigger than defense, bigger than the whole domestic auto industry. . . . In fact, only health care has a larger segment of the American marketplace."

Because the "education market" combines a large problem with a small corporate presence, it is poised, much as health care was thirty years ago, to expand rapidly. In 2001 alone, the number of EMOs in the United States increased by 70 percent. Conservatively, Moe estimates, 10 percent of the $800 billion education industry will be run by for-profit corporations in ten years' time, compared to 1 percent today. Government, much like businesses, wants to outsource its operations, and is likely to transform its role from an "owner-operator of schools . . . to be more of a general contractor." Milton Friedman has been making this case for forty-five years, "and it's in the last five years or so that we've really started to break the ice jam and get moving," he says. Soon, Friedman predicts, corporations like Edison will "develop into enterprises that will run their own private schools," rather than just operating government-owned schools.

Proponents have used political muscle to promote the growth of their industry. Two of Edison's largest investors, Boston financier John Childs and Gap chairman Donald Fisher, recently donated $670,000 and $260,800, respectively, to the Republicans. They must have been pleased when President Bush pledged $3 billion in federal loans to fund new charter schools and subsidize students who wish to attend private schools—policy changes that could significantly expand the EMO markets. Other big-money supporters of the Bush administration also have major stakes in the education industry. Leading businessmen, such as Amway founder Richard De Vos, industrialist David Brennan, and Wal-Mart's John Walton, have supported Bush and spent millions of dollars promoting state voucher systems, which will create lucrative markets for EMOs once they are adopted.

Edison's leaders, like others in the industry, claim to have evidence documenting the educational superiority of for-profit schools. But their assertions have been widely questioned. Independent researchers at Western Michigan University concluded that "Edison students do not perform as well as Edison claims in its annual reports on student performance." The company has also been criticized for inflating the numbers of schools it runs by counting each of the K–5, 6–8, and 9–12 grade divisions as separate schools in settings where they are actually all administered by one principal and housed in one building.

Shares in Edison Schools, which reached a high of $21.68 on the NASDAQ stock exchange, later plummeted to less than $1.00. To save money in running its Philadelphia schools, the company sold off textbooks, computers, lab supplies, and musical instruments. It moved its executives into schoolrooms in the hope of saving $9,000 a month in rent on the corporate offices (upon learning about the move, the school board quickly ordered the executives out of the schools). Edison founder and CEO Chris Whittle further proposed that the company use unpaid Edison students to do the work of paid school employees. "We could have less adult staff," he is reported to have told a group of Edison principals as he described his plan to have each of six hundred students in a school work one hour a day at administrative tasks, thus making the work of seventy-five adults redundant.

Proponents defend privatization as theoretically correct, even when, in the real world, they see it going awry. Playing on people's self-interest in material gain, they say, is the surest route to promoting the public good. "People tend to react to economic incentives as a reason to do things," says Edison Schools financier Jeffrey Fromm, explaining why for-profit schools should outperform their public counterparts. Motivated by a desire to make money, teachers will teach better, administrators will administer better, and corporations will provide their customers—parents, teachers, school boards—with what they want and need. Therefore, says Fromm, "the for-profit incentive can have a positive impact on schools" even though corporations "have to think . . . really only about one bottom line." Corporations can "provide the ability for change to be infused into the educational system," he argues, because the "Darwinism among business in a capitalist economy . . . if unleashed on the education system, will tend to produce better education in the U.S."

Privatization thus makes the most of our inevitably selfish and materialist nature. "We owe our daily bread not to the benevolence of the baker but to his concern for his own interest" is how Milton Friedman, paraphrasing Adam Smith, puts it. By corollary, public institutions are inherently flawed because they rely on an unrealistic—that is, not entirely selfish and materialistic—concept of what motivates us. For Friedman and other advocates of privatization, the idea of civil servants "pursuing the interest of the community at large, rather than their own self-interest," is far-fetched. More than on anything else, the case for privatization rests on the notion of a fundamental difference between the motives of civil servants (lazy, bureaucratic, turf-protecting) and the employees of private companies (driven, dedicated, efficiency-conscious).

The theory fails on its own terms, however, because the alleged public benefits of private ownership depend on managers and executives who see their self-interest tied to company performance. In the corporate world, this equation doesn't necessarily hold, as Edison's own record attests. This is a business that turned only one quarterly profit in ten years as a publicly traded company; its schools were criticized for poor academic performance; and its stock collapse led to shareholder lawsuits—hardly a model of corporate success. Nonetheless, Edison's top executives, especially CEO Chris Whittle and chairman Benno Schmidt, managed to extract millions in salary, stock options, and "loans" from the company. Members of the company's board made tens of thousands of dollars just for showing up at meetings, even as the company's poor financial situation led it to seek an outside buyout. Ultimately, Edison's flailing business was bought up by Florida's state employee pension fund (ironically, the fund that provides pensions for the state's *public-school* teachers), whose board of trustees includes privatization advocate Governor Jeb Bush. The buyout kept Whittle in place as CEO and doubled his salary, despite the fact that his business model appears to have been a complete failure in the only place that corporate ideology says should matter—the marketplace.

Corporate compensation practices in general seem to contradict the image of a private sector that is responsive to its public performance. Clubby corporate boards, not shareholders as a whole or the "market," set salaries for executives. The ratio of CEO pay to the salary of an average worker is now 301 to 1. Despite claims that outlandish pay packages are necessary to attract and retain talented executives, companies are often embarrassed when the actual numbers come to light—as when Richard Grasso's $140 million deal from the New York Stock Exchange raised a furor against the exchange's board.

In the real world, a wide range of motives can be found in both government and private organizations, and sloth, opportunism, and corner cutting do not suddenly vanish when a public function is turned over to the private sector. Even when privatized services might, by some measures and in some contexts, prove more effective than public ones, privatization is nonetheless flawed as a general and long-term solution to society's problems. Philosophically, it rests on a distorted and incomplete conception of human nature. Self-interest and materialistic desire are parts of who we are, but not all. To base a social and economic system on these traits is dangerously fundamentalist.

At a more practical level, privatization is flawed for its reliance on for-profit corporations to deliver the public good. Unlike public institutions, whose only legitimate mandate is to serve the public good, corporations are legally required always to put their own interests above everyone else's. In many cases, in fact, the people who run corporations aren't even able to put their company's interests above their own individual selfishness. The most obvious examples, such as Enron and Tyco, collapsed under the weight of their own executives' greed, hubris, and criminality. Though these companies are now notorious for their arrogant and ethically challenged executives, the underlying reasons for their collapse can be traced to characteristics common to all corporations: obsession with profits and share prices, greed, lack of concern for others, and a penchant for breaking the rules. These companies' downfalls are best understood as showing what can happen when the characteristics we normally accept in a corporation are taken to an extreme. In fact, corporate proponents offer no compelling explanation for why selfishly motivated individuals will stop at anything—including the ruin of the corporation itself—to line their personal pockets. The thought that something approaching the "public good" will necessarily emerge from such an amoral environment is thus implausible.

Even institutions that remain ostensibly public or "nonprofit" are increasingly adopting a corporate model of doing business.

Modern universities are run like corporations, relying on under-paid labor to teach students while pursuing big profits through research programs funded by private industry. New York's Museum of Modern Art, one of the city's great cultural institutions, reopened after its recent renovation with a 67 percent hike in admission prices and a raft of new corporate sponsors—including Target, which sponsors the free Friday-evening admission that is now the only way many visitors can afford to see the art. Boards of trustees of universities, libraries, and museums are being stocked with corporate executives, who pay college presidents and museum directors CEO-level salaries.

Corporations may act in ways that promote the public good when it is to their advantage to do so, but they will just as quickly sacrifice it—as is their legal obligation—when necessary to serve their own ends (as Edison's Philadelphia debacle demonstrates). No doubt privatization opens up new areas for corporations to exploit for profit, which is why they zealously promote it. From the public's standpoint, however, we have to ask what kind of society we create when we put corporations in charge of the very sinews of our society—the institutions that define who we are, that bind us together, and that enable us to survive and live securely.

These concerns are not confined to privatization, however; they also extend to a closely related, though less formal process—the commercialization of society—which also involves corporations infiltrating areas of society from which, until recently, they were excluded. Advertising is now inescapable, whether on our television or computer screens, on huge outdoor billboards and electrical signs, wrapped around buses and subway cars (sometimes covering even their windows), or at museums, concerts, galleries, and sporting events, which increasingly seem like little more than shills for their corporate sponsors. Beyond these tangible signs of encroaching commercialism, however, an even more subtle process is under way: the places where we interact as social beings, our public spaces, are increasingly commercialized.

"PUBLIC SPACE," proclaims a plaque in the AT&T Plaza in New York. "Owned and Maintained by AT&T." The "street"—a term that denotes not only streets but other public places such as plazas and town squares—occupies a central place in the democratic imagination. It is a public urban space, a place where people meet and congregate, where they rally, protest, march, picket, shout through megaphones, convey various forms of information, and simply enjoy their freedom just to be in public. The idea of freedom of speech draws much of its evocative power from the street, whether through images of protesters in Tiananmen Square, soapbox orators at Speakers' Corner in London's Hyde Park, or civil rights and labor marches through downtown streets.

The street, however, is disappearing as suburban town centers give way to shopping malls, and downtown sidewalks are replaced by commercialized skywalks and tunnels. As one commentator observes:

> Sidewalks are changing; they are moving indoors into private property. During the last several decades, [we] have witnessed the erosion of traditional streets where public life transpired. The automobile, the skyscraper, the dispersed residential suburb, and the shopping mall have contributed to the demise of a pedestrian-

oriented, outdoor street life in our city cores. . . . Civic life now occurs indoors on privately owned, publicly used, pedestrian places in the form of above-ground "skywalks" between buildings, ground-level office and retail complexes, atriums and shopping malls, and below-ground shop-lined tunnels.

Almost all of downtown Minneapolis—hundreds of shops and services, four major department stores, government buildings, and corporate headquarters—is connected by more than seven miles of skyways, each segment built, owned, and maintained by the companies (and sometimes government agencies) whose buildings they connect. The skyways are lined with advertising, much of it provided by CityLites USA—the self-proclaimed "providers of skyway advertising," which boasts that its "backlit advertising program [in Minneapolis] makes it possible to reach up to 1,000,000 upscale decision-makers each week."

The trend toward enclosed, privatized "public" space contributes to broader societal inequality and segregation, insofar as corporations exercise their right to exclude anyone unable or unwilling to accede to the corporate code of conduct. While access to public space is open to all citizens, access to privatized space is dependent on one's economic situation and willingness to do business with the corporation. Security guards and surveillance equipment are ubiquitous in urban tunnels and skyways and suburban malls because, as one commentator points out, "the proprietors must maintain an atmosphere conducive to business, which necessitates prohibiting those members of the public and activities they perceive as detracting from this objective"—such as, for example, picketers, protesters, leafleters, and homeless people. Because malls, tunnels, and skywalks are private property, citizens' exercise of rights to free speech and assembly can more easily be curtailed in these places than on comparable public property. They also tend to be decorated and designed in ways that create environments comfortable for middle-class and upscale consumers—but for no one else.

On the residential side, gated neighborhoods, walled off from the surrounding areas and regulated through networks of covenants relating to use and services, are now home to as many as four million people in the United States. They represent, in the words of one study, "a trend away from increased governmental control over land use and governmental provision of services and toward an increased reliance on privately created controls and privately supplied services," and they "provide a new and more potent way to exclude unwanted persons and uses from the company of those rich enough to afford the increased control and privacy supplied in such developments."

"The corporation has essentially replaced the church in terms of who you are," says Edison Schools financier Michael Moe. It wants the same thing as the church, he says: "obedient constituents that . . . pay [their] dues and follow the rules." Human nature is neither static nor universal. It tends to reflect the social orders people inhabit. Throughout history, dominant institutions have established roles and identities for their subjects that meshed with their own institutional natures, needs, and interests: God-fearing subjects for the church, lords and serfs for feudal orders, citizens for democratic governments.

As the corporation comes to dominate society—through, among other things, privatization and commercialization—its ideal conception of human nature inevitably becomes dominant too. And that is a frightening prospect. The corporation, after all, is deliberately designed to be a psychopath: purely self-interested, incapable of concern for others, amoral, and without conscience —in a word, inhuman—and its goal, as Noam Chomsky states, is to "ensure that the human beings who [it is] interacting with, you and me, also become inhuman. You have to drive out of people's heads natural sentiments like care about others, or sympathy, or solidarity. . . . The ideal is to have individuals who are totally dis-associated from one another, who don't care about anyone else . . . whose conception of themselves, their sense of value, is 'Just how many created wants can I satisfy? And how deeply can I go into debt and still get away with satisfying created wants?' If you can create a society in which the smallest unit is a person and a tube, and no connections to people, that would be ideal."

Chomsky says that the "main driving force" behind privatiza-tion is "not just profit for Wall Street" but also reinforcement of the corporation's particular conception of humanity. Privatiza-tion of the Social Security system, for example, he says, is de-signed, in part, "to undermine the very dangerous principle on which Social Security rests, namely . . . that you care about whether a widow down the street has something to eat. You're not supposed to do that. You're supposed to only gain wealth, forget-ting about all but self. . . . Same with schools. [With privatiza-tion] you're undermining the social solidarity that the public system relies on, that is, the idea that I care whether the kid down the street goes to school. Well, make sure to undermine that be-cause you're supposed to be out for yourself and no one else." Adds philosopher Mark Kingwell, "From the point of view of the corporation, the ideal citizen is a kind of insanely rapacious consumer" driven by a "kind of psychopathic version of self-interest."

A democratic society, on the other hand, has another vision of the citizen. The fundamental premise of democracy is that, as citizens, all people are equal, at least within the public sphere. Everyone has one vote, regardless of his or her wealth or social position. But the expansion of privatization at the expense of the public sphere increases the portion of society in which one *dollar*—not one person—equals one vote. The severe and increasing economic inequality that has been described throughout this book means that, in a privatized world, some citizens have many "votes" while others have very few.

The idea that some areas of society and life are too precious, vulnerable, sacred, or important for the public interest to be subject to commercial exploitation seems to be losing its influence. Indeed, the very notion that there is a public interest, a common good that transcends our individual self-interest, is slipping away. Increasingly, we are told, commercial potential is the measure of all value, corporations should be free to exploit anything and anyone for profit, and human beings are creatures of pure self-interest and materialistic desire. These are the elements of an emerging order that may prove to be as dangerous as any fundamentalism that history has produced.

A SELF-PERPETUATING TREND?
Eric Wanner

TOO MUCH TALK about social inequality generally makes Americans uncomfortable. We are, after all, a nation founded on the premise that "all men are created equal," and most Americans see themselves as part of a vast middle class that encompasses the greater part of society. The evident economic differences between rich and poor do not dislodge a popular conviction that America still provides equal opportunities for all. In a free-market economy, open to individual enterprise and ability, some people will inevitably work harder, or get a better education, or invest more fortunately, and as a result, accumulate more resources than others. In principle, these inequalities of outcomes need not threaten equality of opportunity, so long as the children of rich and poor can still start life's race on an equal footing. In fact, of course, an individual's chances in life have always been shaped to some degree by family resources of all kinds—income, education, social connections, and political influence. America's promise of equal opportunity has, at best, been approximated by social reality—much more closely at some periods in our history than others.

The three decades after World War II were a particularly promising time in this regard. Pent-up demand fueled an industrial boom after the war that produced strong economic growth and put Americans back to work, erasing memories of the Great Depression. High rates of unionization reduced wage competition between firms in many industries. American business, with little challenge from abroad, could afford generous labor settlements. Wages for manufacturing workers and others made steady gains, and economic disparities between rich and poor declined. The GI Bill made college available to returning veterans, and the subsequent expansion of state-supported higher education brought college within reach of more families than ever before. The civil rights movement ended legal discrimination and began to pry open educational and economic opportunities for previously excluded groups. Economic mobility rose significantly, and an individual's chances to prosper were less tightly determined by family resources. The great American social project of growing the middle class and broadly sharing prosperity appeared to be an inexorable and irreversible trend. We know now that it was not.

Beginning in the late 1970s, the United States experienced a series of economic shocks and demographic changes that caused economic inequality to rise sharply. Although there are still arguments about exactly how and why this happened, the broad outlines of the story are, by now, familiar. Stagflation in the 1970s, the two oil price crises, and loss of market share to reviving foreign competition led to a period of restructuring in many U.S. industries. The dismantling of regulations and the de facto weakening of labor protections, undertaken to shore up U.S. competitiveness, put strong downward pressure on wages, particularly for male workers with limited education in previously unionized industries. At the same time, the increasing penetration of information technology into all sectors of the economy began to automate many production jobs and substitute computer power for many repetitive, low-skill clerical jobs. The result was declining demand for workers with no more than a high school education, a trend that has persisted ever since. Finally, and most notoriously, globalization—in the form of increased trade with low-wage countries, increased outsourcing of production and service jobs to offshore locales, and increased immigration to the United States of workers willing to accept very low wages—has put American workers, and particularly those with modest skills and training, into competition with a much larger labor pool on a worldwide scale. Not surprisingly, the result has been a long downtrend in wages at the bottom of the labor market.

To be sure, many Americans have benefited from the new economy. Globalization has put downward pressure on prices and made many consumer goods dramatically cheaper. Investments in information technology eventually led to a welcome burst of productivity growth in the 1990s, which ushered in an unprecedented period of low unemployment and low inflation toward the end of the decade. All workers gained ground in the strong economy of the late 1990s, but college-educated workers benefited most. The wage premium paid to male college graduates rose to about 80 percent above the wages of high school graduates. Overall, mean family income grew about 30 percent in real terms from the end of the 1970s to the beginning of the new century. But the distribution of aggregate national income became dramatically more unequal. From 1979 to 2002, families in the top fifth of the income distribution increased their share of the national income from 44 percent to just under 50 percent, with almost all of the gain going to families in the top 5 percent. Every other quintile lost income share, with the losses getting progressively steeper (in percentage terms) going down the income scale. The bottom fifth of all American families saw their meager share of national income decline from 4.3 percent to 3.5 percent.

Although these facts are well known, we still understand very little of their larger social significance. Is the recent burst of economic inequality nothing but a temporary consequence of the transition to a new and more productive economy? Can Americans respond to the increasing economic importance of education by going to college in greater numbers and adapting themselves to computerization and global competition? Or will inequality, once under way, prove difficult to reverse? This might happen if the families who have fallen behind economically also fell behind in other ways that made it more difficult for them, and for their children, to compete with the more advantaged. If, for example, as economic inequality rose over the past twenty-five years, the children of families at the bottom of the income distribution were increasingly likely to live in single-parent families, grow up in distressed neighborhoods, receive substandard child care and health care, attend poor-quality schools, and have less of an opportunity to go to college, then economic inequality might become a self-reinforcing trend. Inequality might also tend to reinforce itself at the other end of the economic spectrum if high-income families become wealthy enough to purchase private substitutes for public goods and withdraw political support for public investments in schools and social insurance systems that benefit the poor.

In 2000, the Russell Sage Foundation and the Carnegie Corporation of New York joined forces in support of a program of research designed to examine whether the recent upturn in economic inequality has in fact exacerbated social inequalities of the kind that might make rising economic inequality more difficult to reverse. Forty-eight social scientists, organized into six working groups, are examining many different dimensions of social life in an effort to determine, from the available social data, the *level* of social inequality observed between rich and poor in each social domain, and the *changes* in levels of inequality that appear to be correlated with the recent rise in inequality. For each social domain, the researchers have asked how the lives of rich and poor changed over the last three decades as economic inequality rose. Did inequality in family structure and investments in children, in educational quality and opportunity, in health care and outcomes, in job quality and satisfaction with work, in political participation and influence, and in many other aspects of social life become more or less pronounced?

Results from the project thus far have yielded a complex view of inequality in many areas of social life. The findings, though varied by social domain, often point to a pattern of self-replicating inequality.

Several social-inequality researchers have been examining family life—a highly salient domain for the immediate well-being of children, and for the eventual economic and social status of the next generation. We know, for example, that growing up in a single-parent family can impair school performance, raise the odds of teen pregnancy and criminal involvement, and depress future employment and earnings. It is therefore particularly worrisome that Harvard University researchers David Ellwood and Christopher Jencks report growing class differences in the incidence of single-parent families. They find that well-educated women are increasingly postponing both childbirth and marriage, but tend to marry when they have children. Less-educated women are also postponing or eschewing marriage, but not childbirth. As a result, nonmarital births have risen much more quickly among less-educated women than among their more educated peers during the past thirty years. Although the causes of these trends are complex, Ellwood and Jencks argue that decisions to marry and bear children have become more a matter of individual choice in the past thirty years because of changing social norms, which have made unwed motherhood more acceptable, and more effective methods of birth control, which enable women to postpone childbirth. As women consider their options, implicitly or explicitly, rising economic inequality may well influence their decisions. Less-educated women may have little economic incentive to marry, given the increasingly limited economic prospects of their likely partners. Nor do they have as much to lose from early childbearing as more educated women with increasingly bright career prospects, so they have less reason to put off having a child.

Education is another dimension of inequality with transparent importance for the next generation. Over the last three decades, the economic value of education has risen dramatically. High school dropouts are marginalized in a very competitive job market, and strong cognitive skills and college credentials are increasingly important to economic attainment. Americans have responded to this rising demand for skill by getting more and better education wherever they can. But do families at the bottom of the income distribution have the opportunity to improve their educational preparation as effectively as more advantaged groups? By and large, the answer appears to be no.

This is most clearly the case at the beginning and end of the formal educational process, where access to educational facilities depends in part on private financing and the ability of individual families to pay for tuition. Research by Marcia Meyers, Dan Rosenbaum, Christopher Ruhm, and Jane Waldfogel shows that the wealthiest fifth of American families spend almost five times as much for preschool child care as the bottom fifth. The type of day care used also reveals inequalities; well-off families are more likely to use regulated day care centers, while poorer families are more likely to rely on informal arrangements. This difference between rich and poor is echoed at the other end of the educational spectrum, where UCLA economist Thomas Kane finds that students from well-off families have been able to increase their enrollment in four-year colleges more rapidly than students from poor families. This is true even after differences in educational preparation between these groups are taken into account. Again, the problem appears to be financial. As tuitions for four-year colleges have outstripped available financial aid, students from poor families have been increasingly unable to keep up with the rich. Since the average lifetime earnings advantage of a college graduate over a high school graduate has more than doubled in the last thirty years, this widening college enrollment gap portends greater and greater inequality in the future.

How has the American political system performed during this period of rising inequality? Political scientists have long held that the democratic process offers a potential check against gross economic disparities, if increasing inequality prompts the poor to mobilize politically in support of redistributive policies. But evidently nothing of this sort has happened in the past thirty years. Instead, the poor have become increasingly inactive and politically ineffectual as their relative economic position has deteriorated. Richard Freeman of Harvard University finds that inequality in voting behavior has increased significantly over the past forty years. While all income and education groups are voting less in presidential elections than they did in 1964, the poor show by far the largest decline. Over this period, the voting rate among the poorest fifth of the population dropped by 14 percent—far more than the decline for any other income group. Furthermore, the political gap between the rich and the poor is not limited to voting behavior. Political scientists Sidney Verba, Kay Lehman Scholzman, and Henry Brady show that the poor participate less in other facets of political life, like volunteering for a campaign, participating in a local governing board, or (of course) making financial contributions to political candidates. Elsewhere in this volume, Theda Skocpol describes how the social gap extends to other elements of civic life, such as group membership. As the gap in political participation between social classes rises and financial resources become more relevant in the

American political system, the voice of the poor will increasingly fall on deaf ears in government.

These changes in family structure, educational attainment, and political participation are subtle, complicated, and pervasive—all correlates of rising economic inequality. We see similar socioeconomic gradients in many other areas of life. As time passes, children from disadvantaged families are more likely to attend public schools that are dilapidated, overcrowded, and staffed by poorly trained teachers with little experience. They are more likely to report low job satisfaction and to work in unsafe environments. They are a lot more likely to become involved with the criminal justice system, and, perhaps not surprisingly, they even report lower general satisfaction with life.

How do all these disadvantages accumulate? How do they aggregate to change life chances for children in the next generation? Do they in fact have an impact on social mobility? Will we find that as inequality goes up, one's chances of going from the bottom to the top—or even from the bottom to the middle—will decrease? We do not yet know whether rising economic inequality is a leading indicator of declining mobility, but there is every reason to worry that small disadvantages will add up to make inequality a stubborn and growing problem.

Part Three

CHANGING THE CONVERSATION

WHO IS THE ELITE?
Betsy Leondar-Wright

FOR HIS THIRTEENTH BIRTHDAY, I bought my nephew an assortment of toilet paper rolls imprinted with George W. Bush's face and malapropisms. It was during the heat of the 2004 presidential campaign. My nephew had become a connoisseur of anti-Bush humor, and I was happy to bring him fresh specimens, including bumper stickers that said "The emperor has no brains," "Somewhere in Texas a village is missing its idiot," and "Any man who can render himself unconscious with a pretzel isn't smart enough to lead the Free World."

As the election drew nearer, however, I lost my enthusiasm for the theme of presidential stupidity. How were all those Bush-is-dumb jokes going to play with the working-class citizens who, according to the polls, made up a large proportion of Undecided America? Not well, I suspected. Once a forwarder of Bush-denigrating e-mails, I began to push the Delete button instead.

Although the election is now long past, some retrospection as well as introspection may be in order. There is an important lesson to be learned from the campaign and the result. To communicate across the legendary red/blue divide, liberals and progressives need to find a new way to talk to America, and, by implication, a new way to present themselves. The Bush-is-dumb jokes played into the opposition's game. They reinforced the impression that while conservatives stood for something, their political adversaries didn't. They depicted us as exactly the kind of people—latte-drinking, Lycra-wearing, snooty out-of-touch elitists—the right had said we were.

The work of George Lakoff, William Gamson, and others has taught us that facts make an impact only in the context of a "frame" with strong cultural resonances. By "frame," they mean a way of presenting an issue that uses consistent vocabulary and imagery to evoke a certain value-laden worldview. Think about the frame suggested by the Bush-is-stupid anecdotes. They simply confirmed the Bush campaign's chosen image of the president as a regular guy—someone voters could relate to, under attack by people who obviously considered themselves better than he was.

The problem is not that President Bush mispronounces words. The problem is that he is beholden to wealthy donors and big corporations. To energize millions of people to advocate for a fairer economy, we have to understand better the frames that shape the political behavior and outlook of large segments of the population. Once we do, it becomes less surprising that we often fail when we try to sell leaders on the basis of superior competence or intelligence. An election is not a contest over whose facts are right. Too often our information-heavy presentations lack the passion, values, and human stories that would inspire people to get involved or to vote as we would wish them to. We pick apart the conservative story instead of giving voters a more compelling story of our own.

Fairer economic rules shouldn't be a hard sell. Even in this age of get-rich-quick lotteries and reality shows, outrage at inequality is everywhere if you listen for it. It shows up in country music lyrics and punk lyrics, in hip-hop culture, and at Bruce Springsteen concerts. Wherever culture isn't too heavily filtered through the corporate gauze, there's outrage at inequality. We have far more potential allies than we realize—enough, in fact, to create a mass movement for a fairer economy.

One of the deepest American myths is that of the underdog taking on corruption in high places. That story permeates our culture. In addition to the Frank Capra version and the Erin Brockovich version, there's an African American version with resistance against racism, and an immigrant version of success in an unwelcoming land. Even in these free-market-worshipping times, almost every issue of *Reader's Digest* has a story of a whistleblower or a little guy overcoming powerful wrongdoers.

So deep-seated and powerful is this story that influential multimillionaires like Bill O'Reilly and George W. Bush feel compelled to paint themselves as down-to-earth good old boys pitted against elitist snobs. Incredibly, they often manage to carry off this act, at least in the eyes of many Americans. What accounts for their success? It helps to have Fox News and the rest of the right-leaning mass media reading from the same script morning, noon, and night. It also helps to have liberals and leftists falling into the roles that conservatives have assigned us. We need to flip the roles. We progressives must learn to present ourselves as the underdogs we are, in order to expose the corporate-funded right for what it is.

Flipping roles is a matter of both substance and style. It begins with a recommitment to issues of justice and fairness. In that context, the otherwise gloomy 2004 election results offer grounds for encouragement. In Florida, a grassroots alliance of church and community action groups led by ACORN collected enough signatures to get a minimum-wage increase on the November 2004 ballot, and turned people out to vote for it. That effort served to shine a spotlight on workers earning poverty wages and on the employers who underpay them. It united Floridians on one of the most universally held American values—that full-time work should lift someone out of poverty. The Florida living-wage referendum won with 72 percent of the vote.

By a somewhat less lopsided margin, Californians decided to impose a special tax on millionaires to fund mental health services. It does not take a sophisticated grasp of statistics to figure out that a great many of those who supported these populist initiatives were simultaneously casting their ballots for George W. Bush. In both cases, they saw themselves as voting for regular folks, against an elite.

To illustrate the stylistic side of the challenge, let me tell a story about the nonprofit advocacy group I work for, United for a Fair Economy. On April 15, 1998, two leading Republican members of Congress, Billy Tauzin and Dick Armey, came to Boston to promote a campaign for a flat tax and a national sales tax. They invited supporters onto the Boston Tea Party ship, a floating tourist attraction, in order to join them in throwing the entirety of the

United States tax code—thousands of pages' worth—into Boston Harbor.

With advance knowledge of their plans, my colleagues and I set out to use the occasion to dramatize the shift in the tax burden—away from rich people, onto working people—that such proposals would inevitably cause. We bought an inflatable raft, named it the *Working Family Life Raft*, and had a young man and woman row it around a nearby yacht. We sent fifteen people in suits and dresses onto the Tea Party ship. With television cameras rolling, the congressmen made their speeches and prepared to dump the tax code into the harbor. In fact, they were poised to do so when our raft crew rowed right under them, shouting: "Don't throw it! You'll flatten us with your flat tax, you'll sink us with your sales tax!"

Meanwhile, our agents on the Tea Party ship chanted, "Throw it! Throw it! Flatten them with the flat tax! Sink them with the sales tax!" The congressmen froze. It must have been hard for them to decide whether to follow through with their plan. But they did. They hurled the mighty tax code overboard, directly onto the inflatable dinghy, which promptly overturned, tossing our two operatives into Boston Harbor. And that's what was shown on CNN over and over, and in newspaper photos: the capsizing of the *Working Family Life Raft*. The congressmen had hoped to come on as the regular people staging a revolt. We wouldn't let them get away with it. We took them out of the role of underdog and put them back in their rightful role as defenders of a self-interested elite.

Flipping the meaning doesn't have to mean getting wet or engaging in public confrontations. Consider the ingenious work of

Billionaires for Bush, with its slogan, "Leave No Billionaire Behind." That resonant message, devised by what started out as a very small spoof group, soon spread to op-eds, picket signs, and bumper stickers because it so aptly captured the hypocrisy of the Bush administration's education bill—the bill that saddled the public schools with new tests, paperwork, and huge underfunded mandates.

Why aren't there more stories like these? What stops progressives from invoking frames with the potential to unite Americans across the red-blue divide in efforts to narrow inequality? There are, of course, many constraining factors. Limits on funding are part of the story; the right's thirty-year ascendancy has been financed with far more millions than the left has ever seen. We, too, need more think tanks, bigger independent media outlets, and an infrastructure to sustain grassroots organizing over time. We need national organizations that bring together progressives of every race and class across the liberal-to-left spectrum. We need to become more savvy about getting into the mainstream media. But none of those advances will make much difference if we do not step out of the elitist role that has been our gift to the right.

It's easy for conservatives to accuse us of being snobs if we act like snobs. When I was researching my book *Class Matters,* I interviewed twenty working-class activists, asking them to complete the sentence "Middle-class activists drive me crazy when they . . ." Over and over again, they complained of being treated condescendingly. Here are three examples:

> White middle-class activists drive me crazy when they believe theirs is the default reality.

Middle-class activists drive me crazy when they think "we know what's best for workers."

Middle-class activists drive me crazy when they make assumptions that other people are having the same experience they are.

In the understandably emotional time after President Bush's reelection in November 2004, Democrats and other progressives wrote a torrent of bitter analysis. In op-ed columns, letters to the editor, and blog entries, a new theme was the stupidity and ignorance not only of the president but, now, of all who had voted for him. "How Can 59,054,087 People Be So DUMB?," London's *Daily Mirror* asked in a headline that crisscrossed progressive America at Internet speed. More than one friend forwarded me H.L. Mencken's prediction: "On some great and glorious day the plain folks of the land will reach their heart's desire at last and the White House will be adorned by a downright moron." Also widely forwarded was a map with the red states labeled "Dumb-fuckistan."

The most extreme example I saw was a deliberately provocative column by cartoonist Ted Rall. To support Bush, "you had to be spectacularly stupid," Rall declared. He claimed a brainpower advantage not only for Kerry supporters over Bush supporters but for coastal Americans over heartland Americans. "Why shouldn't those of us on the coasts feel superior?" he wrote. "We eat better, travel more, dress better, watch cooler movies, earn better salaries, meet more interesting people, listen to better music and know more about what's going on in the world."

It's a sign of the classist dysfunction in parts of the college-educated left that a public debate was actually needed over whether or not millions of Americans are stupid. When millions of people act in unison, it's because an organized movement has spread a set of ideals and encouraged them to act that way. Just a generation ago, a mass movement arose out of ideals of solidarity, civil rights, and freedom among African Americans and their allies. Progressive values have proliferated in college towns thanks to 1960s activists who became professors, and more recently thanks to student organizing for living wages and against sweatshops, the war, and globalization. Union members have experienced worker solidarity and heard messages about economic justice from their unions. These histories explain why these groups have a more liberal voting record.

Republican ideals have been spread through the proselytizing of evangelical denominations, which predominate in the South. The antichoice movement recruited millions at the grassroots level in the South and Midwest and urged them to vote for right-wing Republicans, as Thomas Frank described so vividly in *What's the Matter with Kansas*. Right-wing media, think tanks, and political ads have saturated the rural and red state landscape. We should hardly be surprised by the conservative voting record of these parts of the country.

The groups that have not experienced such systematic ideological recruitment, or which have been influenced by both left-wing and right-wing movements, such as Latinos and Catholics, are the ones that split their votes. Evangelical Christianity doesn't inevitably lead to right-wing politics, as Jim Wallis's progressive evangelical network Call to Renewal demonstrates. It depends on whose message has been heard loudest, most often, most convincingly, and from the most trusted source.

We need to widen our scope, expand the range of our allies and potential allies, and put more time and money into reaching and educating those not already with us. Calling them stupid is not a good way to start.

Where does it come from, this habit of calling people dumb? It's familiar to most Americans from elementary schools, with their tracking systems. Who gets called dumb? Usually it's the kids from low-income families—poor kids of color especially, but working-class white kids too. The more privileged kids, and the few who rise to advanced academic achievement, get told over and over how "smart" they are. In this deep American frame, those who call Bush voters dumb are lashing out against the working class.

The right has made the most of this terrible habit. In one infamous 2004 television ad, the Club for Growth called on candidate Howard Dean to "take his tax-hiking, government-expanding, latte-drinking, sushi-eating, Volvo-driving, *New York Times*-reading, Hollywood-loving, left-wing freak show back to Vermont, where it belongs!"

It's the latte drinker versus Joe Six-Pack, both sides seem to agree. But while our beverage preferences may tend to line up by class, it's not clear that our voting behavior does. To some extent, the class correlation runs the other way. President Bush won in 2004 among people making over $100,000 a year, lost ground compared to 2000 among those earning under $50,000 a year, and lost badly among some distinctly working-class groups such as African Americans and union members. On social issues such as the infamous trio of "gays, guns, and God," there is a class correlation; the higher someone's income, the more socially liberal he or she tends to be. But the same is not true on economic-inequality issues. Polls show that government redistribution efforts are more popular among lower-income people.

And there's no class level at which the majority approve of the Wal-Martizing and Enronizing of our economy. There's no class level at which the majority believe in jobs paying poverty wages, or in prohibitively expensive health care and prescription drugs. When the economist Michael Zweig analyzed occupational data, he found that the majority of employed Americans are in working-class jobs. Just by the demographics, that's where the greatest number of our potential allies can be found. On economic issues, a cross-class and cross-race mass movement for fairness is possible. Widespread underdog cynicism is potential energy for economic justice.

I grew up middle-class, and I know how easy it is for professional middle-class people to remain segregated among people like themselves. Only 27 percent of the adults in the United States have completed four years of college. How many college graduates socialize with people who didn't go to college? When we live segregated lives, economically *or* racially, it's hard for us to understand that our style, habits, and language may offend or baffle people from less privileged backgrounds. In *Politics and the Class Divide,* David Croteau talks about his experience as a young man from a working-class background going to work for a national leftist organization.

> While I had a strong respect and affection for my fellow activists, it became startlingly apparent to me that many of them within

this part of the Left often had no concrete referent in mind when they talked about "the working class." . . . [A]ctivists' notions of "the working class" tended to fall at extreme poles: either workers were the gloriously idyllic proletariat (who one day would smarten up and start doing their revolutionary duty), or they were stupid, fascistic hard hats for whom there was no hope (and who were the easy target of ridicule). Either way, their working class bore little resemblance to the working class I knew.

This ignorance is what makes some of us middle-class progressives oblivious when it comes to choices of language and posture that could win us more allies. A mass movement for a fairer economy would need to communicate its values in as many styles as there are cultural groups in the United States. Progressive material should be made widely available in Spanish, the first language of one-tenth of our country. We need to spotlight leaders under age thirty and adapt our messages to current youth culture. In the South, we need to speak with a southern accent and a southern sense of humor.

Still, no amount of folksiness will get us past the biggest obstacle, which is one of cynicism and hopelessness more than language and style. The reason most people don't get involved is not because they don't want a fairer economy, but because they don't expect it. Just as bread won't rise without yeast, a movement cannot rise without hope. And hope has been hard for many progressives to come by in this new Gilded Age. Neither national party has a platform that would get us even halfway to economic justice, and the party in charge seems intent on rolling us back to the days of sweatshops and robber barons. A major social activity in progressive circles these days is competing to see who can name the most horrific new political developments.

If we want more people to get active, we had better face up to this critical shortage of hope. I used to work as a community organizer, and at one point my job was to knock on doors of low-income tenants to tell them that their housing was in danger of becoming unaffordable after a certain date. I saw firsthand how most people in their fear jumped immediately to individual solutions: "My sister is in Tennessee, maybe she could take us in for a while if we moved there." The most valuable thing I brought to them was the information that other tenants in other towns had gotten together to buy their properties and turn them into permanently affordable housing. I organized three tenant groups that now own and run their apartment complexes. My main contribution to their victories was a sense of informed hope.

In his conversations with working-class people about progressive movements, David Croteau was met with incredulity. The people he interviewed thought that politics was like the weather: it just happened, and they could do nothing but complain. Talk of changing things was met with great skepticism unless the speaker had a concrete plan that sounded realistic.

Hopelessness is at the root of why people grab greedily for individual windfalls. If hard work doesn't pay an honest reward, and political change is impossible, then going to the casino or suing someone seems like the best route. But most Americans aren't pathologically greedy or selfish. Many people, given a measure of hope, would jump at the chance for a fairer economy—

one that would work better not just for themselves, but for everyone else.

And we are surrounded by signs of hope: the prosecution of corporate criminals, victories in service worker organizing, the living-wage movement, the spontaneous rise of a hundred chapters of Billionaires for Bush, towns saying no to Wal-Mart, and on and on.

Those of us who know such hopeful stories, whether from participating in organized efforts for economic justice or from reading history, need to share our understanding of how mass movements can bring about positive change. The current plutocracy is no more difficult to depose than Jim Crow was, or apartheid. It's incumbent on those who know how improbable some past changes seemed, and how they happened despite the odds, to be messengers of hope.

DON'T DRINK THE KOOL-AID
Robert Kuttner

A NUMBER of the other articles in this volume document the shocking increase in inequality in America. My message is simple: It does not have to be that way. It does not have to be that way economically or politically.

The right has a story to tell about inequality. It's a simple story, which has been swallowed whole by elite opinion and a lot of ordinary Americans. If you want an economy that works efficiently, it says, you have to tolerate a great deal of inequality. I've devoted much of my career as an economics writer and a polemicist to disproving that argument. The simplest refutation is to refer back to periods of American history when we had significantly greater equality, both of opportunity and of result, and stronger economic growth; we can also point to other countries that have much less inequality than the United States does, and work better economically.

It's not hard to see why they do. A prosperous economy demands investment in children, in health, in education, in job training, in public systems, in the commons generally. If you have tens of millions of people not living up to their potential as economic beings, by definition your society is going to be less productive than it could be. If you spend almost 15 percent of the gross domestic product on health care because private, profit-motivated insurance companies are taking 30 cents out of every premium dollar, you are not going to have a society that is as healthy as it ought to be.

Equality works. Extreme inequality does not. Out of the grotesque opportunism that we've seen among owners of great wealth in the past ten years has come a colossal waste of financial capital and human energy. The stock market bubble of the late 1990s induced investors to put vast resources into enterprises that never paid back a nickel of return; they only lined the pockets of insiders. If the government squandered money on this scale, conservatives and conservative investment bankers would be up in arms. But they're not, of course. When the government wastes hundreds of dollars, they tell us it's an outrage; when the market wastes trillions of dollars, it's a lamentable glitch. This is not economics. This is ideology, pure and simple.

Why has our society become so much more unequal in the past twenty-five years? It's a trick question. The technical or policy answer involves a systematic weakening of what might be called equalizing institutions, which defend the commonwealth against the forces of wealth and concentrated power. To maintain a social contract of the kind that existed in this country during the postwar decades, you need a government to administer it; to help people climb out of poverty, you have to tax the wealthy and put some of the proceeds into opportunity-making programs. But in a global economy with no global government, there is no entity capable of enforcing rules or effectively collecting taxes and directing public investment. I am a citizen of the United States of America. I am not a citizen of the Republic of NAFTA. There is no Republic of NAFTA, and that is exactly the way big business wants it.

And so, in addition to the alleged economic efficiency of freer trade, business gets another benefit: it wipes away all of the social institutions that have been built through great struggle by ordinary people and their governments over the past hundred years. That is really the insidious influence of globalization. It is not just that jobs move to countries where people are desperate enough to work for starvation wages, or where publics are too powerless to demand environmental standards. No, it is the fact that we are left with no democratically accountable institution capable of setting ground rules. We could have had a brand of globalization in which the ability to sell products to the United States depended on meeting certain social minimums, involving wages, organizing rights, environmental standards, treatment of children, and so on. But because that was not the globalization that corporate America sought, it is not what has evolved.

So the real answer to the question, "Why have we become so much more unequal?" has to be a political answer. The forces that yearn for a restoration of the kind of polity we had in the robber baron era of the late 1800s have become far stronger over the past quarter century; that, in essence, is why organized labor has shrunk since 1970 from 35 percent to 12.5 percent of the American workforce. That's what encourages giant corporations to demand huge tax "incentives" before they move in anywhere, and then to move out with impunity as soon as another jurisdiction offers a better deal. That's why, in so many areas, property rights now take precedence over human rights, social rights, and labor rights. The instruments and institutions that allow us to choose to become a more egalitarian society have simply been removed from the realm of democratic citizenship.

We cannot fully blame this change on one political faction or party. Too often, over the past twenty-five years, both parties have been drinking the same Kool-Aid. Too much of the time, Democrats have presented themselves as the "me too" party. "We do not really like government either," they say. "We love big business, too. Let the free market decide." We heard far too much of that from our last two Democratic presidents.

There are several explanations for this self-defeating rhetoric. First of all, it is the result of money becoming paramount in politics—becoming the medium of politics. If you spend most of your waking hours courting the wealthy, you start talking their language; you instinctively seek to reassure your donors, and you cease paying attention to building, validating, and energizing your base. As the Democrats have become more artful fund-raisers, their message to the base has become muddy, and populism has become a dirty word.

The news media has abetted the process. When I started out in journalism, a reporter was a kind of average person who wore cheap suits and identified with the downtrodden. Today the most influential journalists, who make six- and seven-figure incomes by giving well-paid lectures to trade associations and hobnob with elites, do not identify with ordinary people. One of the daunting tasks that faces us, in addition to taking back American politics, is taking back the American press.

As a magazine editor, I spend much of my time raising money. That means, among other things, trying to persuade the wealthy liberals who give to political candidates that it is equally important to invest in intellectual and media infrastructure. The *American Prospect,* the magazine I edit, depends on the kindness of many strangers, and we are duly grateful; yet there is something a little off about the relationship. America has always had wealthy people who genuinely cared about the commonwealth. Franklin Roosevelt was a class traitor, perhaps the greatest class traitor our country has ever known, and we surely need more like him. For the most part, however, the liberalism of extremely affluent liberals runs out when you move beyond tolerance issues and social issues. Start talking about progressive taxation or national health insurance or a more dramatic equalizing role for the government, and the benefactors will get squeamish; that's when you can expect to be cautioned against the hazards of "populism," which is donor code for articulating the pocketbook interests of working-class and poor Americans. The dependence on wealthy people, even liberal ones, creates a disjuncture between how politicians spend their time—how they get elected and hone their message—and what they need to do to mobilize the Democratic base.

About ten years ago, I was at a local Democratic Party event in an affluent Boston suburb. There were two speakers. The first was our junior senator, John Kerry. The other speaker was me, in my role as a columnist for the *Boston Globe.* "Who among us," Kerry said at one point, "really wants more regulation?" After he had finished, I said, "Excuse me, Senator, but I do. I want more environmental regulation. I want more regulation of corporate misconduct. I certainly want more regulation of health care so the insurance companies do not drop people who have the effrontery to get sick." Kerry backed off. Of course, he was not talking about that sort of regulation. He was talking about bureaucracy and red tape. The point is, a reflexive distancing from government has become second nature among Democratic as well as Republican leaders. It's become part of the party's collective unconscious in a very unfortunate way. I don't think it was any accident that Bill Clinton and Jimmy Carter spent so much of their time disparaging government. It was in the air, because of a quarter century of hard and very effective organizing by the right—the financial right, the business right, the intellectual right, and the political right.

Right-wing foundations, advocacy groups, activists, and politicians tend to march in lockstep, with the same message and the same strategy at all times. There is a huge gulf between their coordinated efficiency and what happens on the liberal side of the fence. There we see wonderful foundations with heroic presidents and program officers (many of these foundations were named after some of the worst robber barons in the history of this country), providing money for good causes but finding themselves whipsawed between their business-dominated boards and the groups they seek to fund. Progressive media organs and advocacy groups not only have less in the way of resources than the right does but have to do a lot more fancy footwork to tap them. The *Weekly Standard* has the same circulation as the *American Prospect*, about sixty thousand, but Bill Kristol, its editor, does not have to go around with a tin cup the way I do. Once a year Rupert Murdoch writes him a check for $12 million. The rest of the time, Bill is free to make his mischief.

The right has vast resources, a well-honed strategy, and enormous discipline. Nonetheless, I think progressives can win this struggle because, ultimately, America is still a democracy. When people get energized, people count for more than money. The writer and scholar Frances Fox Piven spent much of her career celebrating the achievements of activists and movements operating outside the political system. Then, late in midlife, with her husband, Richard Cloward, she became one of the inspirations—maybe the pivotal force—behind the motor voter law. After years as a radical and student of radicalism, Piven came back to realizing that the most radical thing of all in a democracy is the notion of popular rule.

But the people rule only when they are energized. That means we have to look at both sides of the inequality equation: the dynamics of economic inequality and the dynamics of political or participatory inequality, and how the two cross-influence each other. When a political system is dominated by money, the issues that might motivate and change the lives of ordinary voters are effectively removed from the agenda. Ordinary people are not fools; why should they waste their time with a process that holds no practical promise for them? So you have what the political scientist Walter Dean Burnham has called a "politics of excluded alternatives"—a politics in which options that the vast majority of Americans would favor, like universal health care, are not on the agenda. You have a politics in which, to cite another example, high-quality child-development programs—early childhood, pre-kindergarten, after-school—are not an option, despite the fact that, according to every social scientist who has studied the question, they make a crucial difference in whether children grow up to be productive citizens. For about $60 billion a year you could have a comprehensive, universal, development-oriented childhood program. But when money shapes the agenda, the policies that would inspire ordinary people to get involved don't even make it into the discussion, and people tune out.

In 2004, a coalition of groups led by ACORN succeeded in putting an increase in the minimum wage on the Florida ballot. It carried every single county, winning 72 percent of the vote. It got a million more votes than George W. Bush and 1.5 million more than John Kerry. I'd venture to say that if Kerry, who did not actively back the initiative, had been out there visibly campaigning with ACORN, he'd be president.

For the most part, the kinds of instruments that could make this society a more equal polity and a more equal society are not on offer. So many of the things that government could do, like living-wage ordinances and federal minimum-wage laws, or civil-rights protection for union organizers—policies that would transform American society as well as politics—cannot get a hearing.

We need our elected officials to use the power of their offices to change the dominant rhetoric and assumptions. Instead of joining the right in bashing government, let's celebrate what social investment can do. Instead of saying we do not like regulation much either, let's talk about all the bad things corporations do, and about the need to housebreak them with strong public-interest regulation.

Not long ago, at a convention of the Hotel Employees and Restaurant Employees Union (HERE), John Wilhelm, the union's president, summoned to the front of the hall a body of rank-and-file members representing every imaginable ethnic and racial group. They were there to be honored with speeches and slides and music, with a thousand people watching, for the heroic act of organizing a union. In Las Vegas, because of this union, hotel jobs now pay middle-class wages and offer health benefits, and men and women who start out cleaning rooms can hope to enter the ranks of management eventually. As the tribute continued, I found myself indulging in a fantasy: what if, instead of John Wilhelm, it was the president of the United States making a fuss over these men and women? Suppose the President addressed Congress, and we saw, up in the balcony with the First Lady, not the foreign minister of Iraq or a hero who had pulled a survivor from a plane crash, but a collection of ordinary everyday heroes—Americans raising and supporting their families, and holding body and soul together in jobs with wretched pay and no health insurance—struggling against great odds to organize their fellow workers? Imagine the president speaking about what such citizens deserve as Americans, and about our shared responsibility to make this a fairer country. With a series of celebrations like that, we could begin to turn around the rhetoric and the thinking that help account for the growing economic divide. We could begin to discover a new faith in public institutions and the ideal of a more equal society.

But of course you cannot just wait until someone with those values and that kind of courage wins the presidency. First, we have to take back the political process. Progressives often complain that politicians are weather vanes, bending with the winds. It is up to us to change the prevailing wind.

THE LEGITIMIZATION OF INEQUALITY
Robert M. Franklin

I AM A THEOLOGIAN. In my profession, people spend a good deal of time thinking about why and how humans strive to make meaning in their lives. Often, meaning takes the form of myth. The English word *myth* derives from the Greek word *mythos,* which means "story." But a myth is not, as people now commonly assume, a story that is patently untrue; rather, it is a story that conveys meaning and purpose. A myth speaks truth to those who take it seriously.

"We need a story to see in the dark," says the psychiatrist to his patient in Peter Shaffer's play *Equus.* Commenting on that poignant line, my fellow theologian John Westerhoff observes, "We all need such a story. Stories are the means by which we see reality. . . . Without a story we cannot have community. Without a story life makes no sense. The story that is foundational to our life provides us with the basis for our perceptions and for our faith. Stories are the imaginative way of ordering our experience."

Every social system needs what the German social thinker Jurgen Habermas calls a legitimating myth—a narrative that conveys the social system's aspirations and values. Ideally, that myth compels loyalty and inspires devotion. It rouses people to acts of self-sacrifice on behalf of the community. It can even help them learn to accept social injustice by depicting it as a remediable discrepancy or as a temporary means to a greater good. But when the myth no longer persuades—when it no longer mystifies—then, according to Habermas, society experiences a legitimation crisis.

In America, growing economic inequality may be propelling us toward such a crisis. In fact, the crisis may be overdue. Through insidious and calculated mythmaking, we have been numbed into accepting as normal a degree of inequality that is a betrayal of our founding ideals. At the core of the American creed is the conviction—spelled out in the Declaration of Independence and our other constitutive documents—that God made all people equal, and that all are endowed with inalienable rights. This language, which ranks among history's greatest examples of aspirational mythmaking, is thick and complex. It assumes a deity. It assumes a deity who is creative and had something to do with the creation of humans. It assumes and asserts that this deity bestowed or gifted human beings (not just Americans but all humans) with certain goods or rights that are profound, intrinsic, and not subject to negotiation. When Jefferson used the phrase "all men," he meant (as many scholars and historians have been careful to note) white men of property. But over the course of American history, the narrative of equality has been porous and malleable: we have enlarged the meaning of the story to include people of color and women. It is here in the American language of human equality that we find the "primal myth" that inspires faith in our nation and that binds us together as one united American people, regardless of race, creed, or national origin. That is a good and inspiring myth.

But it has always coexisted with—and, in our own time, runs the risk of being displaced by—a parallel myth, which declares that no matter how hard we try, there will be some who thrive and become wealthy, while others, many others, will never rise much above poverty and virtual servitude. This premise goes back to the supposed observation of Jesus of Nazareth that "the poor you will have with you always." Like other words in sacred scripture, their meaning is unclear, even if we assume that Jesus actually spoke them. Nevertheless, over the past several decades this ambiguous statement has become central to an ideology of greed and callousness, and to what I would call a myth of normative inequality. Pragmatically, "normative inequality" means that our system of government can and will thrive despite dramatic disparities in wealth and power. It has done so in the past; why not now? Politically, "normative inequality" suggests that if the poor were truly disgusted with the concentration of power and assets, they would rise up in revolt. Theologically, "normative inequality" asserts that God or the moral universe is content with this arrangement of power, and there is no ethical imperative for redistribution or change.

Because the myth of normative inequality has taken over our political, economic, and media cultures, we will need an equally powerful myth to dislodge this untruth parading as gospel. But the germ for a new, empowering myth could come from a familiar place. At the core of all the great religious or wisdom traditions is the belief that those who are strong have an obligation to assist the weak. From those to whom much has been given, much is required. Never theirs alone, the assets of the privileged are meant to enhance the life prospects of other members of the community. The Catholic bishops have advocated a "social mortgage" in which all citizens share claims to certain basic forms of wealth, challenging exclusive notions of private property and conventional mortgages. This is the underlying assumption of the genteel notion of noblesse oblige.

Wealthy, powerful people have often twisted this moral expectation into a condescending, missionary impulse to help the unwashed masses. Beneath the distortion, however, stands a fundamental truth: We are not autonomous, detached moral agents. In this sense, Immanuel Kant and John Rawls got the moral anthropology wrong. Humans are fundamentally interdependent and responsible for the fabric of society that is shared by all. That's what prompts young soldiers to go far away from home to defend and restore the freedom and rights of innocent people from tyrants. That's the impulse that guides old women and men to plant trees that they will never see or sit under. And in that context, although relatively few legislators and executives are responsible for facilitating the concentration of wealth, we all are obliged to act to change the status quo. As Rabbi Joachim Prinz declared at the 1963 March on Washington, commenting on the social sins of racism and anti-Semitism, "while few are guilty, all are responsible."

The psychologist Erik Erikson tells us that as we move into the later years of the human life span, our maturity should be measured by the extent to which we care for the next generation. (Suburban elders who seek to duck the burden of paying for public education, take note.) Erikson refers to this capacity to prepare the world for the next generation as the virtue of "generativity." Those who are indifferent to the next generation are, in a sense, developmentally arrested. It is fascinating to note how our culture's obsession with immortal youthfulness devalues the virtue of generativity, depriving communities of real grown-ups and of grandparents (actual or fictive) who love children more than golf or shopping. One wonders if the obsessive-compulsive dimension of the Enron executives who stole the assets of fellow employees and investors to buy lavish toys was yet another escape into prolonged adolescence.

Inequality undermines the possibility of creating a community in which all citizens perceive and accept their responsibilities for preserving the social order; the myth of normative inequality insulates us from even trying. Inequality compromises political and economic systems and then thrives on their dysfunction. Psychologically, inequality disables citizens by infantilizing them and making them dependent, while the culture distracts them with entertaining television shows, lifestyle icons, and self-improvement fads. Adults lose their ability to demand respect and justice from systems. They lose their voice. They stop fighting back. They become amnesiacs who cannot remember the struggles or the victories of the past. Normative inequality moves from sociology and economics to psychology and spirituality.

But, as Habermas suggests, a myth begins to lose its power when the deception becomes transparent and it no longer persuades. When people start to realize that the emperor has no clothes, change is more than possible; it is inevitable. When people no longer believe that it is okay to live in a society where the

Bill Gateses, the Donald Trumps, the Ted Turners, and the Waltons (I am referring to the Wal-Mart Waltons, not the TV show family) ostentatiously display their power while families are living in motel rooms and automobiles or begging for quarters on the street, things can happen. When people get mad and (as Bill Moyers has said) get organized, movements can be born. When a movement is born that reaches out into the hinterlands and across Wall Street and the Beltway, then we will witness the remaking of American public life.

The concept of mythmaking is crucial for two reasons. First, the contest for the minds, the trust and the loyalty, of American citizens must go deeper than the force of the better argument ever can—we must tell our story in ways that go beyond marshaling compelling statistics and abstract arguments about democracy's decline. Second, the contest for America's future must reach deeper into the psyche of citizens to show them that the current system is immoral and offensive to American ideals and to the cherished values of their own wisdom traditions. We need to convey to those 93 percent of Americans who claim to believe in a divine being that God is pissed off about our stewardship of the Earth's resources and our failure to take responsibility for building a blessed community.

Support for this claim can be found in the headlines. On June 3, 2004, *USA Today* led with the headline "Churchgoing Closely Tied to Voting Patterns," and followed that with "GOP Capitalizes on Religion Gap; Dems Debate What to Do." The article goes on to say, "Forget the gender gap. The 'religion gap' is bigger, more powerful and growing. The religion gap is the leading edge of the 'culture war' that has polarized American politics, reshaped the coalitions that make up the Democratic and Republican parties and influenced the appeals their presidential candidates are making."

In politics, heavy-handed moralizing can backfire. But while that is a danger for today's Republicans to consider, Democrats should be alert to a different peril: their restraint and civility, born of respect for private moral and religious convictions (or the lack thereof), becomes a liability in our Machiavellian political culture. Karl Rove knows that this silence, ironically, fails to communicate respect, and he has used that wedge to suggest that in the battle for moral leadership, it is the believers against the rest of us.

Progressives, therefore, must find a way to remind America of the core values in all our sacred wisdom traditions that are fundamentally opposed to our culture of inequality. Historic Judaism observed the practices of Sabbath and of Jubilee, which recognized that the laissez-faire economy, left to itself, would exploit and harm poor people, and called for a periodic (every seven or fifty years) readjustment, in which the privileged members of the society were compelled to demonstrate their social righteousness (*tzedekah*) by enabling the poor and vulnerable to improve their lot.

In Islam, usury is not permitted, in order to guard against exploiting those in financial need; *zakat* is the Islamic requirement to contribute a portion of one's wealth toward the aid of the poor and the community. Authentic Islam thus underscores the importance of striving for economic justice through fair and charitable behavior. Needless to say, if American-sponsored globalization appears to be a system in which wealthy nations can further exploit poorer nations, many Muslims will feel obliged to stand up and push back against us.

In Christianity, the first sermon of Jesus emphasized that he was sent to preach good news to the poor, liberty to the incarcerated, recovery of sight to the blind, and liberation to the oppressed. But how often do these vulnerable people appear in the worldview of American churches?

Our task is to reframe the message of inequality, and to deconstruct its enabling myth, for those who are searching for a better alternative. When the legitimation crisis seizes the public imagination, we must have laid the groundwork for another story. Myth and story must come into play because they reach deeper into the core of human motivation and aspiration than rational, cognitive argument. But there is another reason for us to pay more attention to myth, and that is because our political opponents have done so, to awesome effect. The linguist and political thinker George Lakoff, who has written persuasively about the power of language to convey large frames or pictures of reality, reminds us that in 1970, Supreme Court justice Lewis Powell wrote a fateful memo to the National Chamber of Commerce saying that all of the best students were becoming antibusiness because of the Vietnam War and that business leaders needed to do something about it. Powell's agenda included getting wealthy conservatives to set up professorships, and establishing institutes where intellectuals could write books from a conservative business perspective. He urged them to set up conservative think tanks, and they took his advice. The Heritage Foundation was created in 1973; the Manhattan Institute and the American Enterprise Institute followed soon thereafter.

Paul Weyrich, the founder of the Heritage Foundation, estimates that there are now some 1,500 conservative radio talk show hosts. Even if Weyrich overstates slightly, it is a huge number, and they often work together with frightening efficiency. Conservative foundations give large grants year after year to their think tanks; they build infrastructure to get their message out; they hire intellectuals and set aside money to buy a lot of books to get them on the bestseller lists, hire research assistants for their intellectuals so they do well on TV, and hire agents to put them on TV.

By contrast, progressives do not wish to appear too pushy or manipulative. They expect people to connect the dots and see what's going on. Progressives have not framed their message in a catchy, compelling way; they have failed to build the infrastructure to communicate their message. Fortunately, this is beginning to change. Air America, the *American Prospect,* the Center for American Progress, Demos, and others have begun to fill both the message and medium gaps; but much more needs to be done, and it must be sustained.

Meanwhile, conservatives continue to exploit the hot-button issues, and their focus on wedge issues such as abortion and same-sex marriage sets progressives and moderates at war with each other, while the conservative myth of normative inequality goes unchallenged.

How can we hasten the legitimation crisis? How can we pull back the curtain on the "smartest guys in the room" who are selling America poisonous myths? We need to use powerful visual images that allow new stories to be told. It was the sight of dogs unleashed upon innocent citizens in the South that made white Americans realize that their country was still poisonously divided. More recently, it was the video of planes shooting into the World Trade Center that awakened us to our newly vulnerable place in the world. Truth needs to be *seen to be embraced*, not simply heard. In other words, we need to see pictures of inequality—to see the grotesque art that is the daily life of our fellow citizens. We must recover the imaginative and descriptive power of Jacob Riis, Sinclair Lewis, and James Baldwin as we tell the story of inequality in America.

The pictures from Abu Ghraib prison undid the lies of the CIA and Pentagon and forced policy makers and the public to grapple with unbelievable realities; we need equally powerful images to advance this case. What if the American public encountered pictures of families in poverty on television, on posters, on lapel buttons with the simple interrogative "Is this the best that America can do for proud and patriotic Americans? What does God have to say about this distribution of wealth and power?"

"This hour in history needs a dedicated circle of transformed nonconformists," Martin Luther King declared. "The saving of our world from pending doom will come not from the actions of a conforming majority but from the creative maladjustment of a transformed minority."

BUILDING A MORAL ECONOMY
William Greider

CAPITALISM IS A HUMAN CONSTRUCT. It was not inscribed on tablets handed down by Adam Smith or God; it was made by people, and so it can be altered by people. The fact that all of us, whether we like it or not, participate in capitalism suggests that there may be a bit of soul buried there under the manure and greed.

Putting *soul* and *capitalism* into the same sentence provokes snickers and sneers in some of the quarters I frequent. I get more of the same when I talk about building a moral economy. "What's *that*?" people ask in disbelief—the people who haven't already turned the page or left the room. By moral economy, I mean an economy that serves people and society first, providing, as John Maynard Keynes wrote long ago, the material basis for civilization instead of overwhelming society and people with destructive consequences. The word *moral* implies not only the comparatively narrow question of personal ethics, but a society that allows people—propels people—to fulfill their obligations and responsibilities as human beings. Such a society is, by definition, one that encourages the nurture of children and the protection of community; that is aware, every day, of the difference between right and wrong; and that preserves our earthly and cultural inheritance for the benefit of future generations—our grandchildren and theirs. All these things are moral obligations. They are also life's rewards, far beyond material comfort or gains.

In 1932, a conservative minister of the Dutch Reform church, Emil Brunner, described capitalism this way: "The system is contrary to the spirit of service. It is debased and irresponsible. Indeed we may go further and say it is irresponsibility developed into a system."

Irresponsibility developed into a system—sadly, that is the face that capitalism most often shows us. Irresponsibility is our great wound as a society. It's imposed on us by the economic system in ways that make us innocent bystanders and unwitting accomplices. Like it or not, we are complicit in the destruction of family and community, in the evisceration of democracy, in the relentless exploitation of nature; and, yes, in a gross and growing inequality that is not just a contradiction of our values, but makes the fulfillment of our values impossible to imagine.

This is not 1932. The Great Depression was a time of unbelievable want and suffering. The social and political conflicts of those years lie equally far beyond our imagining. People were in the streets, and with reason. Our condition today is almost the opposite. Our problem is abundance—a plenitude of material goods and a fabulous kind of elusive wealth that exists in our society and yet floats away from most people, perversely putting them under a kind of tension that drives them to sacrifice more of their private selves (those moral obligations I referred to) in order to keep the engine roaring, and to keep up with not only what they have assumed is the required devotion to the system of production and consumption, but with what they believe are their material entitlements as Americans. We are a breathtakingly wealthy country in those gross terms—why, then, is our wealth so buried in discontent and so unequally distributed?

The problem of abundance is important for us to absorb, because the images of the Great Depression and the New Deal remain in our heads. They are powerful images, which I don't mean to disparage. But we're in a different situation. Our affluence is an opportunity *and* a burden, yet Pastor Brunner's words still ring true: we are made irresponsible. It is not just the owners and the CEOs who avert their eyes. As workers, as employees, as consumers, we, too, are distanced from the consequences of our actions. As investors, our money is shipped off to some obscure place to perform we know not what mission; often, we don't have a clue what our investment is doing to us, to our neighbors, to our society. When we catch a glimpse of the consequences, we invoke natural law and abjure responsibility.

This uncontrolled and seemingly uncontrollable economy generates terrible inequality of income and wealth, and, more crucially, of power. That is the place for us to begin thinking about change, and it is the place where we have the capacity to effect change—to impose our values, priorities, and sensibilities on the economic system. First, though, we have to locate our power—our leverage within the system—as workers, investors, consumers, citizens, owners, and managers. To do that, we need to broaden our understanding of who's on our side and who's on the other side, because the categories we inherited from the nineteenth and early twentieth centuries no longer capture our circumstances. Some people have shifted roles in ways that allow us to leap over old boundaries, stitch together new relationships, and face some of the contradictions of capitalism that have so easily been dodged in the past.

I am referring to a loose community of what I sometimes playfully call humanist populist capitalists. It sounds like a triple oxymoron, but they exist; I know because I've actually met some of them. They are not what you'd call bleeding-heart liberals; they are practical men and women of business who have decided that the system—their system, our system—is fouled up on its own terms; and they have set out to change their little piece of it. They will tell you that, like other capitalists, they are motivated by profit. But if you push them a little, they will acknowledge that they are also trying to do right by the people and communities around them.

The great reforms enacted from the 1880s through the 1960s were achieved by government correcting capitalism's injustices and excesses, and compensating people and society for their injuries. If we are honest with ourselves, we will acknowledge that many of the best ideas of those years have been blunted or pushed aside, and that the reforms, great as they were, did not in the end fundamentally alter the contours or the operating values of the system. Yet we were left with the idea of government as our protector—as the counterweight to capitalism. That concept continues to anchor our politics to this day, even though many of the great structures of mediation and moderation built by the New Deal have been utterly eviscerated. Like our politics, they don't work.

The government made another brief and narrowly defined attempt to set things right after the corporate meltdown and scandals of the late 1990s. But it didn't come to much. In the last decade or two, it has become clear—it *should* have become clear—that the efforts of government have always fallen short of what is needed. They have not, and perhaps cannot, overcome the originating sources within capitalism of our injury. They have contained it in various ways—they have domesticated it. But the system is still with us. The beast still functions in pretty much the same old delightfully irresponsible way.

That leaves us with a different challenge, which is to confront the American system of capitalism itself and change it in organic ways—reinvent its major institutions and create new ones; reform its operating values by imposing our broader social values on how firms and companies and marketplaces function; and above all, rearrange power within the system so it's not concentrated—either in finance or in corporations or other institutions, including, I would add, the government—within the reach of only a few, opaque and walled off from the voices of the man.

Government is not going to meet this challenge. Even if it wanted to, it wouldn't know how. Government can, I hope, encourage and eventually ratify positive changes that take root in the society at large; government can embed new principles in law. First, though, people have to envision a transformed economic system through the act of transforming their part of it; they need to imagine what society can become. In this effort, we must be a bit grandiose and self-indulgent and allow ourselves to dream a little—of not next year or the year after or even five or ten years from now, but of twenty-five or fifty years from now; we need to ask what we want this country to feel like and look like for our children and grandchildren. We need to entertain the implausible—wallow in it a little—and then work backward, asking: "Where are the lever points; where are the mechanisms that might make these changes possible?"

These visions must be the polestar against which we measure the practical steps that are within our reach today. Many people, it turns out, are already thinking and acting in this way. They start new companies, they reform existing companies, they even start new financial institutions (which are, after all, nothing more than savings pooled together for different purposes), they make new alliances of interest among labor, environmentalists, and business, and they use those alliances to exert serious, often decisive, leverage in the marketplace and the halls of government. Fanciful? Maybe. But I have seen it happen. It is happening in small, fragmented ways in places as diverse as Youngstown, Ohio, Marin County, and Baltimore. These disparate efforts are the beginning of what I suspect will prove to be an important new force. They represent an era of reform that is struggling to find its feet, like a newborn colt.

Let us be honest. Most of us don't really think much about how capitalism works—it's the beast that's out there, and we are running around it like little guerrillas shooting arrows into the belly, hoping for a reaction. I cannot assert with confidence that this new movement will form and gather force over the next generation, but there are believers at work. I have seen them. And I'm excited by them, because they embody the heart and soul of democracy—they are people putting their own self-interest in harness with their idealism and looking for other like-minded people with whom they can connect. They have big ideas—first about themselves and what they can achieve, but also about changing society, which is, after all, the starting gate for every great transformation. Deep change does not begin in the political process or with single issues; it begins among ordinary people deciding to change their circumstances.

I am not urging people to turn away from politics and government and issues. I do suggest, however, that ideas big enough to transform our country will likely not gain authenticity in the political debate, nor the political strength to truly advance, unless and until we have done this hard work of building alternative enterprises that link our values to our livelihoods. I am confident that we can do this if we start out with a sense of mutual respect, and understand that we are going to be patient with each other as well. A recognition of mutuality, and the alliances that follow from that recognition, are crucial. Remember, self-interest and idealism, or love of country, are really the most powerful thing we have got going. Regaining those values and making them manifest in the real world has been the work of all great reform movements, including—as I can't emphasize too strongly—the right over the last thirty or forty years. The convictions of those on the right gave them the patience and persistence to do hard work that produced lasting results.

One reason for taking business more seriously—and taking government, for now, a bit less seriously—is the crucial importance of work in shaping lives and attitudes. The ineffectuality of our democracy has much to do with a wave of resignation and passivity and solemn acceptance of our situation that has swept over Americans during the past few decades. Where did we learn to think so little of ourselves and our possibilities? We learned it at work—at the office as well as on the shop floor. American workplaces have become "factories of authoritarianism polluting our democracy," in the words of Elaine Bernard of the Harvard Trade Union Studies Program. "Citizens cannot spend eight hours a day obeying orders and being shut out of important decisions affecting them," she observes, "and then be expected to engage in a robust critical dialogue about the structure of our society."

This is unexplored territory because it requires us to step back from—not renounce, but step back from—established frameworks of thinking, and begin to appreciate, first, that democratic renewal might have to begin at work as much as at the polls, and second, that the sense of confinement and even loss, personal loss, that people feel at work is not confined to the working poor or the working class (though obviously they have suffered far more severely than others). In this age of triumph for market values and the narrowly smug economics of Milton Friedman and Friedrich von Hayek, you can go quite a ways up the ladder of income and status, and still find much the same stripping away of self-control and self-direction.

In my book *The Soul of Capitalism,* I suggest that despite all our civilized trappings, most of us still function in a feudal remnant known as the master-servant relationship. Everywhere I go—from a trendy bookstore in Silicon Valley to a union hall in Minneapolis or Chicago—that simple phrase rings a bell. It expresses a deep hurt.

The most direct and profound remedy is a simple and familiar touchstone of capitalism: ownership. Supervisors and workers, those in the front office and those on the loading dock, must own their own work. To get a sense of the potential, consider a temp agency in Baltimore called Solidarity. It is owned by the temp workers themselves, and modeled on the network of cooperatives in the Mondragon region of Spain. The company has a young MBA who was idealistic enough to hire on as a manager, and who knows what she is doing. But more important, the workers know what they're doing. They pay themselves a dollar or two an hour more than the other temp agencies in town, and they have health insurance. But the most important quality is that they meet regularly for self-criticism and self-disciplining, and they've come up with some marvelously practical commonsense ideas about, first of all, how to do the work more effectively and responsibly so the contractors will keep hiring them, and also how to develop a relationship among themselves that is actually more self-disciplining than anything a boss would ever have devised. And here comes the punch line: all the workers are African American, most are recovering narcotics addicts, and some of them are recovering drug dealers. Most have been in prison or jail.

While it is easiest to think about ownership of work in simple and nontraditional settings, the concept is no less applicable—or crucial—in the complex setting of a modern industrial organization with diverse ownership and responsibility. Each worker must have some voice in her own work and destiny, and some influence over the bigger decisions of the firm. Each worker must be willing to accept some of the risk and responsibility of production within all the dimensions of the firm: that means making products that people need and are willing to pay for, but also working in ways that are respectful to others and to the community and the environment, and recognizing that when risk is borne by all so must profit be shared by all.

The link between ownership of work and inequality of reward is obvious. The corporation and the employment system are two of the principal engines, maybe the main engines, of enduring inequality in today's world, and the proof of that is the recurring waves of inequality that follow the life of the firm. Gross inequality is somewhat mitigated by rule regulation and contract, yet it persists because when the big decisions are made, only a handful of people are at the table. If we can imagine a firm where everybody has some participating voice and more than just cosmetic power to influence decisions, can we imagine them allowing the outrages of CEO pay that we've seen? I don't think so. I don't think any community of working people organized in such a way would decide that these compensation arrangements were good for the company.

The road to the kind of ownership I am imagining is long and difficult for lots of practical everyday reasons, but especially because people have to change themselves. The master-servant relationship may be grotesque, but we understand it. For workers, owning one's job requires learning powerful new concepts: first, about who must follow and who gets to give orders, and second, about responsibility beyond a set of prescribed tasks. The managers likewise have to recognize that a new day has come: they must learn to collaborate with their fellow workers rather than bang them around.

But Americans may be ready for this now in a way they weren't in the 1930s, in the 1880s, or in 1848—the last time when people talked in such language. Not all Americans, of course. Some are just too scared or too buried in the past to be able to see beyond the system that has been bequeathed to them. But many people—including managers and owners as well as workers—do see, and are ready to imagine something different.

Those temp workers in Baltimore are not going to get rich. In fact, some of them are making less money than they could around the corner, to say nothing of what they used to make dealing drugs. But they have devised a business model and a way of relating to one another and to the economic community that allows them to go to work without checking their humanity at the door. That is a crucial achievement—more important and more promising, perhaps, than anything we can hope to do, for now, through citizenship alone.

A PROPHETIC POLITICS
Jim Wallis

IN THE AFTERMATH of the 2004 presidential election, a badly worded exit poll question set off an enormous and important debate on the place of religion in American politics. Asked to name the most important issue that influenced their vote, 22 percent of voters chose "moral values," just edging out terrorism and the economy. That poll result sparked a firestorm in the media and in Washington's political circles about who gets or doesn't get the "moral values issue." Conventional wisdom holds that the Republicans, attuned to their Christian conservative base, understand moral values in a way that secular Democrats don't. The conventional wisdom also holds that moral values consist of two issues: abortion and gay marriage. The lesson immediately taken from this poll was that the Republicans won because people who cared about moral values voted for them.

But from a Christian perspective, these are hardly the only, or even the most important, moral values. A Christian who cares deeply about peace would likely have checked the war in Iraq (one of the survey choices) instead of "moral values," and the coordinator of a food pantry would likely have chosen the survey's closest thing to poverty, which would have been the economy or perhaps health care. The single "moral values" option was categorically different from the rest of the issues, reducing morality to a couple of hot-button issues and ignoring the moral values inherent in those other concerns. A second important poll taken several days later bore this out, showing that the war in Iraq rated as the issue of highest moral importance for those who voted. The greatest moral "crisis" was named as "greed and materialism," followed closely by "poverty and economic injustice."

America today indeed faces a crisis of inequality and injustice. The top 20 percent of households receive around half of all income, while the bottom fifth divide up less than 5 percent. CEO pay continues to rise to dizzying heights, while millions of Americans struggle just to pull down a living wage. We have both record prosperity and increasing child poverty. Forty-four million Americans lack health insurance; millions more struggle to find affordable housing. The *New York Times* a few years back had a striking illustration of what presidential candidate John Edwards called the "two Americas"—a *Sunday Magazine* cover story spoke of the "invisible poor," while a business-page piece the same week explored the consequences of a new syndrome called "affluenza" on the children of the rich.

Not only are war, poverty, inequality, and economic injustice moral concerns, despite what that famous survey implied; they are issues absolutely central to Christians. In announcing his mission on earth, Jesus said that he had come to bring good news to the poor. He also said, "Blessed are the peacemakers, for they will be called children of God." Saint Peter told a Roman centurion that "God shows no partiality, but in every nation anyone who fears him and does what is right is acceptable to him" (Acts 10:34–35). Yet the version of Christianity offered in so much of American politics today seems like precisely the opposite of the vision suggested in these passages. So those who really know the Bible wonder, how did the faith of Jesus come to be known as prorich, prowar, and *only* pro-American? Such an interpretation of Christianity threatens both our politics and our faith.

One of the most mistaken perceptions of our time is that religious influence in political life equates only to the politics of the religious right. The religious right's grip on public debates about values has been driven in part by media that continue to give airtime to the loudest religious voices rather than to the most representative, leaving millions of Christians and other people of faith without a say in the values debate. But today, many of us who feel that our faith has been stolen want to take it back. Our vision—a progressive and prophetic vision of faith and politics—was not running in the 2004 election. Neither candidate championed the poor as a "moral value" or made the war in Iraq a clearly religious matter. And neither advocated a "consistent ethic of human life" beyond single-issue voting. The ways in which the visions of both parties are morally and politically incomplete must now be taken up by people of faith. That can best be done by reaching into both the conservative Christian communities that voted for George Bush and the more liberal Christian communities that voted for John Kerry.

A new vision of politics—what I call "prophetic politics"—has the potential to build new alliances and coalitions that will break the political deadlock that recent polls and elections have shown our country to be in. At its heart is the integral link between personal ethics and social justice, and it appeals to people who refuse to make the false choice between the two. Prophetic politics would not be an endless argument between personal and social responsibility, but a weaving of the two together in search of the common good. Prophetic politics wouldn't assign all the answers to the government, the market, or the churches and charities; rather, it would patiently and creatively forge new civic partnerships where everyone does his or her share and everybody does what he or she does best, led by a moral compass. Most important, prophetic politics would be dedicated to identifying and solving problems, rather than simply seeking (as most of our politicians do today) to exploit them for electoral advantage.

What would be the substance of this prophetic politics? It would look very different from what passes for biblically based politics in America today. I am an evangelical Christian. *Evangelical*, which comes from the word *evangel* ("good news"), used to be a good word, with progressive connotations. In the nineteenth century, evangelical Christians were leaders in the abolitionist movement, advocates for the poor and oppressed, and activists in the struggle for women's rights. It is a word that, despite what has happened to it in contemporary political discourse, I still proudly claim. It implies a biblically rooted and Jesus-centered faith, and so as an evangelical, I have to be attentive to what the Bible actually says. The primary social issue in the Bible isn't homosexuality —there are about twelve verses in the Bible that touch on that question (none of them spoken by Jesus), and most are very contextual. It isn't abortion either. The first principle of biblical politics is compassion and justice for the poor. Thousands of verses concern the issue of poverty. In the Old Testament, it is the second most prominent theme, after idolatry, with which it is often linked. One out of every sixteen New Testament verses is explicitly about the poor—in the Gospels themselves, the proportion rises to one in ten. Throughout the Bible, God is portrayed as the deliverer of the poor and oppressed.

The biblical prophets frequently spoke to rulers and kings. They spoke to "the nations," and those in charge of things were the ones called to greatest accountability. They taught their people to be suspicious of concentrations of wealth and power, to mistrust ideological rationales that justified subordinating persons to causes, and especially to become sensitive to the poor and the vulnerable. They spoke to a nation's priorities.

Sadly, our own nation's political leaders—even those who profess a strong Christian faith—do not seem to hear or to heed the biblical call to do justice to the poor. As the Bush administration began, I joined a small group of religious leaders to meet with the new president. We encouraged him to commit himself to a concrete and measurable goal in the battle against poverty, such as cutting child poverty by half in ten years, as the British government under Tony Blair had pledged. I thought a Republican president, in the name of "compassionate conservatism," could make new progress on the critical issue of poverty. I supported the president's faith-based initiative, much to the chagrin of Democratic friends, but from the beginning of the Bush presidency have had a very consistent message: significant resources must be committed to serious poverty reduction, not just in a faith-based initiative but more importantly in budget decisions, tax policies, and spending priorities.

Unfortunately, other priorities were more important to the Bush administration than poverty reduction. Tax cuts that mostly benefited the wealthy were more important, the war in Iraq was more important, and homeland security was more important, but without the key recognition of how poverty, despair, family instability, and social disintegration undermine our national security. One result of the lack of White House leadership has been the steady rise of the number of people, families, and children living in poverty in each year of the Bush presidency, according to the U.S. Census Bureau. A budget based on a windfall of benefits for the wealthy and harsh cuts for poor families and children directly conflicts with biblical priorities. And that is a religious issue. If the prophets of the Old Testament were around today, they would surely be preaching against tax and budget policies that enrich the wealthy and make misery for the poor.

Those prophets, such as Amos and Isaiah, lived in a time not unlike our own—one of great prosperity, but prosperity built on corruption and oppression, leading to a great and growing inequality. In such times, they called for radical social justice—in Amos's stirring words, to "let justice roll down like waters, and righteousness like an ever-flowing stream." Yet so much of what passes for "religious" discourse in politics today focuses only on issues of personal morality and piety, without a concern for social justice. Religious conservative leaders such as James Dobson and Gary Bauer define their moral agenda to include school prayer, opposition to abortion, denial of rights to gays and lesbians, elimination of the National Endowment for the Arts, and censoring pornography. They say very little, however, about the biblical and moral imperatives of economic justice. Some Christian conservatives have actively campaigned *against* economic justice, as when the Christian Coalition of Alabama helped to defeat Republican Governor Bob Riley's tax reform plan—itself a biblically influenced proposal that would have relieved the poor of some of the crippling tax burden they face under Alabama's laws.

The religious right, in fact, preaches a politics that is more nationalist than truly evangelical. Listening to its leaders' words and agenda, one hears little about Jesus at all. Their political preference for wealth, power, and military might flies in the face of a gospel that was intended to be good news to the poor and was preached by an itinerant Jewish rabbi who said that it was the peacemakers who would be blessed. The religious right and its allies are guilty not just of bad politics but of bad theology: true Christianity is subverted when wealth and power are extolled rather than held accountable, and when the gospel message is turned upside down to bring more comfort to those on the top of society than to those at the bottom.

In politics, the best interest of the country is served when the prophetic voice of religion is heard—challenging both right and left from consistent moral ground. The best public contribution of religion is precisely *not* to be ideologically predictable or a loyal partisan. Jerry Falwell, Pat Robertson, and other extreme fundamentalists are losing credibility among the faithful by putting loyalty to party before loyalty to scripture. A true prophetic voice would proclaim moral truths regardless of which party or political interest it challenged or offended. It would demand that we always be suspicious of concentrated power—politically *and* economically—either in totalitarian regimes or in huge multinational corporations, which now have more wealth and power than many governments. It would remind us that matters such as the sacredness of life and family bonds are so important that they should never be used as ideological symbols or mere political pawns in partisan warfare. It would never simply endorse the social programs of liberals or conservatives, but would make clear that poverty is indeed a religious issue and that the failure of political leaders to help uplift those in poverty would be judged a moral failing.

This vision of a prophetic politics would also require many liberals and progressives to reconsider some of their hesitation about the language and substance of religion. Just as religious fundamentalists have brought their poor reading of scripture into the political arena, "secular fundamentalists" have fought to keep the language of morality and spirituality out of politics. Many progressives have forgotten their own history—forgotten that every major social movement in America has been fueled in large part by faith. Abolitionism, women's suffrage, laws against child labor, and, most famously, the civil rights movement were all largely faith-based initiatives. Where would we be if the Reverend Dr. Martin Luther King Jr. had kept his faith to himself? We can, and must, support the separation of church and state, but we need not separate public life from personal, moral, and spiritual values. Indeed, our impoverished political process needs the moral direction and energy that spiritual and religious values can contribute to the public debate.

Linking personal ethics and social justice, talking about personal responsibility and social responsibility, can be winning options in American politics. It can be the way to repent of the sins of social and economic injustice, to bring the good news—the "evangel"—to the poor and oppressed, and to bring our nation closer to the vision of the good community that is God's promise in every religious tradition.

What would a prophetic politics be like in practice? At the time of the 2002 elections, I was a fellow at Harvard's Kennedy School of Government. A Republican strategist dropped in one night to give a speech and attend a private dinner afterward. He radiated success, having just won five gubernatorial and Senate races, and he wanted to tell us all how he'd done it—and how his party would go on winning victory after victory. To get working-class people and many middle-class people, he explained, we use abortion, marriage, and family—the social, moral, and cultural issues that Democrats don't understand. By hooking people on those issues, he continued, we get them to vote against their economic self-interest. Since the rich are with us anyway, we win elections.

I raised my hand and asked the following question: What if you were up against a candidate who was solid on moral and family values—who cared about personal responsibility and the environment in which children are brought up, saw abortion as a moral issue and sought common ground in reducing the number of abortions, and would support strengthening families without blaming gay and lesbian people for their breakdown. What if that morally centered candidate, with those values, was also an economic populist, defending working people against corporate

power and talking about the sins of inequality and economic injustice, and an internationalist on foreign policy, preferring international law to preemptive and unilateral war? What, I asked,
would you do with that kind of candidate?

There was a long pause. "We would panic," he said.

DEMOCRACY FIRST

Miles S. Rapoport and David A. Smith

MUCH OF WHAT HAS BEEN SAID in this book will come as no surprise to millions of Americans. The deepening inequality documented here is palpable in everyday life. Housing prices in Manhattan, where we both work, recently reached an average of $1 million, a cost that requires annual earnings of about $400,000 (ten times New York City's median household income) to finance. In the country as a whole, CEOs in the financial sector receive compensation packages in the tens of millions, about five hundred times the median household income. Meanwhile, working families struggle to find public schooling for their children, increasing numbers of people endure two- and three-hour commutes in a desperate search for housing they can afford, the average worker's pay has shrunk in real terms since 1979, and the poverty rate has returned to that of 1973. And across the board, it is people of color who are disproportionately affected.

Our system is entrenching inequality rather than promoting broad upward mobility. As these essays have shown, economic and political inequality are mutually reinforcing. So what can we do to reverse this vicious cycle?

Let's first remind ourselves that there is nothing natural or inevitable about these trends. They are man-made phenomena rooted in a reinforcing mix of public and private actions. Recent policy has rigged the tax code so that it actually increases inequality. We have allowed the minimum wage to erode significantly: by 1999 it had lost more than 20 percent of its 1979 value. Since Congress failed to pass labor-law reform in 1979, the share of private-sector workers protected by union contracts has decreased by 50 percent. Because unionized workers are more likely to receive employer-provided health benefits, the decline in union representation accounts for a significant share of the increased number of uninsured Americans, now an estimated forty-four million.

Trade policy has helped pave the low road for American employers and their international competitors by keeping labor and environmental rights out of trade agreements, advantaging those who are most willing to exploit their workers and degrade the environment. Since making an unprecedented investment in the education of the World War II generation with the GI Bill, we have done so little that today three-quarters of the students at elite universities come from upper-middle-class or wealthy families and only 5 percent from families with household incomes of less than $35,000. The enormous returns to elite education compound the inequality that barred the admissions-office door to lower-income students in the first place.

The good news is that if public policy decisions helped create this problem, we can undo our own work and choose another path. We could begin to restore the equalizing institutions that once characterized our economy: progressive taxation, social investment, and regulation of the market's distortions. We could take steps to ensure that the earnings of working Americans better reflect the value of their work and their essential contribution to our economy. The minimum wage could be increased so that people willing to work full-time do not remain mired in poverty. Labor laws could be reformed to ensure that unions continue to exist as a check against corporate cost-cutting directed at workers' wages and benefits. Low-road employers have learned how to hold down pay for all workers by exploiting the vulnerability of immigrants, so we need a broad legalization program for current undocumented workers and a more realistic policy of legal immigration with full rights. Because asset inequality is even greater than income inequality, we could create new asset-creating mechanisms for poor and working Americans. Other nations, for example, start their citizens on a path of lifelong financial stability by establishing savings accounts for every child at birth. We could support families in acquiring the largest asset most will ever own—their home—by ensuring long-term mortgage availability and by fighting predatory lending.

Investing in the well-being and potential of our citizens would also ease inequality. For all our talk about the critical importance of an educated workforce, this country's support of education remains tepid. Public schools need far more adequate funding; higher education should truly be open to all regardless of their financial condition. A working single-payer health-care system would both stop the drain on incomes caused by the erosion of insurance coverage and equalize access to medical care. Affordable and accessible child care would help working families and relieve another large out-of-pocket cost. In addition to reducing inequality, measures like these would increase productivity and improve the overall health of the economy. Social investment, not "trickle-down" tax cuts, is truly the rising tide that lifts all boats.

Such public outlays would require us to restore federal revenues, which are now at their lowest level as a share of the gross domestic product in six decades, creating a fiscal straitjacket that effectively blocks these and other needed measures. We could boost revenues and, at the same time, establish real tax progressivity by bringing the highest-income tax brackets and the estate tax back up to their 2000 levels. We could enforce the tax laws and close loopholes that allow the wealthy to shift their share of the burden onto everyone else. We could repeal the rate reduction for capital gains and dividends—two income streams skewed dramatically up the income-distribution ladder. Our tax code could be a way to fairly fund the operations of government, instead of a way for some to enjoy the benefits of that government without paying its costs.

It is easy to think of policies that would have an inequality-reducing effect. Sadly, it is far harder to imagine them gaining the support—or even the serious consideration—of Congress, the White House, or the two major political parties in the current political environment. This is not, as many claim, because Americans are indifferent to the problem. That may be true of some Americans, and a few, surely, like the economic reward structure the way it is. A great many others, however, dislike it intensely, but are effectively unpresented in the political process.

This country, as many Americans know, has a conspicuously bad record, by the standards of other democracies, when it comes to political participation. What is not so well known is the close correlation in the United States between voter turnout and economic status. High-income Americans are dependable voters and, as the American Political Science Association report cited by Charles Lewis shows, are likely to engage in other, more active forms of political participation as well. In fact, high-income Americans vote almost as consistently as the high-income citizens of other countries. What sets the United States apart is its very low voter turnout rates for middle- and low-income citizens. That problem, in turn, can be traced to an array of policies and procedural barriers that affect them disproportionately.

In other words, our political system has been infected and disabled by the same pervasive inequality that disfigures our economy. For this reason, we must reform the political system before we can plausibly use that system to bring about significant economic reform. Any effort to combat inequality must begin with the challenge of creating a vibrant and inclusive democracy—eliminating barriers to citizen participation, ending the dominance that moneyed interests and entrenched officeholders now enjoy, and encouraging engagement by the massive number of Americans who are alienated from, or locked out of, the American political debate.

There are two sides to the agenda for effective democratic political reform. The first is to dismantle barriers to full participation, most fundamentally by making it easier for Americans to register and vote. The voter-registration requirement itself is unusual in democratic nations (most democracies register their citizens automatically), and was originally instituted in this country to discourage voting by freed slaves in the South and new and often radical immigrants in the North. If America is not prepared to scrap this requirement altogether, we should at least follow the lead of the handful of states that have made it less burdensome by allowing citizens to register and vote at the polls on election day. In 2004, four of the five states with the highest turnout were among those that allowed election day registration, or EDR; collectively, the EDR states achieved a turnout rate 14.1 percent higher than that of the rest of the country. We can also bring more people into the process by fully implementing the National Voter Registration Act of 1993, which requires state agencies providing human services to register voters. Simple changes in procedure at offices offering food stamps, welfare, Medicaid, or disability benefits could help register millions of the low-income Americans whose voices are now missing from politics.

In addition to making it complicated to register, our system discourages the act of voting itself, as the multihour waits of 2004 in Ohio, Florida, and elsewhere dramatically demonstrated. We get a single day—a working Tuesday, at that—to exercise this fundamental right of a democratic citizen. The civic importance of Election Day should be acknowledged by making it a national holiday; in addition to boosting turnout, that step would allow people to serve as poll workers for the day, educate their children, and get involved in other ways. And Election Day should be a deadline, not an appointment. In 2004, thirty states opened their polling places well in advance, giving citizens a period of days or weeks to cast their ballots. People should be entitled to fill out their ballots at home and mail them in—a privilege already extended to the elderly, the ill, and American citizens overseas. A combination of mail-in balloting, early voting, and the opportunity to register and vote at local polling places on election day would maximize participation.

But neither easier registration nor more accessible voting will help the millions of Americans who are explicitly, and unfairly, barred from voting because of felony convictions. The number of citizens affected by such rules now stands at an appalling 4.7 million, including 30 percent of the African American male population of Florida, Alabama, and other states. To eliminate this massive act of discrimination, we need many more legislative and administrative changes at the state level, as well as federal supervision of the voter-purge lists that have been abused in Florida and elsewhere. In addition, the number of foreign-born noncitizens in this country is now 17.5 million, large numbers of whom wait for extended periods to become citizens. If the naturalization process were more efficient, many people ready for citizenship could become voters.

Taking steps to reduce barriers to full participation, as necessary as that is, only takes care of one side of the democratic reform agenda. Our democracy has become rigged in many other respects, so that even when votes are counted, in all too many cases they do not meaningfully count. Although Americans are narrowly divided in terms of political allegiance, you would never know it from the results of most congressional elections. The House of Representatives is supposed to be the "people's house"—the most direct link between citizens and their national government. But because districts are drawn to ensure the dominance of whichever party is in charge, the outcomes are all too often a foregone conclusion. The trend has reached the point of absurdity: in 2004, only 30 of the 435 House races nationwide were considered competitive, and only seven incumbents were actually defeated. To guarantee voters a real choice, redistricting must be overseen by independent commissions drawing lines according to logic and numbers rather than partisan desire and incumbent protection.

Parties try to control not just who wins, but who is allowed to run. Ballot access rules, again generally crafted by the major parties, are often barriers to candidates, thus limiting voter choice. In many states, requirements for candidates are far too stringent, and the conditions for qualifying as a political party are even more daunting. In the states that allow "fusion," or the cross-endorsement of candidates by more than one party, a minor party can grow and encourage people to join without automatically splintering votes from major-party candidates. Instant-runoff voting, which had a successful 2004 trial in San Francisco, is another way that candidates can compete and people can choose to vote for them without creating "spoiler" situations.

The factor that most distorts our political system's responsiveness, though, is the overpowering role of money. As Charles Lewis has described in this volume, American elections have turned into high-priced television ad wars, allowing wealthy candidates to buy their way into office and wealthy interests to buy a place at the table. To give all Americans a truly equal voice, we must find ways to keep big money from swamping democracy. One obvious step is to restore a credible presidential public-financing system, now that our current system has been dismantled and discarded by both parties. We could reduce the cost of campaigning by, as in Britain, allowing candidates free broadcast time on the public airwaves and by curbing exorbitant charges for political advertising rates. Ultimately, true reform and the health of our democracy require that we expand public funding of campaigns, breaking politicians' dependence on big donors and leveling the playing field for candidates so that the best ideas, not just the loudest ones, prevail.

In arguing for political-process reform as a way of setting the stage for economic reform, we may seem to be substituting one impossible challenge for another. But the landscape is promising in several ways. As a result of controversies involving both the 2000 and 2004 presidential elections, a great many Americans (traditional reformers and newly energized activists alike) have experienced the frailty of the system firsthand and, with widespread attention to these questions from the media, have begun to create the infrastructure of a national democracy reform movement. This effort also benefits from a number of examples of meaningful and successful reform, thanks largely to initiatives taken by the states.

In Maine and Arizona, for example, real public financing has changed the nature of politics, establishing more competitive races and introducing candidates from outside the ranks of wealthy career politicians. Maine has also led the way in enacting Election Day registration, allowing voting rights even for people in prison, and allocating presidential electors according to the proportion of votes each candidate receives. Nevada has been a leader in acquiring effective and auditable electronic voting machines and has accomplished better voter registration in social-service agencies than most other states. Some states have been better known for their failures and controversies than for their successes, and will be under major pressure for change.

Ultimately, however, we cannot be satisfied with a democratic reform that focuses only on what happens once every couple of years on Election Day. The key is to develop a real and ongoing democracy movement—a spirited reform movement to create a democracy that is robust and inclusive, with fuller participation by Americans in elections and in all areas of democratic decision making. That means working at the national and state levels to promote a broad agenda of democracy reforms. It means encouraging democratic participation throughout the year by stimulating community organizing and embedding forms of deliberative democracy in governmental processes at all levels. It even means exercising democracy in the economic sphere itself: working people—who hold significant ownership interests in corporations through public and private pension funds, mutual funds, insurance companies, and trust institutions—can use their power to ensure that they are not disadvantaged by the behavior of the very firms that they own.

This brings us, circularly, back to where we began. Inequality, with all of its consequences, is the result of deliberate political decisions and can be mitigated and ultimately reversed only by reclaiming democratic politics. Only when we have a political system that truly hears its citizens, and citizens who truly embrace the responsibilities of democracy, will we be on the way to a society that understands inequality as the pervasive and poisonous problem that it is.

ACKNOWLEDGMENTS

Organizations as well as individuals came together to create this book. ACORN, the *American Prospect,* Call to Renewal, the Center for American Progress, the Center for Public Integrity, the Century Foundation, the Economic Policy Institute, the Russell Sage Foundation, the Tomales Bay Institute, and United for a Fair Economy all made important contributions. Our work is, to a large extent, their work.

The biggest of our organizational debts is to Demos, a think-and-action-tank that has been out front in its grasp of the connection between rising economic inequality, on the one hand, and eroding opportunity and democracy, on the other.

The editors are grateful to The New Press for its commitment to the subject as well as the book, and to the Quixote Foundation for supporting the "Inequality Matters" conference and our continued work.

We could not name all the people, many associated with the groups cited here, who have had a significant hand in this enterprise. High on the list, though, are Miles Rapoport, the president of Demos; Ellen Adler, our editor at The New Press; Sue Warga and Bonnie Lefkowitz, who checked and revised a portion of the manuscript; and John M. Summers, who helped us and the authors reshape a number of these essays.

Our work would have been much more difficult without the excellent reports that the Century Foundation has published on a number of subjects explored here. In addition, the editors and a number of contributors made abundant use of data and analysis in *The State of Working America, 2004/2005* by Jared Bernstein, Lawrence Mishel, and Sylvia Allegretto. We agree with Simon Head (writing in the *New York Review of Books*) that "this is an indispensable book."

We have found the Web sites maintained by the Center for American Progress (www.americanprogress.org), the Century Foundation (www.tcf.org), United for a Fair Economy (www.faireconomy.org), and Demos (www.demos.org and www.inequality.org) especially useful, and we recommend them to readers seeking additional or updated information.

James Lardner and David A. Smith

NOTES

THE FIGHT OF OUR LIVES *Bill Moyers*

1 **These two stories:** Michael Winerip, "At Poor Schools' Libraries, Time Stops on the Shelves," *New York Times*, March 10, 2004, B1.

2 **Caroline Payne:** David Shipler, *The Working Poor: Invisible in America* (New York: Random House, 2004).

2 **The editorial page:** *Washington Post*, May 19, 2004, A22.

5 **In 1960, the gap:** United Nations Development Programme, *Human Development Report* (New York: UNDP, 1997), 28–29.

6 **After a long career:** Elizabeth Drew, *The Corruption of American Politics: What Went Wrong and Why* (New York: Overlook Press, 1999), 61.

7 **Campaign money:** Jeffrey Birnbaum, *The Money Men: The Real Story of Fund-Raising's Influence on Political Power in America* (New York: Crown, 2000).

7 **When powerful interests:** Donald L. Barlett and James B. Steele, "Big Money & Politics: Who Gets Hurt?" *Time*, February 7, 2000, 38.

9 **The battle strategy:** William E. Simon, *Time for Truth* (New York: Readers Digest Press/McGraw-Hill, 1978).

10 **Thomas Edsall of the *Washington Post:*** Edsall, *The New Politics of Inequality* (New York: W.W. Norton, 1984), 128.

10 **In Daniel Altman's:** Daniel Altman, *Neoconomy: George Bush's Revolutionary Gamble with America's Future* (New York: Public Affairs, 2004).

10 **"If there was a class war":** "Buffett: Dividend Tax Cut Unfair; Benefits the Rich, He Tells Senators," Bloomberg News, March 14, 2003.

10 **In 2003:** "Drop in Number of Wealthy Who Owe Taxes," *New York Times,* October 2, 2004.

12 **His labor secretary:** CNN, *Inside Politics,* February 6, 2004.

12 **You'll find more of these shenanigans:** Eric Moskowitz, Vincent Del Giudice, and James Cordahi, "Citigroup Slapped with $70 Million Fine," Bloomberg News, May 28, 2004. For the NEC story, see Matt Richtel and Gary Rivlin, "NEC Unit Admits It Defrauded Schools," *New York Times,* May 28, 2004.

13 **It was a time:** Frederick Townsend Martin, *The Passing of the Idle Rich* (New York: Hodder & Stoughton, 1911).

WHAT'S THE PROBLEM? *James Lardner*

15 **A generation ago:** Paul Krugman, "The Great Wealth Transfer," *Rolling Stone,* December 2006.

17 **When it comes to mobility:** David Wessel, "As Rich-Poor Gap Widens in U.S., Class Mobility Stalls," *Wall Street Journal,* May 13, 2005, A1.

17 **When people "are ranked":** Alexis de Tocqueville, *Democracy in America* (New York: Library of America, 2004), book 3, chap. 1.

19 **The net effect is an enrollment gap:** Thomas R. Wolanin, ed., *Reauthorizing the Higher Education Act: Issues and Options* (Washington, DC: Institute for Higher Education Policy, 2003). Also see Advisory Committee on Student Financial Assistance, *Empty*

Promises: The Myth of College Access in America (Washington, DC: The Committee, 2002).

20 **Worn down by the pressures:** Arthur Caplan, "Good Health Care: For Rich People Only?" *Newsday,* June 30, 2004, A39.

21 **In 1950, an African American baby:** National Center for Health Statistics, *Health, United States,* 2004 report, tables 19 and 29. See also David R. Williams and James Lardner, "The Doctor's Bill," in this volume.

21 **Yet we design our schools:** Richard D. Kahlenberg, *All Together Now: Creating Middle-Class Schools Through Public-School Choice* (Washington, DC: Brookings Institution Press, 2001), 65–66. See also Kahlenberg, "The Return of Separate but Equal," in this volume.

22 **Meanwhile, millionaires:** Alan I. Abramowitz, Brad Alexander, and Matthew Gunning, "Incumbency, Redistricting, and the Decline of Competition in U.S. House Elections," paper delivered at the Annual Meeting of the Southern Political Science Association, New Orleans, Louisiana, January 6–8, 2005; Charlie Cook, "Looking Back at 1996," *National Journal,* December 18, 2006. On millionaires in the Senate, see Charles Lewis, "Of the Few, by the Few, for the Few," in this volume.

WHAT THE NUMBERS TELL US
Heather Boushey and Christian E. Weller

27 **Between 1968 and 1992, the Gini coefficient:** See Carmen DeNavas-Walt, Robert Cleveland, and Bruce H. Webster Jr., U.S. Census Bureau, *Current Population Reports, P60-221. Income in the United States: 2002* (Washington, DC: U.S. Government Printing Office, 2003), Table A-3, available at http://www.census.gov/prod/2003pubs/p60–221.pdf. The Gini coefficient has remained steady

or slightly increased from its 1992 level; post-1992 numbers aren't directly comparable, however, because of a change in the methodology the Census Bureau uses to collect data on income distribution.

27 **There are other ways to measure inequality:** See Michael Förster and Mark Pearson, "Income Distribution and Poverty in the OECD Area: Trends and Driving Forces," *OECD Economic Studies* 34 (2002), available at http://www.oecd.org/dataoecd/16/33/2968109 .pdf.

29 **The titles of two recent research papers:** Greg Duncan, Ariel Kalil, Susan E. Mayer, Robin Tepper, and Monique R. Payne, "The Apple Does Not Fall Far from the Tree," and Bhashkar Mazumder, "The Apple Falls Even Closer to the Tree Than We Thought: New and Revised Estimates of the Intergenerational Inheritance of Earnings," in *Unequal Chances: Family Background and Economic Success,* ed. Samuel Bowles, Herbert Gintis, and Melissa Osborne Groves (Princeton, NJ: Princeton University Press, 2005).

29 **The economist Thomas Hertz:** Thomas Hertz, "Rags, Riches and Race: The Intergenerational Income Mobility of Black and White Families in the United States," in *Unequal Chances,* ed. Bowles, Gintis, and Osborne.

29 **Among the developed nations:** Gary Solon, "Cross-Country Differences in Intergenerational Earnings Mobility," *Journal of Economic Perspectives* 16, no. 3 (Summer 2002).

30 **From the economic peak in 1979 to the next peak in 1989:** Lawrence Mishel, Jared Bernstein, and Heather Boushey, *The State of Working America, 2002/2003* (Ithaca, NY: Cornell University Press, 2003).

31 **Still, by 2000, the top 5 percent:** Lawrence Mishel, "Waging Inequality: Those at the Top Have Reaped Huge Gains While Regular

Folks Have Just Been Getting by," *American Prospect* online, February 24, 2005.

31 **Recent research using data from tax returns:** Thomas Piketty and Emmanuel Saez, "Income Inequality in the United States," National Bureau of Economic Research Working Paper no. 8467, September 2001.

31 **Today, households at the eightieth percentile have over twice the income:** Carmen DeNavas-Walt, Bernadette D. Proctor, and Robert J. Mills, U.S. Census Bureau, *Current Population Reports, P60-226, Income, Poverty, and Health Insurance Coverage in the United States: 2003* (Washington, DC: U.S. Government Printing Office, 2004).

33 **Among women, the black/white gap:** Peter Gottschalk and Sheldon Danziger, "Wage Inequality, Earnings Inequality, and Poverty in the U.S. over the Last Quarter of the Twentieth Century," Boston College Working Papers in Economics no. 560, May 2003.

34 **The sons of fathers from the bottom:** Earl Wysong, Robert Perrucci, and David Wright, "Organizations, Resources, and Class Analysis: The Distributional Model and the U.S. Class Structure," Wichita State University Working Paper, 2004. See also Bhashkar Mazumder, "Earnings Mobility in the US: A New Look at Intergenerational Inequality," Federal Reserve Bank Chicago Working Paper no. 2001-18, 2001.

35 **Recent research indicates that economic mobility:** See Solon, "Cross-Country Differences in Intergenerational Earnings Mobility." Some of the research on international comparisons of mobility is summarized in Bernard Wasow, "Rags to Riches? The American Dream Is Less Common in the United States than Elsewhere," Century Foundation, New York, March 2004.

36 **In 2001, the richest 5 percent:** Lawrence Mishel, Jared Bernstein,

and Sylvia Allegretto, *The State of Working America 2004/2005* (Ithaca, NY: Cornell University Press, 2005).

36 **Statistics on homeownership:** Ibid.

37 **For some pockets of families:** A.M. Aizcorbe, A.B. Kennickel, and K.B. Moore, "Recent Changes in U.S. Family Finances: Evidence from the 1998 and 2001 Survey of Consumer Finances," *Federal Reserve Bulletin,* January 2003.

39 **Only 12.4 percent of households:** Ibid.

39 **The actual amount of holdings is heavily concentrated:** Mishel, Bernstein, and Allegretto, *The State of Working America 2004/2005,* Figure 4D.

EARTH TO WAL-MARS *Barbara Ehrenreich*

42 **Among my fellow "associates":** According to the 2004 Wal-Mart proxy statement (http://www.walmartstores.com/Files/proxy2004.pdf), Scott received $1.2 million in base salary, $4.2 million in incentive pay, and options to purchase 630,413 shares of stock at $52.12 and another 128,550 shares of restricted stock.

45 **I am not speaking hypothetically:** "Wal-Mart Workers Make History—Say 'Union Yes'!" United Food and Commercial Workers press release, February 18, 2000, http://www.ufcw.org/pressroom/pressreleases2000/wmworkersunionize.cfm (accessed January 11, 2005); "Workers Win Again at Wal-Mart," United Food and Commercial Workers press release, March 15, 2000, http://www.ufcw.org/pressroom/pressreleases2000/wmworkerswinagain.cfm (accessed January 12, 2005); Jill Cashen, assistant to the director for communications, United Food and Commercial Workers, Washington, DC, phone conversation, January 12, 2005.

45 **It took the employees:** Democratic Staff of the Committee on

Education and the Workforce, U.S. House of Representatives, "Everyday Low Wages: The Hidden Price We All Pay for Wal-Mart," February 16, 2004, available at http://edworkforce.house.gov/democrats/WALMARTREPORT.pdf (accessed January 12, 2005), 4, citing Dan Kasler, "Labor Dispute Has Historical Precedent," Scripps Howard News Service, November 3, 2003.

46 **It has been sued:** Steven Greenhouse, "Suits Say Wal-Mart Forces Workers to Toil Off the Clock," *New York Times,* June 25, 2002, A1.

48 **About one out of seven:** Hector Soto, Children's Defense Fund, testimony before a hearing of the federal Office of Children and Family Services, May 23, 2005.

49 **The Economic Policy Institute:** Heather Boushey, Chauna Brocht, Bethney Gunderson, and Jared Bernstein, *Hardships in America: The Real Story of Working Families* (Washington, DC: Economic Policy Institute, 2001).

49 **Wal-Mart provides:** Democratic Staff of the Committee on Education and the Workforce, "Everyday Low Wages," 7.

49 **Employees who opt in:** "The Problem with Wal-Mart," United Food and Commercial Workers Web site, http://www.ufcw.org/worker_political_agenda/where_we_stand/health_care_reform/walmart.cfm (accessed January 11, 2005).

49 **As a result, fewer than half:** Democratic Staff of the Committee on Education and the Workforce, "Everyday Low Wages," 7.

49 **The company well understands:** *NOW with Bill Moyers,* December 19, 2003, transcript available at http://www.pbs.org/now/transcript/transcript247_full.html (accessed January 12, 2005).

49 **In Georgia alone:** Stan Cox, "Wal-Mart's Magic Numbers," *Counterpunch,* April 20, 2004, available at http://www.counterpunch.org/cox04202004.html (accessed January 12, 2005).

49 **You see this sort of thing:** Democratic Staff of the Committee on Education and the Workforce, "Everyday Low Wages," 8–9.

50 **Measured by sales:** Wal-Mart Facts, a Web site maintained by the company. See http://www.walmartfacts.com/newsdesk/wal-mart-fact-sheets.aspx.

50 **Their visits account:** Company information from the Wal-Mart Web site, http://www.walmart.com (accessed January 11, 2005).

50 **Wal-Mart has come a long way:** Wal-Mart Facts Web site.

51 **Sales have leveled off:** Becky Yerak, "Target Thrives; Wal-Mart Wobbles," *Chicago Tribune,* May 22, 2005, C1.

51 **In October 2003:** Dina ElBoghdady and Greg Schneider, "Immigration Officials Raid Wal-Mart Stores," *Washington Post,* October 24, 2003, p. E1.

51 **In June 2001:** "Miss America '92 Uses TV Ads, Internet, Cell Phone Text Messaging in Novel Appeal to Women over Sex Bias by Wal-Mart," WalmartVersusWomen.com press release, May 21, 2003.

51 **Wal-Mart has fought back:** Information about the current status of the lawsuit can be found at the Wal-Mart Class Web site, http://www.walmartclass.com.

52 **Management is worried:** Constance L. Hays, "Wal-Mart Out to Change Image: Retailer Turns to Supporting Public Broadcasting," *New York Times,* August 12, 2004, C1.

THE RETURN OF "SEPARATE BUT EQUAL"   *Richard D. Kahlenberg*

56 **Poor people of color are especially likely:** David Rusk, "Trends in School Segregation," in Century Foundation Task Force on the Common School, *Divided We Fail: Coming Together Through Public School Choice* (New York: Century Foundation Press, 2002).

56 **The equity campaigners point out:** Kevin Carey, "The Funding

Gap 2004: Many States Still Shortchange Low-Income and Minority Students," Education Trust report, Washington, DC, fall 2004, 7, table 3.

57 **This was the lesson of the seminal report:** James S. Coleman et al., *Equality of Educational Opportunity* (Washington, DC: Government Printing Office, 1966).

57 **The fact that poor kids of all races do better:** Gary Orfield and Susan Eaton, *Dismantling Desegregation: The Quiet Reversal of Brown v. Board of Education* (New York: The New Press, 1996), 53.

58 **Classmates provide "a hidden curriculum":** Dr. Charles Pinderhughes, quoted in U.S. Commission on Civil Rights, *Racial Isolation in the Public Schools* (Washington, DC: Government Printing Office, 1967), 1:82.

58 **A middle-class child has a vocabulary:** Betty Hart and Todd R. Risley, *Meaningful Differences in the Everyday Experience of Young American Children* (Baltimore, MD: Paul H. Brookes Publishing, 1995).

58 **On the other hand, a fourth-grade child:** See, for example, Beatrice Birman et al., *The Current Operation of the Chapter 1 Program* (Washington, DC: U.S. Department of Education, 1987), 92–93.

59 **During the 1990s, Wake County:** Walter Sherlin, "N.C. Integration Story Saw Tree, Not Forest," *Education Week,* June 19, 2002, 14.

60 **Teachers in middle-class schools are more likely:** National Center for Education Statistics, *Teacher Quality: A Report on the Preparation and Qualifications of Public School Teachers* (Washington, DC: U.S. Department of Education, 1999), 17 (teaching out of field); John F. Kain and Kraig Singleton, "Equality of Educational Opportunity Revisited," *New England Economic Review,* May–June 1996, 87, 99, 107 (teacher test scores); and Laura Lipmann, Shelley Burns, and Edith McArthur, *Urban Schools: The Challenge of Location and*

Poverty (Washington, DC: National Center for Education Statistics, 1996), 86–88, 96 (experience).

60 **Teacher quality can have a profound effect:** For a summary of studies, see Kati Haycock, "Good Teaching Matters," *Thinking K–16* 3, no. 2 (Summer 1998): 3–13.

60 **Not very many teachers have taken the bait:** Eric A. Hanushek, John F. Kain, and Steven G. Rivkin, "Why Public Schools Lose Teachers," NBER Working Paper no. W8599, National Bureau of Economic Research, Cambridge, MA, November 2001.

60 **When parents volunteer in the classroom:** Esther Ho Sui-Chu and J. Douglas Willms, "Effects of Parental Involvement on Eighth-Grade Achievement," *Sociology of Education* 69 (April 1996): 136.

60 **And socioeconomic status has been found:** Gary Orfield, *City-Suburban Desegregation: Parent and Student Perspectives in Metropolitan Boston* (Cambridge, MA: Harvard Civil Rights Project, 1997), 21.

61 **Middle-class parents are four times more likely:** See, for example, William J. Fowler Jr., ed., *Developments in School Finance* (Washington, DC: U.S. Department of Education, 1995).

63 **In some high-poverty schools today:** James McPartland and Will J. Jordan, "Older Students Also Need Major Federal Compensatory Educational Resources," in *Hard Work for Good Schools: Facts Not Fads in Title I Reform,* ed. Gary Orfield and Elizabeth DeBray (Cambridge, MA: Harvard Civil Rights Project, 1999). Doris R. Entwisle, Karl L. Alexander, and Linda Steffan Olson, *Children, Schools, and Inequality* (New York: Westview Press, 1997).

64 **Minority twelfth-graders read:** National Center for Education Statistics, *NEAP 1998 Reading Report Card for the Nation* (Washington, DC: U.S. Department of Education, 1999), 44, 59.

64 **Students in well-off suburban jurisdictions:** David J. Hoff,

"World-Class Education Eludes Many in the U.S.," *Education Week,* April 11, 2001, 1, 14–15.

THE SNOWBALL AND THE TREADMILL   *Meizhu Lui*

67 **In 2005, white America:** U.S. Census Bureau, Current Population Survey, Historical Income Tables.

67 **In 1968:** Ibid.

68 **Since the early 1970s:** Jerry Landay, "The Apparat," Mediatransparency.org, March 18, 2004.

68 **Although whites have always:** In 2003, poor whites numbered 24 million, blacks 9 million, and Hispanics 9 million, according to U.S. Census Bureau figures.

69 **The typical white family:** Muhammad et al., "State of the Dream 2004," 7. Also see Barbara Robles, unpublished analysis of 2001 Survey of Consumer Finances, University of Texas. Figures converted to 2001 dollars by UFE.

69 **To put it another way:** Melvin Oliver and Thomas M. Shapiro, *Black Wealth, White Wealth: A New Perspective on Racial Inequality* (New York: Routledge, 1995), 87.

70 **Immigrants from India:** Gary Hess, "The Forgotten Asian American: The East Indian Community in the United States," in *Asians in America: The History and Immigration of Asian Americans,* ed. Franklin Ng (New York: Garland Publishing, 1974), 118–20.

70 **The French and British:** Speech given by Massachusetts State Representative Byron Rushing, who is also an African American historian, March 1995.

71 **For a few years, the Freedmen's Bureau:** W.E.B. Du Bois, "The Freedmen's Bureau," *Atlantic Monthly,* 1901.

71 **While the Treaty of Guadalupe Hidalgo:** Ronald Takaki, *A Differ-*

ent Mirror: A History of Multicultural America (Boston: Little, Brown & Co., 1993), 180.

72 **The GI Bill is remembered:** David H. Onkst, "First a Negro, Incidentally a Veteran: Black World War Two Veterans and the G.I. Bill of Rights in the Deep South," *Journal of Social History* 31 (Spring 1998): 517–43.

73 **Homeownership patterns:** Betsy Leondar-Wright, Meizhu Lui, Gloribell Mota, Dedrick Muhammad, and Mara Voukydis, "State of the Dream 2005: Disowned in the Ownership Society," UFE report, January 10, 2005.

73 **One explanation for these gaping disparities:** Nancy McCardle, talk at UFE, June 2004. Also, McArdle and David J. Harris, "More than Money: The Spatial Mismatch Between Where Homeowners of Color in Metro Boston Can Afford to Live and Where They Actually Reside," report prepared for the Metro Boston Equity Initiative of the Harvard Civil Rights Project, January 2004.

73 **In 2000 . . . the median home value:** Thomas M. Shapiro, *The Hidden Cost of Being African-American: How Wealth Perpetuates Inequality* (New York: Oxford University Press, 2004), 122.

74 **The trick:** Isabel Wilkerson, "A Success Story That's Hard to Duplicate," *New York Times,* June 12, 2005.

74 **In *The Hidden Cost:*** Shapiro, *Hidden Cost of Being African-American,* 67–72.

75 **In 2001, 25 percent of whites:** Federal Reserve Board, Survey of Consumer Finances, 2001.

75 **"Lack of income means you don't get by":** Ray Boshara, "Poverty Is More than a Matter of Income," *New York Times,* September 29, 2002.

76 **The racial economic gap:** Dr. Martin Luther King Jr., Sermon at the National Cathedral, Washington, DC, March 31, 1968.

SHREDDING THE RETIREMENT CONTRACT
David A. Smith and Heather McGhee

82 **While median stock and bond values:** The median value of stocks held by households with heads aged fifty-five to sixty-four went from $12,890 in 1983 to $37,500 in 2001. Bonds grew from $22,226 to $60,000, all inflation-adjusted. Source: author calculations from the 1983 and 2001 Survey of Consumer Finances.

82 **Among the general population, stock ownership:** J. Poterba, "Stock Market Wealth and Consumption," *Journal of Economic Perspectives* 14 (Spring 2000): 99–118.

82 **Mutual funds are now held:** Five percent of fifty-five- to sixty-four-year-olds held assets in the category of "nontaxable holdings," which included municipal bonds and shares in certain mutual funds.

83 **By the most conservative measure:** Robert G. Valletta, "Changes in the Structure and Duration of U.S. Unemployment, 1967–1998," *FRBSF Economic Review* 3 (1998): 29–40, available at http://www.frbsf.org/econrsrch/econrev/98-3/29-40.pdf.

83 **And losing a job now sentences workers:** "Displaced Workers Summary," Bureau of Labor Statistics, August 2001.

83 **At the end of the 1975 recession:** Jared Bernstein, Heather Boushey, Elizabeth McNichol, and Robert Zahradnik, *Pulling Apart: A State-by-State Analysis of Income Trends* (Washington, DC: Center on Budget and Policy Priorities / Economic Policy Institute, 2002).

83 **Among families with children:** Elizabeth Warren and Amelia Tyagi-Warren, *The Two-Income Trap: Why Middle-Class Mothers and Fathers Are Going Broke* (New York: Basic Books, 2003).

84 **But they spend 69 percent more:** Ibid.

84 **Revolving consumer debt:** Federal Reserve Board G.19 Consumer

Credit Historical Data. January 1983, revolving consumer debt to-
taled $66,726.23 million (or $66 billion), available at http://www
.federalreserve.gov/Releases/G19/hist/cc_hist_sa. html.

84 **In this time, pricing regulations:** See Demos, "Credit Card Industry Practices: In Brief," New York, June 2004, available at
http://www.demos.org/pub125.cfm.

85 **In 1981, the average family saved:** Warren and Tyagi-Warren, *Two-
Income Trap.*

85 **Demos's** *Retiring in the Red* **reveals:** Heather C. McGhee and
Tamara Draut, "Retiring in the Red: The Growth of Debt Among
Older Americans," Demos briefing paper, New York, February
2004, available at http://www.demos-usa.org/pub101.cfm.

86 **While our national savings rate:** Lillian G. Woo, F. William
Schweke, and David E. Buchholz, "Hidden in Plain Sight: A Look at
the $335 Billion Federal Asset-Building Budget," Corporation for
Enterprise Development report, Washington, DC, Spring 2004.

86 **The federal government now spends:** Elizabeth Bell, C. Eugene
Steuerle, and Adam Carasso, "Retirement Saving Incentives and
Personal Saving," The Urban Institute Tax Policy Center, December
2004.

86 **The Bush administration raised the limits:** "Utilization of Tax Incentives for Retirement Saving," Congressional Budget Office
Paper, August 2003.

THE GROWING COLLEGE GAP *Tamara Draut*

90 **The paradox facing young adults:** Jennifer Cheeseman Day and
Eric C. Newburger, "The Big Payoff: Educational Attainment and
Synthetic Estimates of Work-Life Earnings," U.S. Census Bureau,
July 2002.

91 **In 1944, Congress passed:** The GI Bill cost $5.5 billion per year

over seven years; adjusting for inflation brings the annual amount to $13 billion per year. As cited in Paul Simon, "A GI Bill for Today," *Chronicle of Higher Education,* October 31, 2003.

91 **As a result of this landmark:** Arthur Levine and Jana Nidiffer, *Beating the Odds: How the Poor Get to College* (San Francisco: Jossey-Bass Publishers, 1996), 35.

93 **Between 1991 and 2001:** Donald Heller and Patricia Marin, ed., "Who Should We Help? The Negative Social Consequences of Merit Aid Scholarships," Harvard Civil Rights Project report, Cambridge, MA, August 23, 2002.

94 **The availability of grant aid:** Patrick T. Terenzini, Alberto F. Cabrera, and Elena M. Bernal, "Swimming Against the Tide: The Poor in American Higher Education," College Board Research Report no. 2001-1, New York, 2001.

94 **Given the extraordinary shift:** Advisory Committee on Student Financial Assistance, *Empty Promises: The Myth of College Access in America* (Washington, DC: The Committee, 2002).

94 **The difference in college enrollment:** Thomas R. Wolanin, ed., *Reauthorizing the Higher Education Act: Issues and Options* (Washington, DC: Institute for Higher Education Policy, 2003).

94 **As grant aid has dwindled:** Advisory Committee on Student Financial Assistance, *Empty Promises.*

95 **Today, community colleges:** Daniel J. Phelan, "Enrollment Policies and Student Access at Community Colleges," Community College Policy Center policy paper, Denver, CO, February 2000.

95 **Forty percent of young adults:** Dr. Sandy Baum and Marie O'Malley, "College on Credit: How Borrowers Perceive Their Education Debt. Results of the 2002 National Student Loan Survey," Nellie Mae report, Washington, DC, February 6, 2003.

95 **Nearly six out of ten:** Jean Johnson and Ann Duffett, *Life After High School: Young People Talk about Their Hopes and Prospects*

(New York: Public Agenda, 2005), 15, available at http://www. publicagenda.org/research/pdfs/lifeafterhighschool. pdf.

95 **Of all college entrants:** Richard D. Kahlenberg, ed., *America's Untapped Resource: Low-Income Students in Higher Education* (New York: Century Foundation Press, 2003), 2.

95 **Only about 40 percent:** Richard J. Coley, "The American Community College Turns 100: A Look at Its Students, Programs and Prospects," Education Testing Service policy information report, Princeton, NJ, March 2000.

95 **Other studies find:** Ibid.

96 **Five years after entering:** Gary Hoachlander, Anna C. Sikora, and Laura Horn, "Community College Students: Goals, Academic Preparation, and Outcomes," *Education Statistics Quarterly* 5, no. 2 (2003), available at http://nces.ed.gov/programs/quarterly/vol 5/5_2/q4_1.asp.

96 **Students from low-income families:** Kahlenberg, *America's Untapped Resource,* 22.

96 **Nearly three-quarters of students:** Anthony Carnevale and Stephen Rose, "Socio-Economic Status, Race/Ethnicity and Selective College Admissions," in Kahlenberg, *America's Untapped Resource.*

96 **Black and Hispanic students:** Ibid.

97 **There is also a wage premium:** Ibid.

97 **The same study finds:** Ibid.

98 **Getting a sneak peak:** Marianne Costantinou, "The Great Admissions Race," *San Francisco Chronicle Magazine,* August 10, 2003, 9.

98 **One package includes all the tony:** Prices quoted for the 2004 East Coast tour at http://www.collegecampustours.com.

98 **While the news media:** Fredreka Schouten, "Getting In, with Some Help." *USA Today,* April 30, 2003, 8D.

99 **The average high school guidance counselor:** This statistic is from

the National Association for College Admission Counseling, as cited in Schouten, "Getting In, with Some Help."

99 **Judith Glazer, a scholar:** Judith Glazer, "The Master's Degree: Tradition, Diversity, Innovation," ASHE-ERIC Higher Education Report no. 6, Clearinghouse on Higher Education, George Washington University, Washington, DC, 1986.

100 **Today about 85 percent:** Clifton Conrad, Jennifer Grant Haworth, and Susan Bylard Millar, *A Silent Success: Master's Education in the United States* (Baltimore, MD: Johns Hopkins University Press, 1993).

100 **The demand for graduate degrees:** Earned degrees conferred, projections to 2012, Department of Education, National Center for Education Statistics.

100 **Numerous studies have found:** Catherine Millett, "How Undergraduate Loan Debt Affects Application and Enrollment in Gradate Degree or First-Professional Schools," *Journal of Higher Education* 74, no. 4 (July–August 2003).

101 **The traditional college-age population:** Advisory Committee on Student Financial Assistance, *Empty Promises.*

101 **By 2015, 43 percent:** Population growth estimates from U.S. Census Bureau, "U.S. Interim Projections by Age, Sex, Race and Hispanic Origin," March 18, 2004, available at http://www.census .gov/ipc/www/usinterimproj/.

101 **The Advisory Committee:** Advisory Committee on Student Financial Assistance, *Empty Promises.*

COLD TRUTHS ABOUT CLASS, RACE, AND HEALTH
David R. Williams and James Lardner

102 **But medicine has not been the driving force:** Thomas McKeown, *The Role of Medicine: Dream, Mirage, or Nemisis?* (London:

Nuffield Provincial Hospitals Trust, 1976); Richard Lewontin, "Death of TB," letter to the editor, *New York Review of Books*, January 25, 1979; S. Leonard Syme, "Understanding the Relationship Between Socioeconomic Status and Health: New Research Initiatives," in *Income, Socioeconomic Status, and Health: Exploring the Relationships*, ed. James A. Auerbach and Barbara Kivimae Krimgold (Washington, DC: National Policy Association, 2001).

103 **"It is one of the great and sobering truths":** Theodore Cooper quoted in John K. Iglehart, "Health Care Cost Explosion Squeezes Government Programs, Insurers," *National Journal* 7, no. 38 (1976): 1319–28.

103 **In 2001:** 2001 figures from Uwe E. Reinhardt, Peter S. Hussey, and Gerard F. Anderson, "U.S. Health Care Spending in an International Context," *Health Affairs* 23, no. 3 (2004): 10–25.

103 **The 293 million people:** Ibid.; population estimates from *CIA—The World Factbook*.

104 **Yet, you could listen:** According to a 1999 survey by the Kaiser Family Foundation, over half the U.S. population, and half of African Americans and Hispanics, were unaware of health disparities by race/ethnicity. Perhaps this may have begun to change with more recent studies and passage of the Minority Health and Health Disparities Research and Education Act of 2000 (P.L. 106-525). See Institute of Medicine, *Unequal Treatment: Confronting Racial and Ethnic Disparities in Health Care* (Washington, DC: National Academies Press, 2002), and U.S. Department of Health and Human Services, National Healthcare Disparities Report (Washington, DC: DHHS, 2004). However, note the sparse attention paid to this topic during the 2004 presidential campaign.

104 **In 2000, the World Health Organization:** World Health Organization, *The World Health Report 2000—Health Systems: Improving Performance* (Geneva: WHO, 2000).

104 **The relationship between class:** G. Davey-Smith, J.D. Neaton, and J. Stamler, "Socioeconomic Differentials in Mortality Risk Among Men Screened for the Multiple Risk Factor Intervention Trial: White Men," *American Journal of Public Health* 86 (1996): 489–96; J.S. House et al., "The Social Stratification of Aging and Health," *Journal of Health and Social Behavior* 35, no. 3 (1994): 213–34.

105 **Class and race are inextricably linked:** Ichiro Kawachi, Norman Daniels, and Dean E. Robinson, "Health Disparities by Race and Class: Why Both Matter," *Health Affairs* 24, no. 2 (2005): 343–52; David R. Williams, "Race, SES and Health: The Added Effects of Racism and Discrimination," *Annals of the New York Academy of Sciences* 896 (1999): 173–88.

105 **On average, white Americans:** National Center for Health Statistics, *Health United States, 2004* (Hyattsville, MD: U.S. Department of Health and Human Services, 2004), 10 and table 29.

105 **During the 1980s:** R.S. Levine et al., "Black-White Inequalities in Mortality and Life Expectancy, 1933–1999: Implications for Healthy People 2010," *Public Health Reports* 116, no. 5 (2001): 474–83.

105 **But despite overall reductions:** National Center for Health Statistics, *Health, United States, 1998, with Socioeconomic Status and Health Chartbook* (Hyattsville, MD: U.S. Department of Health and Human Services, 1998), 84.

105 **Nor have most racial disparities:** National Center for Health Statistics, *Health United States, 2004,* tables 19 and 29.

106 **Between 1968 and 1978:** D.R. Williams and P.B. Jackson, "Social Sources of Racial Disparities in Health," *Health Affairs* 24, no. 2 (2005): 325–34. See also Office of the President, *Annual Report of the Council of Economic Advisers* (Washington, DC: Government Printing Office, 1998); and R.S. Cooper et al., "Improved Mortality

Among U.S. Blacks, 1968–1979: The Role of Anti-racist Struggle," *International Journal of Health Services* 11, no. 4 (1981): 511–22.

106 **For example, rates of hypertension:** R.S. Cooper et al., "The Prevalence of Hypertension in Seven Populations of West African Origin," *American Journal of Public Health* 87, no. 2 (1997): 160–68.

107 **In Latinos:** For example, see G.K. Singh and S.M. Yu, "Adverse Pregnancy Outcomes: Differences Between U.S.- and Foreign-Born Women in Major U.S. Racial and Ethnic Groups," *American Journal of Public Health* 86, no. 6 (1996): 837–43.

107 **People without health insurance:** Kaiser Commission on Medicaid and the Uninsured, "Health Insurance Coverage in America: 2003 Data Update," Kaiser Family Foundation Publication no. 7153, December 8, 2004.

108 **Because poor people and people of color:** National Center for Health Statistics, *Health, United States, 1998,* 13; Marsha Lillie-Blanton and Catherine Hoffman, "The Role of Health Insurance Coverage in Reducing Racial/Ethnic Disparities in Health Care," *Health Affairs* 24, no. 2 (2005): 398–408.

108 **But insurance isn't the only determinant:** Dan Hawkins and Michelle Proser, "A Nation's Health at Risk: A National and State Report on America's 36 Million People Without a Regular Health Care Provider," National Association of Community Health Centers Special Topics Issue Brief #5, Washington, DC, March 2004; David R. Williams and Chiquita A. Collins, "Racial Residential Segregation: A Fundamental Cause of Racial Disparities in Health," *Public Health Reports* 116, no. 5 (2001): 404–16; A.T. Geronimus et al., "Inequality in Life Expectancy, Functional Status and Active Life Expectancy Across Selected Black and White Populations in the United States," *Demography* 38, no. 2 (2001): 227–51.

108 **Even when the availability of care:** See, for example, M.G. Marmot et al., "Contribution of Job Control and Other Risk Factors to So-

cial Variations in Coronary Heart Disease Incidence," *Lancet* 350 (1997): 235–39.

109 **Imagine two car accidents:** Institute of Medicine, "The Uninsured Are Sicker and Die Sooner," in *Care Without Coverage: Too Little, Too Late* (Washington, DC: National Academies Press, May 2002).

110 **Here, too, class is compounded by race:** Institute of Medicine, *Unequal Treatment;* U.S. Department of Health and Human Services, *National Healthcare Disparities Report.*

110 **Commenting on the results of these efforts:** National Center for Health Statistics, *Health, United States,* 1998, 25.

111 **"When you have eliminated the impossible":** Appears in so many words in at least three Sherlock Holmes stories: "The Sign of the Four," "The Bruce-Partington Plans," and "The Blanched Soldier."

112 **Thus, Greece, where GDP:** GDP from Reinhardt, Hussey, and Anderson, "U.S. Health Care Spending in an International Context"; World Bank, "Greece at a Glance," http://www.worldbank.org/cgi-bin/sendoff.cgi?page=/ data/countrydata/aag/grc_aag.pdf.

112 **By the same token, Costa Rica:** World Bank, "GNP per Capita: All Regions, Whole World," http://www.worldbank.org/depweb/ english/modules/economic/gnp/datanot.html; World Bank, "Costa Rica at a Glance," http://www.worldbank.org/cgi-bin/sendoff.cgi? page=/data/count rydata/aag/cri_aag.pdf.

112 **The 25 percent of metropolitan areas:** J.W. Lynch et al., "Income Inequality and Mortality in Metropolitan Areas of the United States," *American Journal of Public Health* 88, no. 7 (1998): 1074–80.

112 **Inequality and poverty together:** G.A. Kaplan et al., "Inequality in Income and Mortality in the United States: Analysis of Mortality and Potential Pathways," *British Medical Journal* 312 (1996): 999–1003.

112 **While the reasons may be debatable:** For a summary of work on

stress, see Richard Wilkinson, *The Impact of Inequality: How to Make Sick Societies Healthier* (New York: The New Press, 2005), chapter 5.

113 **Using the Green Line:** Patricia Cohen, "Forget Lonely. Life Is Healthy at the Top," *New York Times,* May 15, 2004.

113 **To reduce health disparities:** S. Leonard Syme, Bonnie Lefkowitz, and Barbara Kivimae Krimgold, "Incorporating Socioeconomic Factors into U.S. Health Policy: Addressing the Barriers," *Health Affairs* 21, no. 2 (2002): 113–18.

OF THE FEW, BY THE FEW, FOR THE FEW *Charles Lewis*

116 **In 2004 the average cost of winning:** The average winning Senate candidate in 2004 spent $7,790,852; the average winning House candidate spent $1,032,956. Calculated from data gathered by the Center for Responsive Politics, see http://www.opensecrets.org/overview/bigspenders.asp?cycle=2004.

118 **In fact, 40 percent of U.S. senators are millionaires:** The 40 percent figure is based on financial disclosure statements filed by members of the 108th Congress.

118 **America's political donors represent a tiny segment:** David Donnely, Janice Fine, and Ellen Miller, *Money and Politics: Financing Our Elections Democratically* (Boston: Beacon Press, 1997).

118 **Those who give significant sums:** Adam Lioz, "The Role of Money in the 2002 Congressional Elections," U.S. Public Interest Research Group Educational Fund, Washington, DC, July 2003, available at http://www.uspirg.org/reports/roleofmoney2003.pdf.

119 **You might think that corporations would strive to conceal:** See the letter from Bush fund-raiser Thomas R. Kuhn to other contributors detailing the importance of using industry "tracking num-

bers," in the Center for Public Integrity's *The Buying of the President, 2004* (New York: HarperCollins, 2004), 8–9.

119 **The always-quotable Bob Dole describes:** Center for Public Integrity, *Buying of the President, 2004,* 473.

120 **A special report by some of America's:** The American Political Science Association Task Force report, "American Democracy in an Age of Rising Inequality," is available at http://www.apsanet.org/inequality/taskforcereport.pdf.

120 **The 2004 presidential race offered several illuminating examples:** More detail on the bankrollers of all the major 2004 presidential candidates is in *The Buying of the President, 2004.*

121 **The contracting process in the rebuilding:** For much more on political favoritism in postwar contracting, see the Center for Public Integrity's "Windfalls of War" project, available at http://www.publicintegrity.org/wow.

122 **As David Cay Johnston documents:** In addition to Johnston's excellent work in *Perfectly Legal: The Covert Campaign to Rig Our Tax System to Benefit the Super Rich—and Cheat Everybody Else* (New York: Portfolio, 2003), see the Center for Public Integrity's investigation of tax cheats in *The Cheating of America: How Tax Avoidance and Evasion by the Super Rich Are Costing the Country Billions—and What You Can Do About It* (New York: HarperPerennial, 2002).

123 **But it is not just our wallets:** See especially chapter 8 of the Center for Public Integrity's *The Buying of the Congress* (New York: Avon Books, 1998), and chapter 7 of Micah Sifry and Nancy Watzman, *Is That a Politician in Your Pocket? Washington on $2 Million a Day* (Hoboken, NJ: John Wiley & Sons, 2004).

WHY DO SO MANY JOBS PAY SO BADLY? *Christopher Jencks*

129 **The American economy turned out:** *Economic Report of the President, 2005,* tables B-2 and B-34.

129 **About one American worker in six:** Lawrence Mishel, Jared Bernstein, and Sylvia Allegretto, *The State of Working America 2004/2005* (Ithaca, NY: Cornell University Press, 2005), table 2.6.

131 **Yet if we use the same price index:** *Economic Report of the President, 2005,* Tables B-7 and B-47.

131 **Among men without any college education:** Mishel, Bernstein, and Allegretto, *State of Working America, 2004/2005,* table 2.18.

131 **Partly for that reason:** *Economic Report of the President, 2005,* tables B-34 and B-35.

131 **The best trend data:** Congressional Budget Office, "Effective Federal Tax Rates, 1997 to 2003," Washington, DC, August 2003.

132 **The Luxembourg Income Study:** The LIS data is available at http://www.lisproject.org/keyfigures/ineqtable.htm.

133 **Computer use and sales spread:** Dan Devroye and Richard B. Freeman, "Does Inequality in Skills Explain Earnings Inequality Across Advanced Countries?" National Bureau of Economic Research Working Paper no. 8140, Cambridge, MA, February 2001.

136 **In retailing, for example:** Michael Forsythe and Rachel Katz, "Costco, Wal-Mart Duel in Political Arena," Bloomberg News, July 21, 2004; Stanley Holmes and Wendy Zellner, "Higher Wages Mean Higher Profits," *Business Week,* April 12, 2004.

HOW THE MIDDLE CLASS IS INJURED BY GAINS AT THE TOP
Robert H. Frank

139 **For a glimpse of the possible downside:** Dirk Johnson, "Where Money Is Everything, Except Hers," *New York Times*, October 28, 1998, A1.

139 **Writing more than two centuries ago:** Adam Smith, *The Wealth of Nations* (New York: Random House, 1937), chap. 2.

141 **Two small midwestern cities:** Robert H. Frank, Bjornulf Ostvik-White, and Adam Seth Levine, "Expenditure Cascades," Cornell University mimeograph, 2005.

143 **Your adaptation to a long trip:** Meni Koslowsky, Avraham N. Kluger, and Mordechai Reich, *Commuting Stress* (New York: Plenum, 1995).

143 **A large increase in background noise:** David C. Glass, Jerome Singer, and James Pennegaker, "Behavioral and Physiological Effects of Uncontrollable Environmental Events," in *Perspectives on Environment and Behavior,* ed. Daniel Stokols (New York: Plenum, 1977).

143 **If the noise is not only loud:** Ibid.

143 **This pattern has been seen:** N.D. Weinstein, "Community Noise Problems: Evidence Against Adaptation," *Journal of Environmental Psychology* 2 (1982): 82–97.

143 **The prolonged experience of commuting stress:** Anita DeLongis, Susan Folkman, and Richard S. Lazarus, "The Impact of Daily Stress on Health and Mood: Psychological and Social Resources as Mediators," *Journal of Personality and Social Psychology* 54 (1988): 486–95; Daniel Stokols, Raymond W. Novaco, Jeannette Stokols, and Joan Campbell, "Traffic Congestion, Type A Behavior, and Stress," *Journal of Applied Psychology* 63 (1978): 467–80; Koslowsky, Kluger, and Reich, *Commuting Stress,* chap. 4.

144 **The incidence of these and other illnesses:** P. Taylor and C. Pocock, "Commuter Travel and Sickness: Absence of London Office Workers," *British Journal of Preventive and Social Medicine* 26 (1972): 165–72; Meni Koslowsky and Moshe Krausz, "On the Relationship Between Commuting, Stress Symptoms, and Attitudinal Measures," *Journal of Applied Behavioral Sciences* 9 (December 1993): 485–92.

144 **and lower still among noncommuters:** European Foundation for the Improvement of Living and Working Conditions, *The Journey from Home to the Workplace: The Impact on the Safety and Health of the Community/Workers* (Dublin: European Foundation for the Improvement of Living and Working Conditions, 1984).

144 **Among rush-hour travelers:** David Schrank and Tim Lomax, *The 2002 Urban Mobility Report*, Texas Transportation Institute, College Station, June 2002, available at http://mobility.tamu.edu/.

144 **The Federal Highway Administration:** Charles S. Clark, "Traffic Congestion," *CQ Researcher,* May 6, 1994, 387–404.

145 **Can we attribute this to rising inequality?:** Frank et al., "Expenditure Cascades."

145 **Analyzing international data:** Samuel Bowles and Yongjin Park, "Emulation, Inequality, and Work Hours: Was Thorstein Veblen Right?" Santa Fe Institute mimeograph, 2002.

145 **American families carry an average:** Stephen Brobeck, "Recent Trends in Bank Credit Card Marketing and Indebtedness," Consumer Federation of America report, 1998.

146 **Nationwide, more than 50 percent:** For citations of the relevant supporting studies, see Robert Frank, *Luxury Fever: Money and Happiness in an Era of Excess* (New York: The Free Press, 1999), chap. 4.

146 **Americans spend less:** Elliot D. Sclar, *You Don't Always Get What*

You Pay For: The Economics of Privatization (Ithaca, NY: Cornell University Press, 2000).

147 **Although spending on public education:** Ibid.

THE VANISHING COMMONS   *Jonathan Rowe*

150 **Southern planters faced a major dilemma:** Steven Hahn, *The Roots of Southern Populism* (New York: Oxford University Press, 1983), 241.

152 **The Massachusetts Colonial Ordinance:** Joseph L. Fernandez, "Untwisting the Common Law: Public Trust and the Massachusetts Colonial Ordinance," *Albany Law Review* 62 (1998): 623–30.

153 **Benjamin Franklin had a sharp eye:** Benjamin Franklin, *Autobiography* (New Haven: Yale University Press, 1964), 192.

153 **Thomas Edison, America's trademark inventor:** Robert Conot, *Thomas A. Edison: A Streak of Luck* (New York: DaCapo Press, 1979), 75.

154 **Not to mention the many competitors:** Ibid., 469.

154 **Representative Dan V. Stephens:** W. Elliot Brownlee, "Wilson and Financing the Modern State: The Revenue Act of 1916," *Proceedings of the American Philosophical Society* 129, no. 2 (1985): 185.

155 **When the city of Philadelphia:** See, among other articles, Cynthia L. Webb, "Telecoms Winning the WiFi War," *Washington Post,* December 1, 2004.

156 **But those who doubt the impact:** Robert Frank, "New Luxury Goods Set Super-Wealthy Apart from Pack," *Wall Street Journal,* January 14, 2004, 1.

157 **Community gardens:** Food Project Web site, http://www.thefoodproject.org.

158 **In 1943, in the midst of World War II:** Amy Bentley, *Eating for Vic-*

tory: Food Rationing and the Politics of Domesticity (Urbana: University of Illinois Press), 1998.

158 **In Philadelphia, urban gardeners save:** Katherine H. Brown and Anne Carter, "Urban Agriculture and Community Food Security in the United States: Farming from the City Center to the Urban Fringe," Community Food Security Coalition report, Venice, CA, October 2003, 13.

160 **Peter Barnes:** Peter Barnes, *Who Owns the Sky: Our Common Assets and the Future of Capitalism* (Washington, DC: Island Press, 2001).

161 **Both Congress and the courts:** James Surowiecki, "Patent Bending," *New Yorker,* July 14, 2003, 36.

162 **Under the antiquated Mining Law of 1872:** Green Scissors Campaign, "Green Scissors 2002: Cutting Wasteful and Environmentally Harmful Spending," Washington, DC, April 2002, available at http://www.greenscissors.org/publications/gs2002411.pdf.

163 **Warren Buffett:** Chuck Collins, Mike Lapham, and Scott Klinger, *I Didn't Do It Alone: Society's Contribution to Individual Wealth and Success* (Boston: United for a Fair Economy, 2004).

163 **The income of ordinary working Americans:** Clifford Cobb and Jonathan Rowe, "The Worst Tax: How Payroll Taxes Have Hurt America's Working Class," *Washington Monthly,* July–August 1997, 17.

164 **When Winston Churchill:** Cobb and Rowe, "The Worst Tax," 17.

THE GREAT TAX SHIFT   *David Cay Johnston*

165 **When the tax burden shifted to the wealthy:** For a good analysis of this historical connection see Maureen B. Cavanaugh, "Democracy, Equality, and Taxes," *Alabama Law Review* 54 (Winter 2003).

166 **As a Pennsylvania congressman said:** These quotes appear in Jonathan Rowe and Clifford Cobb's insightful essay "How the In-

come Tax Became a Tax on Labor," available at http://www
.inequality.org/incometaxlabor.html.

167 **Factor in all the unreported income:** See Daniel Altman, "Dou-
bling Up of Taxation Isn't Limited to Dividends," *New York Times,*
January 21, 2003.

167 **Between 1970 and 2000, economic productivity:** This figure is
based on nonfarm business sector productivity; statistics are available at the Bureau of Labor Statistics Web site, http://www.bls.gov.

167 **In 1970, the average American in the bottom 90 percent:** The statistics on unequal income growth are from Thomas Piketty and
Emmanuel Saez, "Income Inequality in the United States,
1913–1998 (series updated to 2000)," National Bureau of Economic Research Working Paper no. 8467, September 2001.

168 **And a still smaller elite, the top four hundred:** The IRS released its
first data analysis on the four hundred highest-income Americans
in 2003; that analysis is available at http://www.irs.gov/pub/irs-
soi/00in400h.pdf.

172 **By the year 2000, the audit rate:** Data on audit rates is available at
http://trac.syr.edu/tracirs/index.html.

172 **Former IRS commissioner Charles Rossotti:** Rossotti's book on
his time at the IRS is *Many Unhappy Returns: One Man's Quest to
Turn Around the Most Unpopular Organization in America* (Cambridge, MA: Harvard Business School Press, 2005).

174 **By the year 2000, it was collecting over 70 percent:** See Leonard E.
Burman, William G. Gale, Jeffrey Rohaly, and Benjamin H. Harris,
"The Individual AMT: Problems and Potential Solutions," Urban-
Brookings Tax Policy Center Discussion Paper no. 5, September
2002, available at http://www.taxpolicycenter.org/UploadedPDF/
410561_AMT-DP-final.pdf.

176 **But while campaigning for the statehouse:** Susan Pace Hamill's
paper "An Argument for Tax Reform Based on Judeo-Christian

Ethics" (*Alabama Law Review* 54, fall 2002) is available at
http://www.law.ua.edu/pdf/hamill-taxreform.pdf.

AMERICA DISCONNECTED   *Theda Skocpol*

178 **It was also the pivotal force:** Michael J. Bennett, *When Dreams
Came True: The G.I. Bill and the Making of Modern America* (Washington, DC: Brassey's, 1996).

179 **Indeed, the country's largest:** Theda Skocpol, "Civic Transformation and Inequality in the Contemporary United States," in *Social
Inequality,* ed. Kathryn Neckerman (New York: Russell Sage Foundation, 2004). For details of this research on the largest U.S. voluntary associations, see Theda Skocpol, *Diminished Democracy: From
Membership to Management in American Civic Life* (Norman: University of Oklahoma Press, 2003), especially 26–28, table 2.2, and
130–31, table 4.1.

179 **Political scientists Alan Gerber and Don Green:** Alan S. Gerber
and Donald P. Green, "The Effects of Canvassing, Telephone Calls,
and Direct Mail on Voter Turnout: A Field Experiment," *American
Political Science Review* 94, no. 3 (2000): 653–63.

183 **In the years between 1960 and 1990:** Data come from recurrent
editions of the national *Encyclopedia of Associations* (Detroit: Gale
Research Company). For details, see Skocpol, *Diminished Democracy,* 146–47, table 4.2.

185 **It was the otherwise staunchly conservative American Legion:** In
addition to Bennett, *When Dreams Came True,* see Davis R.B. Ross,
Preparing for Ulysses (New York: Columbia University Press, 1969),
plus the analysis and references in Theda Skocpol, "The G.I. Bill
and U.S. Social Policy, Past and Present," *Social Philosophy and Policy* 14, no. 2 (1997): 95–115.

185 **In the eloquent phrasing of Karen Paget:** Karen Paget, "Citizen

Organizing: Many Movements, No Majority," *American Prospect,* June 1990, 115–28.

185 **Perhaps the most intriguing evidence:** Jeffrey M. Berry, *The New Liberalism: The Rising Power of Citizen Groups* (Washington, DC: Brookings Institution Press, 1999), 57.

187 **The shift from mass-membership federations:** For data on the privileged social background of supporters of advocacy groups, see Theda Skocpol, "Voice and Inequality: The Transformation of American Civic Democracy," *Perspectives on Politics* 2, no. 1 (March 2004): 12, figure 3.

CORPORATIONS UNBOUND *Joel Bakan*

188 **Carlton Brown, a normally unflappable commodities broker:** Interview with Carlton Brown.

189 **The corporation, too, is all about creating wealth:** Indeed, like Carlton Brown and his clients, corporations have exploited September 11, 2001, for profit. See, for example, Jim Lobe, "Post–September 11, the Rich Get Richer in the US," *Asia Times Online,* November 8, 2001; Michael Moran, "Cashing In on September 11," MSNBC News, July 9, 2002.

189 **To *exploit,* according to the dictionary:** *The New Lexicon Webster's Dictionary of the English Language* (New York: Lexicon Publications, 2004).

189 **In their 1932 book *The Modern Corporation and Private Property:*** Adolf A. Berle and Gardiner C. Means, *The Modern Corporation and Private Property* (New York: Harcourt, Brace & World, 1968), 14–17.

190 **No public function has been immune:** For discussions of the general scope of privatization and some examples, see David Bollier, *Public Assets, Private Profits: Reclaiming the American Commons in*

an Age of Market Enclosure (Washington, DC: New America Foundation, 2001); Reason Public Policy Institute, *Privatization 2002: Putting the Pieces Together,* 16th Annual Report on Privatization (Los Angeles: Reason Public Policy Institute, 2002); Pamela Winston, Andrew Burwick, Sheena McConnell, and Richard Roper, "Privatization of Welfare Services: A Review of the Literature," Mathematica Policy Research, Washington, DC, 2002; Alex Tysbine, *Water Privatization: A Broken Promise* (Washington, DC: Public Citizen, 2001); American Federation of State, County and Municipal Employees, *Government for Sale: An Examination of the Contracting Out of State and Local Government Services* (Washington, DC: AFSCME, AFL-CIO, 2002); Mark Cassell, *How Governments Privatize: The Politics of Divestment in the United States and Germany* (Washington, DC: Georgetown University Press, 2002); Maude Barlow and Tony Clarke, *Blue Gold: The Fight to Stop the Corporate Theft of the World's Water* (New York: The New Press, 2003); Vandana Shiva, *Water Wars: Privatization, Pollution, and Profit* (Boston: South End Press, 2002); R. Mokhiber and R. Weissman, "Smithsonian for Sale?" *Multinational Monitor,* November 19, 1997; Robert Kuttner, *Everything for Sale: The Virtues and Limits of Markets* (New York: Alfred A. Knopf, 1997); Allison Campbell, Andrew Coyle, and Rodney Neufeld, eds., *Capitalist Punishment: Prison Privatization and Human Rights* (Atlanta: Clarity Press, 2003); Brian Forst and Peter K. Manning, *The Privatization of Policing: Two Views* (Washington, DC: Georgetown University Press, 1999).

190 **The privatizers have an ambitious agenda:** Interviews with Milton Friedman, William Niskanen, and Michael Walker.

191 **"The classic investment opportunity":** Interview with Michael T. Moe. See also Maude Barlow and Heather Jane-Robertson, *Class*

Warfare: The Assault on Canada's Schools (Toronto: Key Porter Books, 1994).

191 **It's "almost unimaginably vast":** Interview with Benno Schmidt.

191 **Because the "education market":** Interviews with Michael T. Moe and Milton Friedman. Expansion will likely continue beyond 10 percent after the next decade to as high as 30 percent, according to another Edison financier, Jeffrey Fromm, in an interview.

192 **Proponents have used political muscle:** Michael Scherer, "Schools: Some of Bush's Largest Donors Stand to Profit from Privatizing Public Education," *Mother Jones,* March 5, 2001, available at http://www.motherjones.com/web_exclusives/special_reports/mojo_40 0/schools.html (under "Web Exclusives").

192 **But their assertions have been widely questioned:** Gary Miron and Brooks Applegate, "An Evaluation of Student Achievement in Edison Schools Opened in 1995 and 1996," Evaluation Center, Western Michigan University, Kalamazoo, MI, December 2001, as cited in Gerald Bracey, "The Market in Theory Meets the Market in Practice: The Case of Edison Schools," Education Policy Research Unit, College of Education, Arizona State University, Tempe, February 2002.

192 **The company has also been criticized:** Wyatt Edward, "Challenges and the Possibility of Profit for Edison," *New York Times,* January 1, 2001, cited in Bracey, "The Market in Theory Meets the Market in Practice."

193 **Shares in Edison Schools:** Doug Sanders, "For-Profit US Schools Sell Off Their Textbooks," *Globe and Mail* (Toronto), October 30, 2002, A1.

193 **"People tend to react to economic incentives":** Interview with Jeffrey Fromm.

194 **"We owe our daily bread":** Interview with Milton Friedman. For

an excellent account of why skilled, professional, and public-minded civil servants are not only possible but also essential for a functioning democracy, see Ezra N. Suleiman, *Dismantling Democratic States* (Princeton, NJ: Princeton University Press, 2003).

194 **This is a business that turned:** Christopher Bryson, "Edison Schools Flunks," *New York Post*, May 6, 2002, 31.

195 **Ultimately, Edison's flailing business was bought:** Helen Huntley, "State Fund Buys School Operator," *St. Petersburg Times*, September 25, 2003.

195 **The ratio of CEO pay:** Sarah Anderson, John Cavanagh, Chris Hartman, Scott Klinger, and Stacey Chan, "Executive Excess 2004: Campaign Contributions, Outsourcing, Unexpensed Stock Options and Rising CEO Pay," Institute for Policy Studies and United for a Fair Economy report, available at http://www.faireconomy .org/press/2004/EE2004.pdf.

197 **Modern universities are run like corporations:** See Derek Bok, *Universities in the Marketplace: The Commercialization of Higher Education* (Princeton, NJ: Princeton University Press, 2003).

197 **New York's Museum of Modern Art:** See the FrEE MoMA Web site, http://freemoma.org.

197 **Corporations may act in ways:** For further examples, see Karen Bakker, David Cameron, and Adele Hurley, "Don't Tap into the Private Sector," *Globe and Mail* (Toronto), February 6, 2003, A17; Linda McQuaig, *All You Can Eat: Greed, Lust and the New Capitalism* (Toronto: Penguin Books, 2001); Elliott D. Sclar, *You Don't Always Get What You Pay For: The Economics of Privatization* (Ithaca, NY: Cornell University Press, 2001); P.W. Singer, *Corporate Warriors: The Rise of the Privatized Military Industry* (Ithaca, NY: Cornell University Press, 2003); Gerald W. Bracey, *The War Against America's Public Schools: Privatizing Schools, Commercializing Education* (Boston: Allyn and Bacon, 2001), and Bracey, *What You*

Should Know About the War Against America's Public Schools (Boston: Allyn and Bacon, 2002); Brenda Cossman and Judy Fudge, eds., *Privatization, Law, and the Challenge to Feminism* (Toronto: University of Toronto Press, 2002); Martha Minow, *Partners, Not Rivals: Privatization and the Public Good* (Boston: Beacon Press, 2002).

198 **"PUBLIC SPACE," proclaims a plaque:** A picture of the sign appears on the cover of Herbert Schiller, *Culture Inc.: The Corporate Takeover of Public Expression* (New York: Oxford University Press, 1989). I also refer to it in Joel Bakan, *Just Words: Constitutional Rights and Social Wrongs* (Toronto: University of Toronto Press, 1997), 68, where I argue that the encroaching privatization of public space erodes free speech rights. See also Jerold S. Kayden, New York City Department of City Planning, and the Municipal Art Society of New York, *Privately Owned Public Space: The New York City Experience* (New York: John Wiley & Sons, 2000). This paragraph is a modified version of one that appears in Joel Bakan, "Beyond Censorship: An Essay on Free Speech and Law," in *Interpreting Censorship in Canada,* ed. Klaus Petersen and Allan C. Hutchinson (Toronto: University of Toronto Press, 1999).

198 **As one commentator observes:** Jeffrey Hopkins, "Excavating Toronto's Underground Streets: In Search of Equitable Rights, Rules and Revenue," in *City Lives and City Forms,* ed. John Caulfield and Linda Peake (Toronto: University of Toronto Press, 1996), 63.

199 **The skyways are lined with advertising:** See the CityLites USA Web site, http://citylitesusa.com.

199 **"the proprietors must maintain an atmosphere":** Hopkins, "Excavating Toronto's Underground Streets," 70–71.

200 **Because malls, tunnels, and skywalks are private property:** See Bakan, "Beyond Censorship," and Bakan, *Just Words.* As Schiller states in *Culture Inc.,* 100: "To the extent that private-property

owners legally can decide what kind of activity is permissible in their malls, a vast and expanding terrain is withdrawn from serving as a site of public expression."

200 **They also tend to be decorated:** This paragraph is a modified version of one that appears in Bakan, "Beyond Censorship." See also Margaret Crawford, "The World in a Shopping Mall," in *Variations on a Theme Park,* ed. Michael Sorkin (New York: Noonday Press, 1992), 27, and Mike Davis, "Fortress Los Angeles: The Militarization of Urban Space," in Sorkin, *Variations on a Theme Park,* 169.

200 **On the residential side, gated neighborhoods:** This paragraph is a modified version of one that appears in Bakan, "Beyond Censorship." The quote is originally from Mary Massaron Ross, Larry Smith, and Robert Pritt, "The Zoning Process: Private Land-Use Controls and Gated Communities: The Impact of Private Property Rights Legislation, and Other Recent Developments in the Law," *Urban Lawyer* 28 (1996): 801–17, 802–3.

200 **"The corporation has essentially replaced the church":** Interview with Michael Moe.

201 **The corporation, after all:** Interview with Noam Chomsky.

201 **Adds philosopher Mark Kingwell:** Interview with Mark Kingwell.

A SELF-PERPETUATING TREND? *Eric Wanner*

205 **The wage premium:** Eileen Appelbaum, Annette Bernhardt, and Richard J. Murnane, *Low-Wage America: How Employers Are Reshaping Opportunity in the Workplace* (New York: Russell Sage Foundation, 2003), 3, figure 1.1.

205 **Overall, mean family income:** Carmen DeNavas-Walt, Robert W. Cleveland, and Bruce H. Webster Jr., *Current Population Reports, P60-221, Income in the United States: 2002* (Washington, DC: U.S. Government Printing Office, 2003), 17, table A-1.

206 **From 1979 to 2002:** Ibid., 25, table A-3.

210 **Instead, the poor:** Richard B. Freeman, "What, Me Vote?" in *Social Inequality,* ed. Kathryn M. Neckerman (New York: Russell Sage Foundation, 2004), 724, table 18.7.

210 **Furthermore, the political gap:** Sidney Verba, Kay Lehman-Schlozman, and Henry Brady, "Political Equality: What Do We Know About It?" in Neckerman, *Social Inequality.*

WHO IS THE ELITE? *Betsy Leondar-Wright*

216 **The work of George Lakoff, William Gamson:** George Lakoff, *Don't Think of an Elephant! Know Your Values and Frame the Debate: The Essential Guide for Progressives* (White River Junction, VT: Chelsea Green Publishing, 2004); William A. Gamson, *Talking Politics* (New York: Cambridge University Press, 1992).

220 **When I was researching my book:** Betsy Leondar-Wright, *Class Matters: Cross-Class Alliance Building for Middle-Class Activists* (Gabriola, BC: New Society Publishers, 2005).

221 **The most extreme example:** Ted Rall, "Confessions of a Cultural Elitist," Universal Press Syndicate, November 9, 2004.

222 **The antichoice movement recruited millions:** Thomas Frank, *What's the Matter with Kansas? How Conservatives Won the Heart of America* (New York: Metropolitan Books, 2004).

222 **Evangelical Christianity doesn't inevitably lead:** Jim Wallis, *God's Politics: Why the Right Gets It Wrong and the Left Doesn't Get It* (San Francisco: Harper SanFrancisco, 2005).

DON'T DRINK THE KOOL-AID *Robert Kuttner*

230 **The forces that yearn:** Edward Wong, "New Labor Realities," *New York Times,* April 17, 2003, C4.

234 **So you have what the political scientist Walter Dean Burnham:** Walter Dean Burnham, *Critical Elections and the Mainsprings of American Politics* (New York: W.W. Norton, 1970).

235 **For about $60 billion a year:** Committee for Economic Development, *Preschool for All* (Washington, DC: The Committee, 2002).

235 **In 2004, a coalition of groups:** Jackie Hallifax, "Voters Pass Minimum Wage Measure," Associated Press, November 3, 2004.

THE LEGITIMIZATION OF INEQUALITY   *Robert M. Franklin*

237 **Commenting on that poignant line:** Quoted in Richard T. Hughes, *Myths America Lives By* (Urbana: University of Illinois Press, 2003).

237 **Every social system needs:** Jürgen Habermas, *Legitimation Crisis,* trans. Thomas McCarthy (Boston: Beacon Press, 1975).

240 **The Catholic bishops have advocated:** The National Conference of Catholic bishops issued a letter on the economy detailing the concept of a "social mortgage," elaborated in Karen Lebacqz, *Six Theories of Justice: Perspectives from Philosophical and Theological Ethics* (Minneapolis, MN: Augsburg Fortress Press, 1986).

240 **The psychologist Erik Erikson:** Erik H. Erikson, *Childhood and Society* (New York: W.W. Norton, 1993).

243 **Karl Rove knows:** Michael Lindsay and George Gallup Jr., *Surveying the Religious Landscape: Trends in U.S. Beliefs* (Harrisburg, PA: Morehouse Group, 2001); George Bishop, "What Americans Really Believe: And Why Faith Isn't as Universal as They Think," *Free Inquiry* 19, no. 3 (1999), available at http://secularhumanism.org/library/fi/bishop_19_3.html.

244 **But there is another reason:** George Lakoff, *Moral Politics: How Liberals and Conservatives Think* (Chicago: University of Chicago Press, 2002), and check the Web site for the Rockridge Institute, a

nonpartisan research institute working to reframe the terms of democratic debate: www.rockridgeinstitute.org.

BUILDING A MORAL ECONOMY *William Greider*

248 **In 1932, a conservative minister:** *Soul in Society: The Making and Renewal of Social Christianity* (Minneapolis, MN: Fortress Press, 1995).

254 **Where did we learn:** Elaine Bernard, "Workplace Democracy Through Labor Law," *Dollars and Sense,* September–October 1999.

255 **To get a sense of the potential:** William Greider, *The Soul of Capitalism: Opening Paths to a Moral Economy* (New York: Simon & Schuster, 2003).

A PROPHETIC POLITICS *Jim Wallis*

258 **The lesson immediately taken:** See, for example, the exit poll conducted by Mitofsky Edison for a consortium of television networks and the Associated Press that was widely reported.

259 **A second important poll:** Zogby International Poll, "American Voters Say Urgent Moral Issues Are Peace, Poverty and Greed," November 12, 2004.

259 **The top 20 percent of households:** Jared Bernstein, Lawrence Mishel, and Heather Boushey, *State of Working America 2004/2005* (Ithaca, NY: Cornell University Press, 2004), chap. 1.

259 **The *New York Times:*** James Fallows, "The Invisible Poor," *New York Times Magazine,* March 19, 2000; Abby Ellin, "Preludes: Money, Money, Money. Guilt, Guilt, Guilt." *New York Times,* March 19, 2000, C14.

263 **Religious conservative leaders such as:** Duane Shank, "Missing Moral Issues," *Sojourners,* September–October 1998.

264 **Some Christian conservatives:** See, for instance, an August 25, 2004, editorial from *Oldspeak,* a publication of the Rutherford Institute, Charlottesville, VA.

DEMOCRACY FIRST   *Miles S. Rapoport and David A. Smith*

268 **Housing prices in Manhattan:** The income figures are from the U.S. Census Bureau, 2000 Census; the housing costs numbers have been widely reported—see "New York Real Estate Stars Reap Millions Among Record Prices," Bloomberg News, July 7, 2005.

268 **Meanwhile, working families struggle:** U.S. Census Bureau, Current Population Survey 2003.

269 **We have allowed the minimum wage:** Ibid.

269 **Since Congress failed:** Lawrence Mishel, Jared Bernstein, and Sylvia Allegretto, *The State of Working America 2004/2005* (Ithaca, NY: Cornell University Press, 2005).

269 **Because unionized workers are more likely:** Ibid.

269 **Since making an unprecedented investment:** See "The Growing College Gap," the chapter in this book by our colleague Tamara Draut, for an extended discussion of this issue.

271 **Such public outlays would require us:** Isaac Shapiro, Center on Budget and Policy Priorities, occasional paper, Washington, DC, October 21, 2003.

273 **In 2004, four of the five states:** "High 2004 Turnout for States with Election Day Registration," Demos press release, January 10, 2005.

274 **The number of citizens affected:** Alec Ewald reviews this data in detail in "Punishing at the Polls: The Case Against Disenfranchising Citizens with Felony Convictions," Demos report, New York, Sep-

tember 2003, available at http://www.demos-usa.org/pubs/FD_Punishing_at_the_Polls.pdf.

275 **The trend has reached the point of absurdity:** Campaign Finance Institute, "CFI's Post-Election Analysis," Washington, DC, November 5, 2004.

CONTRIBUTORS

Joel Bakan teaches constitutional law at the University of British Columbia. He is the author of *Just Words: Constitutional Rights and Social Wrongs* (1997) and *The Corporation: The Pathological Pursuit of Profit and Power* (2004). He was the writer and co-producer of the accompanying documentary, *The Corporation.*

Heather Boushey is an economist at the Center for Economic and Policy Research, specializing in U.S. labor markets, social policy, and work and family issues. She is co-author of *The State of Working America 2002–3* with Larry Mishel and Jared Bernstein, and of *Hardships in America: The Real Story of Working Families* with Chauna Brocht, Bethney Gundersen, and Jared Bernstein.

Tamara Draut is director of the Economic Opportunity Program at Demos, and the co-author of the Demos reports *Millions to the Middle: Three Strategies to Grow the Middle Class, Retiring in the Red: The Growth of Debt Among Older Americans,* and *Bor-*

rowing to Make Ends Meet: The Growth of Credit Card Debt in the 90s. Her book, *Strapped: Why America's 20- and 30-Somethings Can't Get Ahead,* will be published by Random House in 2006.

Barbara Ehrenreich is a journalist, commentator, and the author, most recently, of *Nickel and Dimed: On (Not) Getting By in America.*

Robert H. Frank is the H.J. Louis Professor of Management and Professor of Economics at Cornell's Johnson School of Management, and the author of *Luxury Fever* and (with Philip Cook) of *The Winner-Take-All Society.* He is a monthly contributor to the "Economic Scene" column in the *New York Times.*

Robert M. Franklin is Presidential Distinguished Professor of Social Ethics at Candler School of Theology, Emory University. He provides commentary for *All Things Considered* on National Public Radio and is the author of two books, *Liberating Visions: Human Fulfillment and Social Justice in African-American Thought* and *Another Day's Journey: Black Churches Confronting the American Crisis.*

William Greider is the author of *One World, Ready or Not, Who Will Tell the People?,* and, most recently, *The Soul of Capitalism: Opening Paths to a Moral Economy.* He is the national affairs correspondent for the *Nation* magazine.

Christopher Jencks is the Malcolm Wiener Professor of Social Policy at Harvard's John F. Kennedy School of Government and a member of the editorial board of the *American Prospect*. His most recent books are *The Black-White Test Score Gap* (with Meredith Phillips) and *Rethinking Social Policy*.

David Cay Johnston is a Pulitzer Prize–winning financial reporter who covers tax issues for the *New York Times*. He is the author of *Perfectly Legal: The Covert Campaign to Rig Our Tax System to Benefit the Super-Rich—and Cheat Everybody Else*.

Richard D. Kahlenberg is a senior fellow at the Century Foundation and the author of *The Remedy: Class, Race, and Affirmative Action*.

Robert Kuttner is co-editor of the *American Prospect* and a syndicated columnist in addition to being the author of *Everything for Sale: The Virtues and Limits of Markets*. He is working on a book about deregulation and the stock market collapse.

James Lardner is the founder of Inequality.org and a senior fellow at Demos. As a journalist, he has written articles for the *Washington Post*, the *New Yorker*, the *Nation*, and the *New York Times Magazine*, among other publications. He is the co-author, with Thomas Reppetto, of *NYPD: A City and Its Police*.

Betsy Leondar-Wright is communications director for United for a Fair Economy, the author of *Class Matters: Cross-Class Alliance Building for Middle-Class Activists* (2005), and a co-author of *The Color of Wealth: The Story Behind the Racial Wealth Divide*.

Charles Lewis is the president of the Fund for Independence in Journalism in Washington, and co-author of five books, including the bestselling *The Buying of the President 2004*. A onetime investigative reporter for ABC and for CBS's *60 Minutes*, he founded and for fifteen years was executive director of the Center for Public Integrity, a nonprofit, nonpartisan investigative reporting organization.

Meizhu Lui is executive director of United for a Fair Economy. A former food service worker and AFSCME activist, she was the first Asian president of a local union in Massachusetts. As a community organizer for Health Care for All, she led one of the first challenges to business that led to a community benefits agreement.

Heather McGhee is a co-author of the recent Demos reports *Borrowing to Make Ends Meet* and *Retiring in the Red: The Growth of Debt Among Older Americans*. She has worked as a public policy associate at the Social Policy Action Network in Washington, DC, and as a researcher at Harvard's Kennedy School of Government.

Bill Moyers is president of the Schumann Center for Media and Democracy. His independent production company, Public Affairs Television, has been responsible for more than four hundred hours of acclaimed programming. He is the author or editor of several bestselling books, including *Moyers on America: A Journalist and His Times*.

Miles S. Rapoport is the president of Demos and a longtime leader in the fight for democracy reform. Prior to joining Demos,

Mr. Rapoport was a representative in the Connecticut legislature for ten years before serving four years as the Secretary of State of Connecticut. He founded and serves on the boards of Northeast Action, a political reform organization in New England, and DemocracyWorks, an advocacy organization which promotes democratic values to create a fairer, inclusive, and vibrant society. Mr. Rapoport also is a board member of the Paul J. Aicher Foundation and the Center for Policy Alternatives.

Jonathan Rowe is director of the Tomales Bay Institute and a contributing editor at the *Washington Monthly* and *YES!* magazines.

Theda Skocpol is Victor S. Thomas Professor of Government and Sociology and director of the Center for American Political Studies at Harvard University. Her most recent book is *Diminished Democracy: From Membership to Management in American Civic Life* (University of Oklahoma Press, 2003).

David A. Smith has written and lectured widely on issues of development, labor, tax, and income policy. Before joining Demos, where he is a senior fellow, he was the director of the Public Policy Department at the AFL-CIO in Washington. He has also served as commissioner of business development and senior deputy budget director for the city of New York, as an aide to Senator Edward M. Kennedy, and as a senior economist at the Joint Economic Committee of the United States Congress.

Jim Wallis was a founder of Sojourners—Christians for justice and peace—more than thirty years ago and continues to serve as the editor of *Sojourners* magazine, covering faith, politics, and culture. In 1995, Wallis was instrumental in forming Call to Renewal, a national federation of churches, denominations, and faith-based organizations from across the theological and political spectrum working to overcome poverty. His most recent book is *God's Politics: A New Vision for Faith and Politics in America* (2005).

Eric Wanner is president of the Russell Sage Foundation, where he has led the way in developing research programs on poverty and inequality in the United States, on the economic and social impacts of immigration, and on the causes and consequences of the accelerating changes in the nature of work. With a doctorate in psychology from Harvard University, Wanner served on the faculties at Harvard University, Rockefeller University, and the University of Sussex before turning to foundation work. His own research centered on the development of computer models of speech processing and language learning.

Christian E. Weller is a senior economist with the Center for American Progress in Washington, DC. He specializes in retirement income security, international finance, and macroeconomy and the labor market. Dr. Weller holds a PhD in economics from the University of Massachusetts at Amherst.

David R. Williams is a sociologist whose work focuses on the causes of ill health, including social circumstances, race/ethnicity, and discrimination. He is a senior research scientist and professor at the University of Michigan's Institute for Social Research. Among Williams's most recent papers is "The Health of Men: Structured Inequalities and Opportunities" in the May 2003 issue of the *American Journal of Public Health.*